BAKING BLUE RIBBONS

Stories and Recipes
from the Iowa State Fair
Food Competitions

Kay Fenton Smith with Carol McGarvey

Copyright © 2022 Kay Smith and Carol McGarvey. All rights reserved.

Published in partnership with the Iowa State Fair Blue Ribbon Foundation. Des Moines, Iowa.
To order, please visit the State Fair Store at: blueribbonfoundation.org.
All proceeds benefit the Iowa State Fair Food Department.

Produced and printed by Sigler. Ames, Iowa.
Cover and book design by Michelle Stephenson and Jenny Butcher at Sigler.

ISBN: 978-0-578-29435-3
Library of Congress Control Number: 2022908431

Iowa State Fair images and *Iowa State Fair Cookbook* recipes printed with permission from the Iowa State Fair. Photo credits and copyrights, page 245.

Dedicated to everyone who has been a part of the Iowa State Fair Food Competitions since 1854.

THANK YOU TO OUR CONTRIBUTORS.

Baking Blue Ribbons would not have happened without the generous support of Denny and Candy Elwell and their family. They shared State Fair stories and encouraged us from the start, and we cannot thank them enough. We also extend our gratitude to the many contributors who helped bring the history, stories, and recipes of our Iowa State Fair Food Department to life.

Best of Fair — $2,500 and above

JAMIE BUELT OF POLK CITY AND EN Q STRATEGIES

CAROL AND TOM MCGARVEY OF DES MOINES

KAY AND ELLIOTT SMITH OF DES MOINES,
IN MEMORY OF SAM GANSHAW AND MARYLIN AND EVAN SMITH

Sweepstakes — $1,000–$2,499

BRET AND AMY DOERRING OF NEWTON

EILEEN GANNON OF DES MOINES,
AND SUNDAY NIGHT FOODS

Reserve Sweepstakes — $250–$999

JIM AND PATTY COWNIE OF DES MOINES

IOWA BEEF INDUSTRY COUNCIL

NATIONAL SOCIETY OF THE COLONIAL DAMES OF AMERICA, DES MOINES BOROUGH

JOAN FENTON SEABROOK OF DES MOINES, IN MEMORY OF HAROLD FENTON

MELVIN AND KATHY WEATHERWAX OF ANKENY

ANNIE AND MICHAEL WILLIAMS OF NEW YORK, IN MEMORY OF MARK FENTON GANSHAW

Blue Ribbon — Up to $249

MARTA BURKGREN OF AMES, IN MEMORY OF MARJORIE BURKGREN

MARY BURR OF IOWA CITY

CAROL DAHLSTROM OF ANKENY

LESTER AND SUSAN DAVIS OF JOHNSTON

RICHARD AND NANCY DEGNER OF ANKENY

NANETTE EVERLY OF BATAVIA

F. B. PURNELL SAUSAGE CO. INC. OF SIMPSONVILLE, KENTUCKY

ROBERT AND KAREN HENDERSON OF WAUKEE

WILL AND DIXIE HOEKMAN OF DES MOINES

CALEB AND JULIA HUNTER OF DES MOINES

IOWA POULTRY ASSOCIATION

BRIAN KEUL OF WEST DES MOINES

JAMES AND THERESA LIEWER OF ANKENY

MARJORIE AND HAROLD MAGG OF SPIRIT LAKE

DAVID AND JOY MCFARLAND OF TINGLEY, IN MEMORY OF BARB KIBURZ

DENNIS AND KAREN MCKILLIGAN OF AMES

CONNIE MEESTER OF DES MOINES

DELPHA MUSGRAVE OF DES MOINES

SUZANNE NELSON OF JOHNSTON

MATTHEW PHOENIX OF ANKENY

LOUISE PIPER OF GARNER

ANNE REHNSTROM OF URBANDALE

DAVID AND PAMELA REYNOLDS OF NORWALK

DIANNA ZAIGER SHEEHY OF AUDUBON

ROSA SNYDER OF CLIVE

ROBIN TARBELL-THOMAS OF CENTERVILLE, IN MEMORY OF MILDRED PHILLIPS

MOLLY THOMAS OF CENTERVILLE, IN MEMORY OF OLIVE JEAN TARBELL

TERRI TREFT OF SIOUX CITY

DENNIS AND JANICE TROMETER OF JAMAICA

ROBERT WAGNER OF WEST DES MOINES

JEAN WAITE OF PALO

ILEEN WALLACE OF COUNCIL BLUFFS

TOM AND LOLA ZIMMERMAN OF WEST DES MOINES

Table of Contents

Introduction	xiv
1800s: First Fair to the Closing Century Exposition	2
1800s Recipe List	3
Recipes from Then and Now	19
Early 1900s: Celebrating 20th-Century Cooks and Winning the War with Food	34
Early 1900s Recipe List	35
Early 1900s Stories and Recipes	40
1920s–1930s: Iowa's Rise to the Top	52
1920s–1930s Recipe List	53
1920s–1930s Stories and Recipes	60
1940s–1950s: Wonder Bakers and Champion Judges	80
1940s–1950s Recipe List	81
1940s–1950s Stories and Recipes	90
1960s–1970s: Cookout Kings and Watergate Cake	106
1960s–1970s Recipe List	107
1960s–1970s Stories and Recipes	116
1980s–1990s: A Match Made in Food Heaven	140
1980s–1990s Recipe List	141
1980s–1990s Stories and Recipes	151
Building a Blue Ribbon Dynasty: Five Generations of the Tarbell-Thomas Clan	174
Stepping Behind the Blue Curtain: Words of Wisdom from Iowa State Fair Food Judges	179
Tips and Tricks	182
Advice for First-Time Judges	184
2000s: The Sweetest Gift and A Look to the Future	186
2000s Recipe List	187
2000s Stories and Recipes	194

A Tribute to Margaret and James "Bud" Elwell — 194

Eileen Gannon's 7 Secrets to Beautiful Cakes — 215

How to Enter the Iowa State Fair Food Contests — 237

What I Saw at the Fair, by Geraldine Tait — 238

Acknowledgments — 239

Meet the Authors — 241

Bibliography and Source Notes — 242

Photo Credits — 245

Recipe Table of Contents

APPETIZER
Basil Tomato Tart	198
Egg Roll in a Bowl Hot Dip	197
Nacho Dip	199
Santa Fe Rice Cups	199

SALADS, SOUPS, AND SIDE DISHES
All-American Bacon Cheeseburger Soup	203
Easy Summer Slaw	201
Great-Grandma's Refrigerator Beets	204
Peas De Resistance Salad	200
Roasted Peach and Brown Sugar Soup	202
Summer in Iowa Salad	200
Sweet and Savory Confetti SPAM Salad	155
Swiss Turkey Salad	120
Watergate Salad	127

YEAST BREADS
All-Purpose Yeast Dough	180
Best Bread in Iowa	92
Caraway Rye Bread	60
Lemon Cherry Coffeecake	90
Christmas Braid	118
Cornmeal Buns	63
Daily Bread	20
Date Nut Yeast Bread	62
Golden Wheat Batter Bread	118
Homemade Yeast, (1876)	20
Kolaches	119
Orange Sunshine Rolls	94
Oatmeal Bread	196
Pulled Pork Cinnamon Rolls	153
Soft Pretzels	176
Walnut Yeast Bread	92
Yeast-Rising Bread, (1870)	21

QUICK BREADS
Apple Crunch Muffins   65
Applesauce Muffins   152
Banana Macadamia Nut Bread   151
Bran Bread, (1917)   51
Boston Brown Bread, (1895)   19
Boston Brown Bread   19
Cinnamon Coffee Rolls, (1918)   49
Corn Bread with Rye Flour, (1918)   49
Corn Bread with Honey   116
Dark Fruit Cake   73
Date Pecan Quick Bread   63
Holiday Fruit Bread   178
Nut Quick Bread   62
Oatmeal Bread, (1918)   49
Oatmeal Date Muffins   66
Pumpkin Bread   181
Quick Bake Cinnamon Doughnuts   67
Raisin Buns Bettina, (1918)   50
Yankee Maple Corn Muffins   152

MAIN DISHES AND GRILLING
Asian Pork Burgers   124
Bacon Mac and Cheese   211
Bacon-Wrapped Barbeque Chicken   125
Beef Fillets Supreme   157
Beef Ribs Barbeque Sauce   123
Big Mama's Iowa Nachos   205
Bolognese with Homemade Noodles   210
Bubble Pizza   126
Chicken Pie and Sauce, (1900)   37
Chorizo Hot Cheese Torte   158
Daddy's Drumsticks   122
Dreamfields Tomato Feta Pasta   212
Fruit-Stuffed Pork Chops   125
Heartland Stew   160
Iowa Farmhouse Barbeque Baskets   209
Lasagna   161
Lasagna for 12   207
Low-Sodium Stuffed Peppers   160
Pork Rib Seasoning   121

Quail on Toast, (1893)	22
Salmon Croquettes, (1893)	21
Southwestern Sunrise Breakfast Casserole	213
Spaghetti Sauce	156
Tailgatin' Chili	208
Turkey Patties with Pears	159
Waffle Sausage Strata	214

CAKES

Almond Cake Roll with Raspberry Sauce	70
Angel Food Cake	41
Applesauce Cake	74
Apricot Picnic Cake	101
Best of the Best Lemon Cheesecake	220
Bird's Nest, (1900)	37
Carrot Cake	128
Chocolate Cake, (1900)	40
Chocolate Cake	40
Chocolate Praline Layer Cake	164
Closing Century Pineapple Cake, (1899)	30
Coconut Cake	44
Coconut Love Cake	163
Election Day Cake	68
Fairy Cupcakes, (1917)	46
Fig Cake, (1900)	37
Honey-Glazed Buttermilk Coffee Cake	48
Jelly Cake, (1880s)	25
Lady Baltimore Cake	95
Lavender Lemon Cake	216
Lemon Layer Cake	72
Mandarin Orange Bundt Cake	97
Marble Cake, (1913)	45
Orange Sponge Cake	24
Pear Walnut Upside-Down Cake	71
Pineapple Wow Cake	30
Pound Cake, (1876)	23
President Bill Clinton's Hope Cheesecake	165
Red Velvet Cake	217
Rhubarb Bundt Cake	129
Salted Caramel Mocha Cupcakes	218
Spice Cakes, (1900)	37

Spice Cake	100
Sponge Cake, (1856)	24
Sunshine Cake, (1916)	47
Three-Loaf Pound Cake	23
Today's Jelly Layer Cake	26
Unbeatable Gingerbread	99
Vanilla Strawberry Cheesecake	221
Washington Loaf Cake	25
Watergate Cake	126

PIES

All-Iowa Rhubarb Pie	166
Butterscotch Meringue Pie	168
Key Lime Pie	130
North 40 Berry Pie	136
Orange Crunch Pumpkin Pie	132
Peach Apricot Blueberry Pie	171
Pillsbury Rustic S'more Pie	223
Rhubarb Cream Pie	134
Senator Bob Dole's Double Chocolate Cream Pie	172
Stone Fruit Pie	169
Strawberry Rhubarb Pie	224

COOKIES

Best of Fair Molasses Cookies	178
Best of Fair Peanut Butter Cookies	177
Caramel Apple Cookies	226
Chocolate Chip Cookies	103
Classic Brownies	28
Coconut Cookies	77
Gingerbread Boys	176
Gingerbread House Dough	228
Gluten-Free Monster Cookies	227
Honey Chocolate and Peanut Butter Candy Bars	230
Iowa Potato Chip Cookies	172
Lemon Ice Box Cookies	76
Luck of the Irish Brownies	29
Orange Drop Cookies	138
Palmer House Brownies, (1893)	27
Party Animal Cookies	229
Pineapple Layer Bars	138

| Refrigerator Pyramid Cookies | 137 |
| World War II Victory Snaps | 102 |

CANDIES, SNACKS, AND DESSERTS
Cherry Crispy Rice Treats	232
Classic Vanilla Fudge	173
Divinity Cream Candies	51
Fruit Clouds	139
Fruity Tofu Energizer	173
Mocha Mousse	235
Modern Lemon Bread Pudding	27
Penuche	78
Plain Bread Pudding, (1893)	26
Reese's Peanut Butter Fudge	231

BUTTERS AND PRESERVES
Apricot Butter	32
Apricot Jam	104
Chow Chow, (1887)	33
Fruit Jelly and Plain Lemon Jelly, (1893)	31
Peach Butter	31
Rhubarb Jelly	32
Piccallili, (1899)	33
Violet Jelly	236

Introduction

BAKING BLUE RIBBONS
STORIES AND RECIPES FROM THE IOWA STATE FAIR FOOD COMPETITIONS

CELEBRATING IOWA'S GREATEST TREASURE IN FOOD

The Iowa State Fair has celebrated the best of Iowa since 1854. The first Exhibition of the Iowa State Agricultural Society took place on a 6-acre plot in Fairfield with a budget of about $320. The purpose was to educate farmers on the latest agricultural practices. According to reports of the day, upwards of 8,000 people came on foot, by horse and wagon, and by two-wheeled oxen carts. Organizers of that first gathering could not have known that this would be the most important event in Iowa's early history or that it would go on to become an internationally acclaimed exposition and one of the largest and best state fairs in America. They had no idea that their Fair would one day attract everyone from Iowa families to future Presidents of the United States, or that Iowa's most famous cow would be sculpted from 600 pounds of butter and displayed in a refrigerated room with glass walls.

Today the Fair remains the state's biggest single event. More than a million people from Iowa and around the world stream through the gates each August to be a part of the grand celebration. They come for corn dogs and concerts, stock shows, midway rides, and contests of every kind. For State Fair fans, this is the best 11 days of the year—a magical world where Iowa's past, present, and future come together. It would be impossible to pick the one best attraction from more than 160 years of Iowa State Fairs, but there is one thing that weaves them all together.

Food.

AMERICA'S #1 STATE FAIR FOOD DEPARTMENT

From agricultural production and preparation to celebrating the bounty of an Iowa harvest—growing, making, and eating food has been at the heart of the Fair since opening day in Fairfield.

There is no better way to celebrate Iowa's greatest culinary treasure than through the history, stories, and recipes of the Iowa State Fair Food Competitions. Today the Elwell Family Food Center is home to America's #1 state fair food department with thousands of entries each summer and prize money that has topped $75,000 annually.

In these pages we pay homage to Iowa's culinary traditions and the cooks and bakers who keep them alive, from pioneers who rose their bread on the tops of salt barrels in wagons to modern-day home cooks.

BEYOND BAKING

"Baking" embodies the steps that all cooks follow. In *Baking Blue Ribbons*, we reach beyond this to include stories and recipes of Iowa State Fair cooks in many food categories. A Fair food contestant gathers ingredients, follows a process, and presents a food exhibit that combines flavors with the contestant's unique flair.

Here you will find some of your favorite foods and new ones to try. You will meet winning cooks and learn the stories behind their recipes. You'll see the dedication of farmwives who won the first premiums for cakes and preserves in 1854 and those who saved butter and sugar rations and kept the contests going after two world wars. You will meet modern men who became Iowa's Cookout Kings and young chefs who have mastered everything from Bundt cakes to monster cookies. You'll learn from expert food judges who share tips and techniques.

MORE THAN A LIST OF INGREDIENTS

As every cook knows, a blue ribbon winner is more than a list of ingredients and step-by-step instructions. It begins with the hunt for that perfect recipe. Maybe it was handed down from your great-grandmother, or maybe you found it on your favorite baking blog and added your own spin. No matter how it came to be, there is an indescribable knowledge of all that went into its creation, something that a recipe card cannot capture by itself. It is an intangible element that comes from sharing the story behind the recipe and meeting the cook who brought it to life. It's a slice of pie, a moment in time, a brand-new creation, or one that has been made the same way for decades.

RECIPES BRIDGE GENERATIONS

In these pages we highlight vintage recipes next to modern-day winners, which show how recipes have changed and stayed the same.

The recipes of each era illustrate how the Iowa State Fair Food Competitions evolved. The 1800s and early 1900s emphasized food preservation with jellies, catsups, butters, and canned goods alongside a smaller number of breads, cakes, and candies. By the 1920s and 1930s, baking competitions included cookies, fancy cakes, and many more quick breads. It wasn't until the 1960s and '70s that food divisions like main dishes, appetizers, and salads became popular. In the 1980s and beyond, contest sponsors and culinary trends opened up a new world with food competitions and events, including healthy creations, and kid-favorites like the Ugly Cake contest, which are still going strong today. In the 2000s, the story continues with new divisions, contests, and events added every year.

It is amazing that the greatest culinary exhibition in the country began in the Pantry Department with $15 and a firkin of butter. We are glad that you have joined us on this journey through the Iowa State Fair culinary experience. We hope that these stories and recipes will inspire you to create blue ribbon winners of your own.

Kids' Ugly Cake Contest

xvii

1800s

FIRST FAIR TO THE CLOSING CENTURY EXPOSITION

RECIPES

BREADS
Boston Brown Bread, 1895, *Mrs. Angeline Turner* **19**
Boston Brown Bread, *Robin Tarbell-Thomas* **19**
Homemade Yeast, 1896, *Mrs. C. H. Atkins* **20**
Daily Bread, *Mrs. Don Taylor* **20**
Yeast-Rising Bread, 1870, "receipt" and tips **21**

MAIN DISHES
Salmon Croquettes, *Mary B. Hancock* **21**
Quail on Toast, *Mrs. Whiting S. Clark* **22**

CAKES & DESSERTS
Pound Cake, 1876, *Mrs. E.P. Chase* **23**
Three-Loaf Pound Cake, *Judy Kinney* **23**
Sponge Cake, 1856, Inspired by *Mrs. E. Andrews* **24**
Orange Sponge Cake, *Ruby Groen* **24**
Modern Washington Loaf Cake **25**
Jelly Cake, 1880s **25**
Today's Jelly Layer Cake **26**
Plain Bread Pudding, 1895, *Mrs. Angeline Turner* **26**
Modern Lemon Bread Pudding, *Mary J. Johnson* **27**
Palmer House Brownies, 1893, *Mrs. Bertha Palmer* **27**
Classic Brownies, *Cheryl Ashwill* **28**
Luck of the Irish Brownies, *Ann Gillotti* **29**
Closing Century Pineapple Cake, 1899 **30**
Pineapple Wow Cake, *Joy McFarland* **30**

BUTTERS & PRESERVES
Fruit Jelly and Plain Lemon Jelly, 1895, *Mrs. Jessie Young* **31**
Peach Butter, *Cindy Anderson* **31**
Apricot Butter, *Judy Arnold* **32**
Rhubarb Jelly, *Louise Piper* **32**
Piccalilli **33**
Chow Chow **33**

1854: THE FIRST FAIR

The first Iowa State Fair began on October 25, 1854, in Fairfield. The small town swelled to thousands for the three-day event. Tents sprang up along roads and in surrounding fields as farmers, families, and pioneers gathered. It wasn't the modest 6-acre plot or nearly $1,000 in cash prizes, known as premiums, that sparked such enthusiasm. This was Iowa's chance to educate farmers in the latest agricultural practices. There had never been a bigger opportunity to showcase the state as an emerging agricultural powerhouse. As one farmer put it, "Every live farmer who can possibly be present will be there."

The Fair opened with a stock show where the biggest boar and bull, the finest draft and carriage horses, and even the best pet hog received first-place premiums ranging from $3 to $15. The latest farm equipment dotted the grounds, and the coveted best state crop awards were announced. According to the *Fairfield Sentinel*, about 350 official premiums were given out. The officers of the newly formed Iowa State Agricultural Society (ISAS) reached into their own pockets to increase the purse in key agricultural contests. Society president, Judge T. W. Clagget of Lee County, donated the biggest prize of all for a surprise exhibition that left the crowd breathless, which we'll get to in a moment.

The first Fair didn't have corn dogs, concerts, or food on a stick, but inventions from the latest daguerreotype to a newly patented washing machine, collections of preserved birds and snakes, and the latest in artificial teeth drew curious crowds to Industrial Hall.

As one farmer put it, "Every live farmer who can possibly be present will be there."

An artist's sketch of the first Iowa State Fair at Fairfield (1854)

4 BAKING BLUE RIBBONS

1800s baking at Living History Farms.

LADIES OF THE FAIR

The men won most of the premiums on the first day, but on day two the ladies transformed the Industrial Hall for the Household and Manufactured Goods exhibition. This included the first food department, known as the Pantry Division. As a reporter from the *Muscatine Tri-Weekly Journal* described it, long rows of quilts and coverlets, embroidered shawls, paintings, ornamental boxes and frames for needlework, and other fine crafts attracted much admiration. Amidst the imposing array of the beautiful and fanciful, the more substantial exhibits of the Pantry Division were numerous. Loaves of bread; cake; jars of preserves, jellies and pickles; rolls of butter, white and yellow; along with boiled hams and cheeses varying in diameter from 6 inches to 3 feet crowded the tables. The largest cheese, weighing approximately 400 pounds, was presented to the Honorable J.W. Grimes, Iowa's Governor-elect.

THE FIRST BEST CAKES

According to the *Burlington Tri-Weekly Journal*, the Pantry Division awarded a total of $15. Mrs. C. Baldwin earned the first $1 premium for the best pound cake, Mrs. E. Andrews for sponge cake, and Mrs. L. F. Boerstler won $2 for butter in the dairy class, along with $1 each for tomato preserves, jelly, and apple and peach butters.

A dollar may not seem like much incentive to bake a cake and transport it by horse and buggy halfway across the state. For these pioneering women and those who would follow, the joy of leaving chores behind, socializing for several days, and exhibiting at the very first Iowa State Fair was the best prize of all. And the ladies were just getting started.

OUT OF THE PANTRY AND INTO THE SADDLE:
THE GREATEST EVENT OF THE FAIR

On the second day, Fairgoers gathered at the makeshift track for an event that elevated the 1854 Iowa State Fair from an ag exhibition to entertainment with universal appeal. There was no budget for horse racing—and certainly not for a ladies' event. To everyone's surprise, Judge Clagget offered his gold watch to the boldest and most graceful equestrienne in the most memorable competition of the Fair.

As the story goes, 10 ladies competed. Most of them rode well-trained horses, but Miss Eliza Jane Hodges of Iowa City stole the show on a borrowed stallion. The others rode without incident, but Miss Hodges fought to keep her horse under control when it cleared a ravine that cut through part of the track. Onlookers cheered as she held the reins steady and sped around the course, but the judges awarded the gold watch to a more "graceful" rider. The crowd was not pleased.

Men sprang up across the field. Within minutes nearly $200 was collected for "the poor and unlettered child," along with a scholarship for three terms at the Female Seminary at Fairfield and one term at Mount Pleasant, according to the *Muscatine Tri-Weekly Journal*. President Clagget awarded the other ladies gold rings.

The prizes for this unofficial ladies' event far surpassed any of the men's contests and set the bar for future State Fair entertainment. The competition was so popular they staged it again the following day. Newspapers as far away as Montgomery, Alabama, featured the story. At the 1954 centennial, it was regaled as the most memorable event of the first Fair.

Today, the spirit of Miss Eliza Jane Hodges and the trailblazing women and men of the inaugural Iowa State Fair live on as a recipe for success.

The 1854 equestriennes inspired future female riders, like Miss Lucille Mulhall, who performed at the Iowa State Fair in the early 1900s. – Sioux City Journal, September 25, 1915.

BAKING BLUE RIBBONS

Farmers worked hard in preparation for the Fair.

1850s–1870s: IOWA'S TRAVELING SHOW

After the equestriennes stole the show in 1854, the Iowa State Fair remained in Fairfield for another year. Starting in 1856, it moved every two or three years among towns in the eastern half of the state before it landed on the west side of Des Moines in 1879 in an area known as Brown's Park, between 38th and 42nd streets. It moved to the city's east side in 1886, where it remains today.

During that time the Pantry Division gradually expanded with some ups and downs. In 1855, premiums doubled from $1 for a few cakes to $2 for first place and $1 for second in contests that included fruit jelly, sponge and pound cakes, along with several types of breads, many preserves, the best keg of butter, and water crackers.

Weather was a big factor in the Fair's early success. A heavy rain and muddy roads made traveling in wagons and on horseback difficult. Occasionally the event was closed early or extended an extra day to make up for lost attendance.

1854–1879: IOWA STATE FAIR HOST TOWNS

1854–1855: Fairfield

1856–1857: Muscatine

1858–1859: Oskaloosa

1860–1861: Iowa City

1862–1863: Dubuque

1864–1866: Burlington

1867–1868: Clinton

1869–1870: Keokuk

1871–1873: Cedar Rapids

1874–1875: Keokuk

1876–1878: Cedar Rapids

1879–1885: Des Moines, Brown's Park

1886–Today: Des Moines, 3000 E. Grand

FROM ONE PANTRY TO TWO

Muscatine hosted the fourth Fair in 1857, formally known as the Assembly of the State Agricultural Society. Food entries were divided into two classes: Pantry #1 included the best five rolls of butter, cheese, barrel of flour, salt-rising bread, and yeast bread. Pantry #2 featured preserves, jellies, pickles, catsup, butters, jams, sorghum syrup, airtight peaches, and honey. In 1858 and 1859 Oskaloosa hosted the event with a dedicated Household Arts building for pantry items and a variety of locally produced flours and grains.

Back then, women brought just about anything from their kitchens to be judged, even if no premium was awarded. The committee, made up mostly of men, often gave certificates for exhibits that looked like winners. Sampling the food didn't happen until much later. As one judge said in 1859, "There were 180 entries and nobody could scarcely try to taste, judge, and compare so many things."

1860s: YOUTH EXHIBITORS AND THE CIVIL WAR

In 1861, the Pantry Department attracted young ladies by offering a whopping $8 premium for the best loaf of yeast-rising bread accompanied by a pound of butter made by a girl under the age of 14. Bread and butter seem basic today, but in the 1800s, farmwives and daughters scheduled their days around cooking and baking. They made their own yeast before baking their daily bread, not to mention milking cows, collecting eggs, and churning fresh cream into butter. The idea of special premiums for youth exhibitors soon developed into a separate girls' department.

In 1862, during the Civil War, Iowa held one of the few state fairs in the "Northwest." Bad weather and war hurt attendance and receipts. Exhibitors voted to accept half of their premiums, and for the first time they had to pay an extra fee on all entries that were judged.

Dubuque hosted the tenth anniversary Fair in 1863. The Pantry Department had four cake contests and 29 different preserves competitions, each receiving $2 for first place. Total premiums had grown to nearly $200 for the department.

Bread and butter seem basic today, but in the 1800s, farmwives and daughters scheduled their days around cooking and baking.

Preserves have been a major contest since the first Iowa State Fair.

1870s AND 1880s: SUPER EXHIBITORS

In 1873, the Iowa State Fair celebrated its 20th anniversary in Cedar Rapids. By then the Dairy, Pantry, and Kitchen Department offered a combined $634 in premiums. Fancy cakes became its own separate class with nine contests and over $30 in prizes. Delicate cakes, coconut (also known as cocoanut), and a basket of fancy cakes were added to the new baking class.

During the 1880s, more women entered and won an unusually large number of pantry contests. "Super Exhibitors" like Mrs. L. Knapp of Cedar Falls and Miss Cellie Keene from Illinois took home nearly every prize for butters, jams, pickles, jellies, and preserves, each winning more than 40 premiums in 1883. Mrs. Knapp's walnut and cucumber catsups also earned first place. She perfected her piccalilli and chow chow relish so that nothing in her kitchen garden went to waste.

Mrs. Knapp and Miss Keene earned about $66 each, well over $1,000 today. Since the jars were not opened for judging, they took their winners home to enjoy on a cold winter's night—with sweet memories of a profitable trip to the Fair.

1885: MRS. KELLYER'S CAKES

On September 3, 1885, another Super Exhibitor, Mrs. R. Kellyer, was up late in her Des Moines kitchen putting the finishing touches on 21 cakes and cookies for the State Fair. She baked some of the heartier recipes the day before, like fruit cake and mountain cake, which kept well in tins and flour sack towels. Others, like her finely decorated Best State Fair Cake and jelly cake with homemade raspberry preserves, would be finished in the morning and loaded onto a wagon or two and driven to the Fairgrounds. Perhaps she opted to take a trolley car with friends and loaded baskets.

However she did it, preparing nearly two dozen cakes in 1885 with a wooden spoon, rotary egg beater, and a wood-burning stove is an impressive feat. Imagine collecting roughly 8 dozen eggs, churning 15 pounds of butter, and creaming it with at least 29 cups of sugar to come up with that many cakes, plus decorations and frosting whipped with sugar and egg whites—on top of making the best basket of State Fair cookies.

Mrs. Kellyer must have won a prize for every cake and cookie she entered. The Iowa State Fair opened on September 4 with 22 cake contests. Coconut was the only one in which she did not win a premium. In total, the 1885 baking champion won 16 first prizes and five second-place awards.

Our hats off to Mrs. Kellyer and the pioneering women who baked the cakes and breads, preserved the foods, and built the foundation of the Iowa State Fair Food Department.

A BAKER'S DOZEN

TIPS FOR BLUE RIBBON CAKES IN THE 1800s

1. Do not attempt to make cake without having complete control of the fire.

2. Never add fuel to the stove while your cake is baking.

3. Line baking tins with buttered paper.

4. Slow, even heat for rich cakes, quick heat for plain.

5. Whenever you buy a broom, break off a few of the splints; tie them up and lay them away safely to use as cake testers. It is not pleasant to think of using a splint from a broom that has been used in sweeping a kitchen floor, or any other floor, no matter how nicely kept.

6. Do not allow the oven to cool while the cake is in it, or it will certainly be heavy.

7. Cake made with molasses burns more easily than any other.

8. Thin cakes should bake from 15 to 20 minutes, thicker loaves from 30 to 40 minutes, very thick cake 1 hour, and fruit cake requires 2 to 3 hours.

9. Bake thick cakes in an oven in which you can hold your hand to a count of 25 and not a moment longer.

10. If a cake rises in the middle, stays up, and cracks open, it is mixed too stiff.

11. When "new process" flour is used, take one-eighth less than any recipe calls for.

12. Cakes stay fresh longer when kept in their original baking pan; but if it is necessary to remove it, place it on the top of a sieve until quite cold. Frost if desired and store in a large stone pot or cake safe covered with clean linen.

13. Steam stale cake and serve with a nice hot sauce, and you have a very good pudding.

—"Daughters of America," The Daily Times, (Davenport), September 6, 1888.
The Courier, (Waterloo), July 7, 1870.

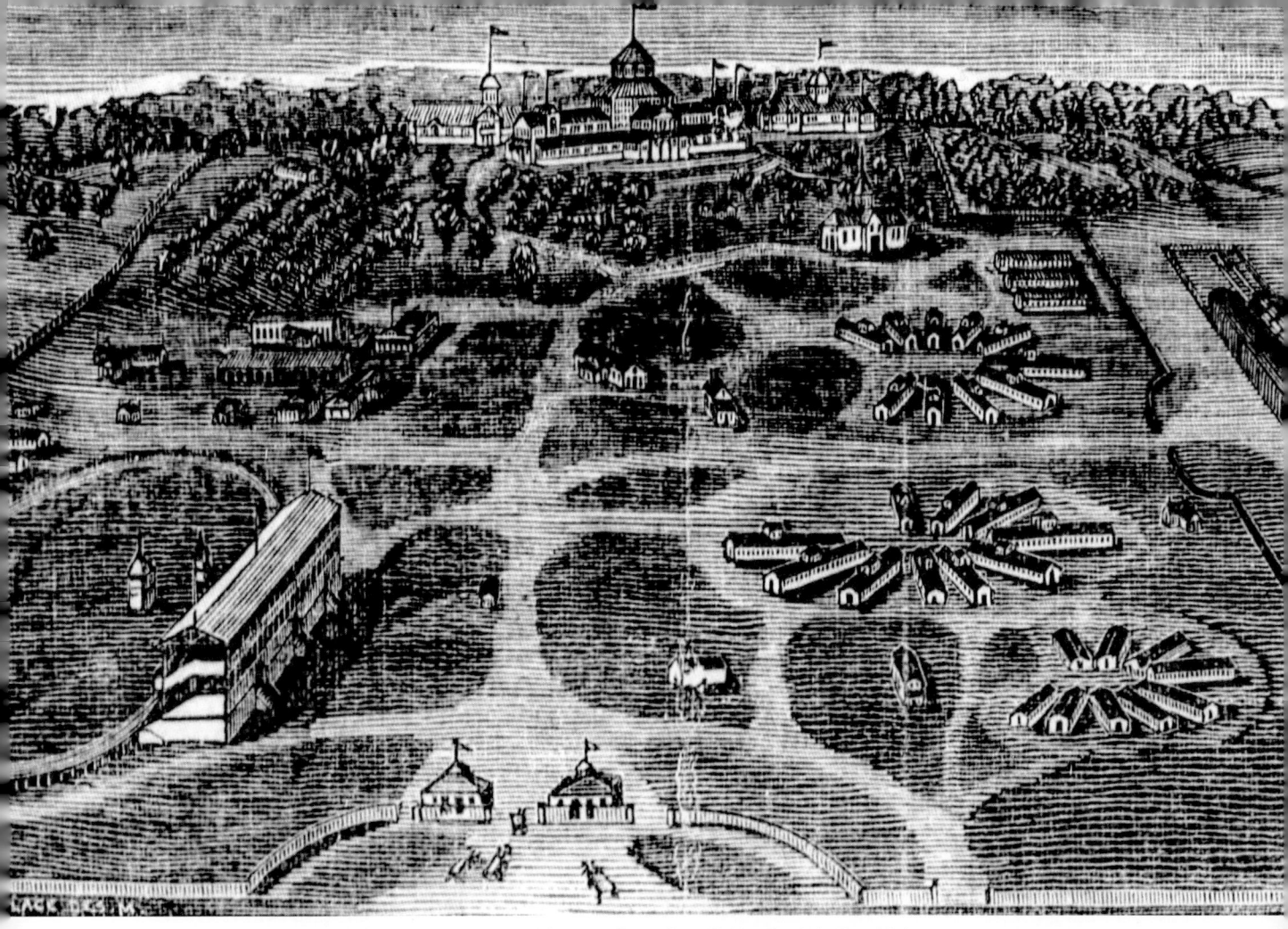

1886: Aerial drawing of the new Iowa State Fairgrounds in Des Moines.

1886: PERMANENT FAIR-GROUNDS

In 1886, Fairgoers in Des Moines hopped on streetcars and headed to the grand opening of the Iowa State Fairgrounds on the east side of the city. Booths, buildings, and tents with colorful banners covered the acreage where a farm had stood a few months before.

Reporters gushed over the grand landscape and the main Exposition Hall illuminated with 4,000 ground-glass lights. Chariot races and speed trials were held each afternoon. Despite a few days with rain, attendance was strong. Neighboring states, like Illinois, soon made plans for their own permanent fairgrounds to compete with Iowa's fabulous 266-acre State Fairgrounds.

1880s Iowa State Fair party.

RISE OF STATE FAIR FOOD SPONSORS

The 1886 Pantry and Kitchen Department offered premiums worth $790 and prizes from outside companies.

The late 1800s gave rise to the battle of the baking powders and the beginning of food contest sponsorships. Baking powder had been around since the 1850s, but competition became fierce as more brands entered the market. Andrews' Pearl Baking Powder was one of the earliest food contest sponsors.

Pantry and Kitchen premiums ranged from $1 to $3, but the 1886 Andrews' cake contest offered a purse worth more than $200. Awards for a single cake ranged from $35 for the best overall State Fair cake to two prizes of $30 each for first place, two $25 awards for second, and cash premiums all the way to sixth place. The company also appealed to Iowans' sense of charity with State Fair cake auctions that drew large crowds and raised money for children in Des Moines.

First-place ribbons were red, second-place ribbons were white, and third-place ribbons were blue when the Iowa State Fair began.

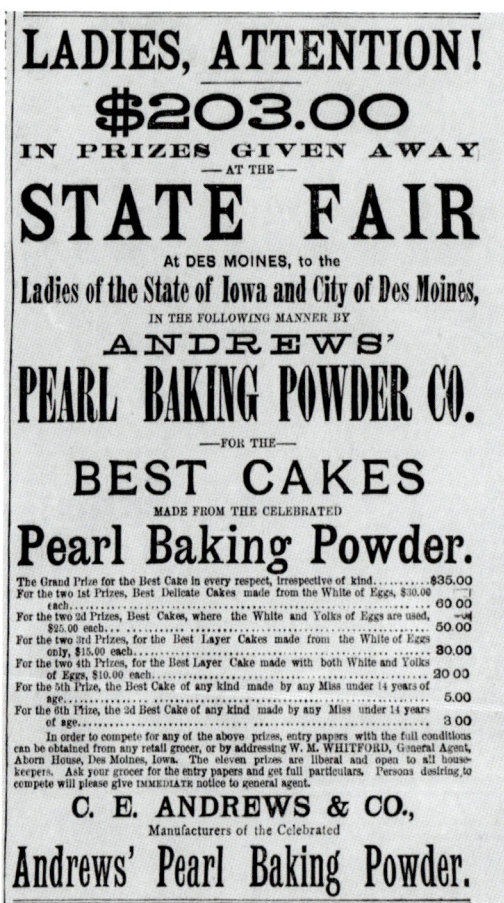

Andrews' Pearl Baking Powder was one of the earliest and most generous Food Department sponsors. Their cake prizes of $203 in 1886 would be worth about $6,000 today—a rich purse in any era.
©The Des Moines Register – USA TODAY NETWORK, 1886.

According to the *Sioux City Journal*, more than 300 cakes were entered in the 1886 Andrews' special premium contest.

Baking champion Mrs. R. Kellyer became an early spokesperson for Andrews' Pearl Baking Powder when the company discovered that all of her prize-winning cakes were made with their product. Print ads proclaimed that "The cake display was one of the leading attractions of the Fair, and a splendid testimonial to the excellent qualities of the incomparable Pearl by the thousands that thronged the halls during the Fair." (*Sioux City Journal*. March 8, 1887)

Andrews' sponsorships opened the door for brands like Royal Company Flour in the 1890s and Crisco Shortening, Omar Wonder Flour, and others in the early 1900s.

While Andrews wooed customers with generosity, Climax Baking Powder raised cakes—and eyebrows—with a different advertising strategy leading up to the 1891 State Fair. *(right)*

Quad-City Times, September 15, 1891.

What could be better than winning a blue ribbon at the Fair? How about one hundred dollars in gold?

In the 1890s, more food sponsors, like R. T. Davis Royal No. 10 Flour, competed to win customers at the Iowa State Fair. Back then there were several small flour companies in the Midwest and no better place to get the attention of homemakers than the Pantry and Kitchen Department.
—The Daily Iowa Capitol, August 30, 1892.

THE 1800s   13

THE UPS AND DOWNS OF THE 1890s

The 1890 Iowa State Fair brought the largest crowd yet with 50,000 attendees and the first electric lights at the Fairgrounds. Unfortunately, this bright start to the new decade did not last for Iowa or the country.

IOWA AT THE 1893 WORLD'S FAIR

By 1893, the declining U.S. economy had turned into the worst financial crisis to date. Farm prices plummeted and economic unrest added to the bleak outlook in the Midwest and the nation. This and competition from the 1893 World's Columbian Exposition in Chicago sent the Iowa State Fair into crippling debt. Many of the state's biggest farm operations took their ag exhibits to Chicago instead of Des Moines. It took years for the State Fair to recover, but with the bad news came a silver lining.

Iowans who made the trek to Chicago could not have been prouder. The Hawkeye State earned awards in agriculture to education on the world stage. The Iowa Building looked like a Midwestern palace with flags and streamers flying from numerous turrets. According to a later report by Iowa historian Bruce E. Mahan, every surface of the hall except the floor was covered in corn and grains that depicted the state's resources and prosperity in mosaic patterns. "The sheer beauty of Iowa's exhibition hall never failed to elicit praise from the thousands of visitors who came to see what Iowa had to offer," Mahan wrote.

Beyond the Iowa State Building, visitors admired the main Court of Honor, which became known as the White City. Inventions, including the Ferris wheel, moving sidewalks, and myriad new uses for electricity, along with automatic dishwashers and zippers were launched at the 1893 World's Columbian Exposition.

TOP: Iowa State Building entrance at the 1893 World's Columbian Exposition in Chicago

BOTTOM: Exhibition hall of the Iowa State Building, 1893 World's Columbian Exposition in Chicago

The 1893 Chicago World's Fair introduced an early version of brownies for Fairgoers' picnic baskets. The "White City" set an unparalleled standard for future fairs. Iowa State Building pictured.

THE BIRTH OF THE BROWNIE

From a culinary standpoint, Fairgoers got their first taste of all-American foods such as hamburgers, hot dogs, and Cracker Jack. For chocolate lovers, the best souvenir was a dense, fudgy treat that became known as the brownie. Bertha Palmer, of Chicago's Palmer House Hotel, had an idea for a small dessert to add to ladies' picnics. Her pastry chef developed a recipe for thick chocolaty cookies that were baked in a shallow tin and cut into squares. Many variations have emerged, but the basic recipe remains largely unchanged. Through the generations, brownies have claimed a permanent spot on State Fair premium lists nationwide.

IOWA RECIPES FOR THE HOME QUEEN

In addition to brownies, Bertha Palmer and the Board of Lady Managers of the Chicago World's Fair collected more than 2,000 recipes from across the United States in *The Home Queen, World's Fair Souvenir Cook Book.* Leading Iowa ladies, including Mrs. Whiting S. Clark, Mrs. Jessie Young, and Mrs. Angeline Turner from Des Moines, and Miss Mary B. Hancock of Dubuque contributed recipes such as Boston Brown bread, Quail on Toast, Plain Bread Pudding, and Salmon Croquettes.

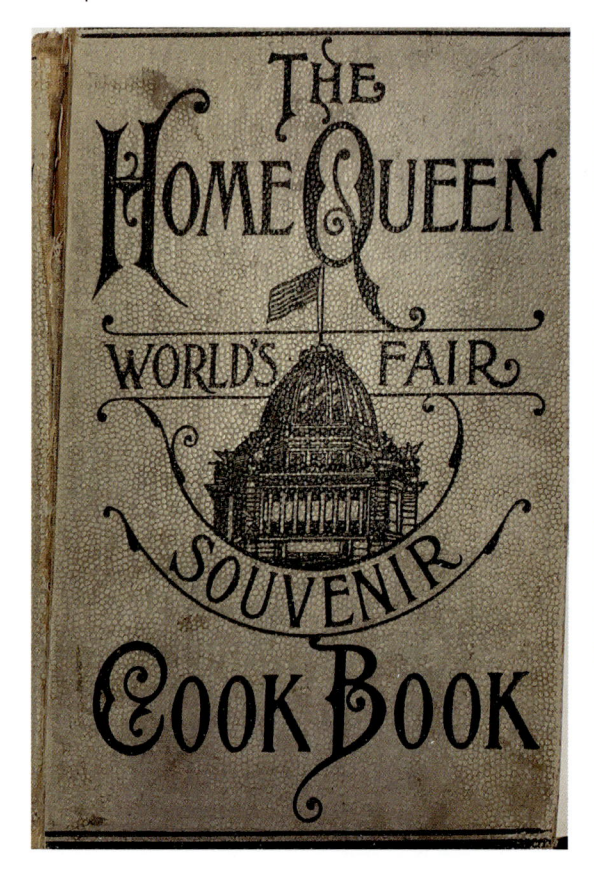

Mrs. Potter (Bertha) Palmer, President of the Board of Lady Managers of the Chicago World's Fair, collected over 2,000 recipes from across America for The Home Queen, World's Fair Souvenir Cook Book. *1895, Boston Book Company.*

Mrs. Whiting S. Clark

Miss Mary B. Hancock

BAKING BLUE RIBBONS

SAVING THE FAIR

After the 1893 World's Columbian Exposition, the Iowa State Fair spent the rest of the decade trying to break even. In 1896, Iowa painted its buildings white to create its own Great White City, but nothing compared to the grandeur of Chicago. The Iowa State Fair went deeper into debt. Many state and county fair organizers wondered if old-fashioned agricultural fairs would survive.

In 1898, the Iowa State Fair was canceled during the Spanish-American War and due to competition from the Trans Mississippi and International Exposition in Omaha. Something big had to happen in 1899, or the "Best Fair in the Northwest" would end before the new century began.

In 1896, exhibitors tickets were sold in addition to regular admission. An extra 10% was also deducted from cash premiums to save money.

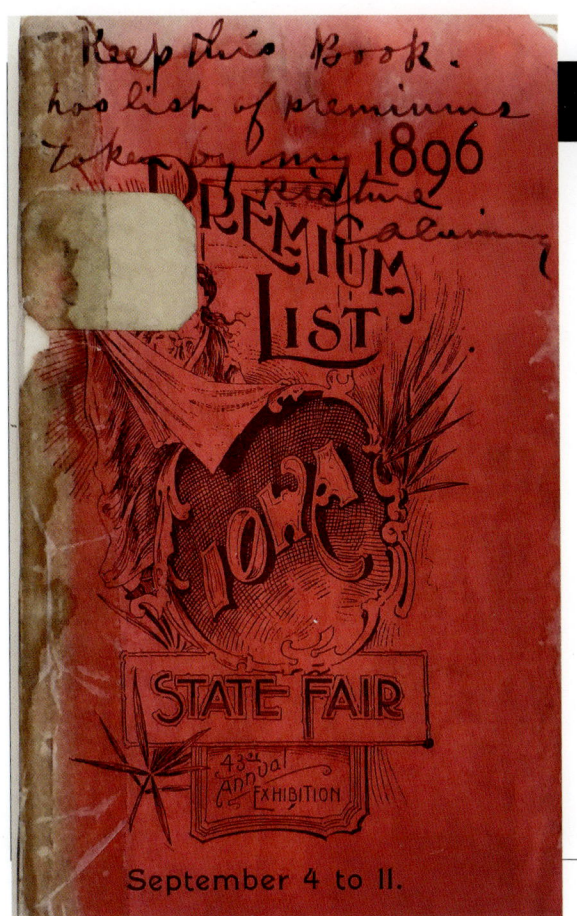

Premium List Cakes Only

By 1897, housewives could no longer enter whatever cake or bread they pleased. Pantry and Kitchen superintendent A. L. Plummer announced that every entry would be classified; and cards had to be attached for specific classes. To this he added an encouraging quote:

> "A good cook is one of nature's noblest works. Bring some of the good things along and enter the lists for some premiums."

—A. L. Plummer, 1897 Pantry & Kitchen Superintendent.

THE 1800s

1899: THE CLOSING CENTURY EXPOSITION

In a last-ditch effort to boost the Fair, the Iowa State Agricultural Society turned the event into "The Closing Century Exposition of 1899—a celebration of Iowa that could not be missed!" This turned out to be a brilliant and inexpensive theme. Iowans gathered in Des Moines to mark the progress of the state's first 50 years and looked to the future with a renewed sense of optimism. Even the weather cooperated.

The 1899 exposition had record-breaking attendance and receipts that took the Fair from $25,000 in debt to a surplus of at least $10,000. Everyone agreed that the quality and quantity of exhibits, the speed contests, stock shows, entertainment, and virtually every aspect of the event had never been better.

In the Pantry and Kitchen Department, the winning pineapple cake captured the sunny mood of the exposition. The recipe from the summer of 1899 was ahead of its time and gave way to myriad pineapple confections that are Fair favorites today.

1800s
RECIPES FROM THEN AND NOW

Breads

BOSTON BROWN BREAD, 1895

Boston Brown Bread from Mrs. Angeline Turner in *The Home Queen, World Columbian Exposition Souvenir Cook Book of 1895* is followed by a modern version from the Iowa State Fair "Blue Ribbon Queen," Robin Tarbell-Thomas, which took first place in 1985.

> **Boston Brown Bread.**
> One cup Graham flour, 1 cup wheat flour, 1 cup rye flour, 1 cup corn meal, 1 cup molasses, 3 cups sweet milk, 1 teaspoon saleratus, 2 eggs, a little salt; steam 3 hours; lastly set in the oven a few minutes to dry off.
>
> *Mrs. Angeline Turner, Des Moines, Iowa.*

BOSTON BROWN BREAD

1 cup white flour
1 teaspoon baking powder
1 teaspoon baking soda
1 teaspoon salt
1 cup yellow cornmeal
1 cup whole wheat flour
¾ cup molasses
2 cups buttermilk
1 cup raisins

Sift white flour, baking powder, baking soda, and salt. Stir in cornmeal and whole wheat flour. Add remaining ingredients; beat well. Divide batter among 4 greased and floured 1-pound food cans. Cover tightly with foil. Place on rack in a deep kettle. Pour in boiling water to 1-inch depth. Cover kettle; steam 3 hours, adding more boiling water if needed. Preheat oven to 450°F. Carefully remove cans from kettle. Remove foil from cans. Bake 5 minutes. Remove bread from cans. Makes 4 loaves.

Robin Tarbell, Centerville
First Place, Quick Bread Other Than Named
1985 Quick Breads Contest Reserve Sweepstakes Winner

HOMEMADE YEAST

Today we are lucky to have instant yeast in premeasured packets. In the 1800s, women made it from scratch and stored it in jugs. The yeast that is added to this recipe would likely have been made from "feeding" a bowl of water, flour, and wild yeast additional water, flour, and sugar each day, like a yeast starter.

AN UNFAILING YEAST.

MRS. C. H. ATKINS.

Put a handful of hops into a bag and drop it into two quarts of boiling water; while steeping, wash, peel and grate six medium sized potatoes; take out the hops, put in the potatoes and boil a few minutes, stirring continually; add a half tea-cup of white or light brown sugar, the same of salt. When cool, stir in a tea-cup of yeast; let it rise till it becomes a mass of foam, then stir down and jug it tight.

"76." A Cook Book. Edited by the Ladies of Plymouth Church, *Des Moines, Iowa. Mills & Company Printers and Publishers, 1876.*

DAILY BREAD

White bread is one of the maiden baking contests that has been entered at every Iowa State Fair. Mrs. Don Taylor of Creston won the coveted contest in 1960 with this generous recipe that makes four loaves, plenty to give and put in the freezer. Along with her recipe, she shared two bread-baking tips that are different from what Mrs. Kellyer would have advised.

1) To quicken the rising process, Mrs. Taylor placed her bread on an electric heating pad, set on warm—a great solution for a cold kitchen counter. 2) She also recommended adding a teaspoon of sugar to any yeast mixture for quicker proofing action.

½ cup warm water
2 packages dry yeast
3½ cups warm milk (or water)
¼ cup sugar
2 tablespoons salt
¼ cup shortening
11 or 12 cups sifted flour

Soak yeast in ½ cup warm water for about 5 minutes. Combine liquid, sugar, salt, and shortening. Beat in yeast mixture with 4 cups flour until smooth. Add remaining flour until dough leaves the sides of the bowl. Turn out on a lightly floured board. Knead until dough becomes smooth and elastic and isn't sticky. Place in a bowl, grease top of dough, and cover with cloth. Let rise in a warm place (80–85°F) until double in bulk, at least an hour. Punch down and let rise again until nearly double. Divide into 4 parts and shape each into a loaf. Place each in a 9x5-inch loaf pan. Cover and let rise again in a warm place until the dough reaches the top of the pans. Preheat oven to 400°F while dough rises. Bake for 15 minutes, then reduce heat to 375°F and bake for another ½ hour. Makes 4 loaves.

Mrs. Don Taylor, Creston
First Place, 1960 Iowa State Fair White Bread

YEAST-RISING BREAD AND TIPS

In the 1800s, recipes or "receipts" were more like baking suggestions, like this "helpful" advice in *The Courier* from 1870.

> BREAD MAKING.—A lady writes to the *Country Gentleman*: I should like to have all lovers of good bread try my mode of making. For three loaves, I put two quarts of flour in a pan, and pour boiling water on it, stirring it briskly until it is as thick as hasty pudding; let it stand and cool until it is lukewarm, add yeast and salt, knead thoroughly and set to rise. When very light, knead over and put in pans to rise; when well risen, bake. I think this will be pronounced superior to any other method.

Main Dishes

Main dish cooking contests did not happen at the Iowa State Fair until the 1960s. A few Iowa ladies were ahead of their time with recipes, like these, that made it into *The Home Queen, World's Columbian Exposition Souvenir Cook Book*, published in 1895. Recipes were collected from across the country to celebrate the 1893 World's Fair in Chicago.

SALMON CROQUETTES

Salmon Croquettes.

Cover the contents of a can of salmon with vinegar, and let it stand in an earthen dish 2 hours. At the end of this time, drain off the vinegar and mince the salmon very fine. For 1 large cup minced salmon work in a table-spoon melted butter, 1 egg beaten, and a tea-spoon lemon juice and anchovy sauce. Put these ingredients in a sauce pan over a slow fire, and stir in ½ cup sifted bread crumbs, salt, pepper, a little nutmeg, and a gill of cream. Shape into croquettes; egg and bread crumb them, and fry in hot lard.

Mary B. Hancock
Alternate Lady Manager
World's Fair,
Dubuque, Iowa.

We modified Mary Hancock's original recipe by using 15 oz. of canned salmon and skipped the vinegar step. We added a generous ½ cup of diced sweet red pepper and swapped the anchovy sauce for ⅓ cup mayonnaise. Fry in a cast-iron skillet in hot butter and serve with salad for a light dinner any night of the week. Thank you, Mrs. Hancock.

QUAIL ON TOAST

Iowa Lady Managers of the 1893 World's Columbian Exposition were high-society women, like Mrs. Whiting S. Clark of Des Moines, who contributed this recipe for Quail on Toast to *The Home Queen, World's Columbian Exposition Souvenir Cook Book*. While this dish may have been trendy in big-city eateries in the late 1800s, the preparation was down-home Iowa.

Quail on Toast.

Wash the birds and wipe dry; split them down the back and broil over bright coals till done and browned lightly, turning often to prevent charring; season with butter, pepper and salt; lay on slices of buttered toast and serve immediately.

Mrs. Whiting S. Clark
Lady Manager World's Fair,
Des Moines, Iowa.

Cakes & Desserts

BEST OF FAIR POUND CAKES

Pound cake ingredients have not changed much since the 1800s, but instructions have come a long way. Here is an example of a recipe that first-place winner Mrs. Baldwin might have used in 1854, followed by an updated version from 1986 State Fair champ Judy Kinney.

1876 POUND CAKE

One pound of butter, one pound of sugar, one pound of flour,
Nine eggs leaving out two yolks, grated peel of one lemon.

Beat the whites to a stiff froth. Beat the butter to a cream. Add the sugar and the yolks and beat until very light. Then add the flour and egg whites, alternately. Bake in a moderate oven.

Mrs. E.P. Chase

"76." A Cook Book. Edited by the Ladies of Plymouth Church, *Des Moines, Iowa. Mills & Company Printers and Publishers, 1876.*

THREE-LOAF POUND CAKE

2 cups butter
3 cups sugar
6 eggs
4 cups flour, sifted
1 teaspoon baking powder
1 cup milk
2 teaspoons vanilla

Preheat oven to 300°F. Butter, eggs, and milk should be at room temperature. Sift flour and baking powder together. In a large mixer bowl cream butter until very light and fluffy. Gradually add sugar, beating constantly. Add eggs, one at a time, beating well after each addition. Combine milk and vanilla. Add flour mixture alternately with milk, beating well after each addition. Pour batter into 3 greased 9x5x3-inch loaf pans. Bake for approximately 90 minutes. Cool in pan 10 minutes. Remove from pan. Cool on wire rack. Makes 3 loaves.

Judy Kinney, Knoxville
First Place, 1986 Cakes, Pound
Mid-America Farms/Prize of Iowa Butter Award
Best Pound Cake of Fair

SPONGE CAKES THEN AND NOW

Mrs. E. Andrews, the first Iowa State Fair sponge cake winner, knew how to bake her cake without instructions, as in this 1856 recipe from the *Quasqueton Guardian*.

1856 SPONGE CAKE

> SPONGE CAKE.—Six eggs—beat the whites alone, the yolks with a cup and half of powdered sugar; rub a teaspoonful of cream tartar in a pint of flower; dissolve half a tea-spoonful of soda in a tablespoonful of water; season with essence of lemon.

ORANGE SPONGE CAKE

Super Exhibitor Ruby Groen of Spencer won many food contests, including the State Fair cake sweepstakes during the 1970s and 1980s. She became the head of her county fair's culinary division in 1979 and won at the state level with this fresh citrusy take on sponge cake in 1988.

9 egg yolks
½ cup cold water
¼ cup orange juice
1 tablespoon grated orange peel
2¼ cups sugar
1 teaspoon vanilla extract
½ teaspoon lemon extract
½ teaspoon orange extract
2¼ cups cake flour
½ teaspoon salt
9 egg whites
1½ teaspoons cream of tartar

This beautiful unadorned cake is the way Ruby Groen made hers. Our State Fair champion cake tester, Ann Gillotti, recommends adding thin orange slices or a light frosting drizzle if you plan to enter it in the Fair.

Preheat oven to 325°F. Beat egg yolks until thick; add water, juice, and peel and continue beating until very thick. Gradually beat in sugar and extracts. Fold in flour sifted with salt. Beat egg whites until foamy; add cream of tartar and beat until moist, glossy peaks form. Fold whites into egg yolk mixture. Pour into ungreased 10-inch tube pan. Bake 60 minutes or until done. Invert pan over long-necked bottle and cool. Makes 12–16 servings.

Ruby Groen, Spencer
First Place, 1988 Cakes, Sponge

BAKING BLUE RIBBONS

MODERN WASHINGTON LOAF CAKE

Washington Cake was a popular contest in the late 1800s with Super Exhibitors like Mrs. R. Kellyer. A cousin of pound cake, the Washington version features warm spices and dried fruits for a moist dessert that stands on its own. Here is a modern take that would make Mrs. Kellyer proud.

1½ cups flour
1 teaspoon baking powder
1 teaspoon cinnamon
½ teaspoon cloves
½ teaspoon nutmeg
½ teaspoon salt
1 cup butter, softened
½ cup sugar
½ cup brown sugar, packed
4 eggs
¼ cup heavy whipping cream
3 tablespoons brandy or orange juice
2 teaspoons vanilla extract
2 cups of your favorite dried fruits in any combination, such as raisins, currants, cranberries, or chopped apricots.

Preheat oven to 325°F. Grease a 9x5-inch loaf pan and line with greased parchment. Sift the flour, baking powder, salt, and spices together. Beat the butter in a large bowl until smooth.

Slowly add the sugars and beat until light and fluffy. Add the eggs, one at a time, and beat well for about 1 minute after each addition. Add the cream, brandy, and vanilla. Gently fold in the flour mixture in three or four additions until no streaks of flour remain. Stir in the dried fruits.

Pour into prepared pan and bake for about 75 minutes or until a toothpick inserted near the center comes out clean. Allow to cool for 5–10 minutes, then turn out onto a wire rack to cool completely. Makes 1 loaf or approximately 12 slices.

Washington Cake adapted from 1800s- and 2000s-era recipes.

1880s JELLY CAKE

This 1880s version makes two 3-layer cakes filled with fruit preserves and sprinkled with powdered sugar before loading into the wagon.

The Courier, Waterloo, Iowa. May 19, 1880

> —Jelly Cake.—One and one-half cups of sugar, one-half cup of butter, one-half cup of milk, two and one-half cups of flour, three eggs, well beaten, two teaspoonfuls of cream of tartar and one teaspoonful of soda. Cook in pans bought for the purpose, using six. When done, turn out on a cloth to cool. Now take your jelly, and with a knife stir it up and spread it on your cake the thickness you desire, not putting it on the top of them. This will make two cakes of three layers.

TODAY'S JELLY LAYER CAKE

1 cup butter, softened
1¾ cups sugar
4 eggs
2½ cups self-rising flour
1 cup milk
1 teaspoon vanilla extract
1 small jar of your favorite seedless fruit jelly
Powdered sugar for dusting
Fresh fruit for garnish

Preheat oven to 350°F. Grease three 9-inch round cake pans and line bottoms with parchment paper. Beat butter and sugar together until creamy and light. Add eggs one at a time, mixing between each addition. In a separate bowl combine milk and vanilla. Add the milk mixture alternately with the flour, mixing after each addition. Pour batter into prepared pans and bake for approximately 20 minutes or until cakes are golden brown and a toothpick inserted near center comes out clean. Allow to rest for several minutes, then turn cakes out onto wire rack. Cool completely before spreading fruit jam between each layer and dusting the top with powdered sugar. Garnish with fresh fruit if desired. Makes approximately 14-16 servings.

Jelly Layer Cake adapted from 1800s- and 2000s-era recipes.

PLAIN BREAD PUDDING

Kay's nana used to make the best bread pudding and never wasted a single crust of bread. This timeless comfort food is still delicious with just bread, milk, and a little nutmeg. Or add flavors with whatever you have on hand, from raisins to chocolate chips. It never goes out of style, like this base recipe from Mrs. Angeline Turner in the 1895 *Home Queen Cookbook*.

Plain Bread Pudding.

Upon a pint of broken pieces of bread pour a pint of scalded milk, with a piece of butter ½ size of an egg; cover and let stand until quite cool, then add 3 well-beaten eggs, a small cup sugar and nearly a pint of cold milk and a little nutmeg; bake ½ hour. This is nice with pudding sauce.

Mrs. Angeline Turner, Des Moines, Iowa.

MODERN LEMON BREAD PUDDING

Angeline Turner's bread pudding gets a citrusy makeover in this 2002 winner, which was one of the most creative twists on the old classic that we found. We often think of bread pudding as a winter treat, but with a hint of coconut and a lemony sauce, it's perfect for spring.

2 eggs
2 cups warm milk
4 tablespoons butter
¾ cup sugar
¼ teaspoon salt
1 teaspoon cinnamon
⅛ teaspoon allspice
¼ teaspoon nutmeg
1 teaspoon vanilla
3 teaspoons lemon extract
¼ teaspoon coconut extract
5 cups raisin bread cubes
½ cup raisins

Preheat oven to 350°F. In large bowl beat eggs lightly. Combine milk and butter. Add to eggs along with sugar, spices, vanilla, coconut, and lemon extract. Add bread cubes and raisins. Stir and pour into greased 9-inch square baking dish. Bake 40 minutes. Serve with Lemon Sauce. Makes 9 servings.

LEMON SAUCE
1 cup sugar
1 tablespoon flour
½ cup half-and-half
½ cup butter
3 teaspoons lemon extract
½ teaspoon vanilla

In saucepan, combine all ingredients except vanilla. Boil 2 minutes. Add vanilla; mix well.

Mary J. Johnson, Des Moines
First Place, 2002 Essence of Extracts

1893 PALMER HOUSE BROWNIES

Bertha Palmer had no idea what a hit she and her chef came up with for the 1893 World's Fair. This is a version of the original 1890s Palmer House Brownie recipe, followed by two modern-day Iowa State Fair winners.

BROWNIES
14 ounces semisweet chocolate
2 cups butter (4 sticks)
1½ cups sugar
½ cup flour
8 eggs
1 teaspoon vanilla extract
12 ounces crushed walnuts
Glaze

Preheat oven to 300°F. Melt chocolate and butter in a double boiler. Mix the sugar and flour together in a medium bowl. Stir chocolate and flour mixtures until flour is fully incorporated. Add eggs and vanilla and continue mixing until thoroughly combined. Pour mixture into a 9x12-inch rimmed baking sheet. Sprinkle walnuts on top and press down slightly into the mixture. Bake 30–40 minutes until brownie edges begin to crisp and a toothpick inserted into the center has gooey crumbs. Brownies should be about ¼ inch thick.

GLAZE
1 cup apricot preserves
1 cup water
1 teaspoon unflavored gelatin

For the glaze, mix ingredients in a saucepan and bring to a boil. Brush hot glaze on brownies while still warm and allow brownies to cool completely before cutting into squares. These are especially great served cold since they are like a cross between brownies and fudge. Makes approximately 24 servings.

Adapted from original 1893 Palmer House Brownie recipe.

THE 1800s

CLASSIC BROWNIES

Everyone needs a go-to brownie recipe. In 1989, this classic version with chocolate frosting was unbeatable. It is still tops today, thanks to Cheryl Ashwill of Des Moines.

6 tablespoons butter, cut in pieces
3 ounces unsweetened chocolate, coarsely chopped
1 cup sugar
2 eggs
1½ teaspoons vanilla
½ cup cake flour, sifted
¼ teaspoon baking powder
⅛ teaspoon salt
¾ cup coarsely broken walnuts

Preheat oven to 325°F. In top of double boiler over hot water, melt butter and chocolate, stirring frequently until smooth. Remove from heat. Transfer chocolate mixture to mixer bowl. Beat sugar into chocolate mixture; mix 30 seconds until smooth. Blend in eggs and vanilla. Sift together flour, baking powder, and salt; add to chocolate mixture. Fold in nuts. Pour batter into greased 8-inch square baking pan. Bake 25 to 30 minutes or until done. Cool on wire rack 30 minutes. Let stand 2 hours. Frost. Makes 12 squares.

CHOCOLATE FROSTING
1 egg
2 cups powdered sugar
4 tablespoons butter, softened
2 ounces unsweetened chocolate, melted
1 teaspoon vanilla

Beat egg until frothy. Gradually beat in sugar. Mix in remaining ingredients, beating until smooth. Frost cooled brownies.

Cheryl Ashwill, Des Moines
First Place, 1989 Cookies, Brownies

LUCK OF THE IRISH BROWNIES

Modern-day cake winner Ann Gillotti also makes incredible brownies. Her Luck of the Irish recipe took top honors at the 2019 State Fair. Ann's Irish Cream ganache lifts these fudgy delights to a new level.

BROWNIES
¾ cup Guinness Stout Beer
2 cups sugar
¼ cup vegetable oil
½ teaspoon vanilla extract
¼ cup butter, melted and cooled
2 large eggs
1 cup all-purpose flour
⅔ cups Hershey's Dark Cocoa

Preheat oven to 350°F. Grease a 9x9-inch baking pan and line with parchment paper. Mix the oil, Guinness, sugar, and vanilla together in a large bowl. Add butter and mix until combined. Then add eggs and beat well. In a medium bowl whisk together the cocoa and flour. Add cocoa mixture to the wet ingredients and mix until blended well. Pour batter into baking pan and bake for 35–38 minutes or until a toothpick comes out clean with a few crumbs. Cool completely before frosting.

GANACHE FROSTING
1 cup semisweet chocolate chips
⅓ cup heavy cream
⅓ cup Bailey's Irish Cream
1 tablespoon butter

Combine chocolate chips, cream, Irish Cream, and butter in a small saucepan. Stir over low heat until smooth. Remove from heat and cool until slightly warm but pourable. Pour the ganache over the brownies and place in the refrigerator to set. Remove from refrigerator at least 30 minutes prior to serving. Makes approximately 12–14 brownies.

Ann Gillotti, Ankeny
First Place, 2019 My Best Brownies
First Place, 2019 Vera Towne's Chocolate Frosted Brownies—Chocolate Brownies with Chocolate Frosting

THE 1800s

CLOSING CENTURY PINEAPPLE CAKE

Here is a Pineapple Cake recipe from 1899, followed by a blue ribbon version by perennial State Fair winner Joy McFarland.

> Pineapple Cake—Pineapple cake is a most delicate and dainty dessert. Take two eggs, one cup of white sugar, one tablespoonful of butter, one-half cup of sweet milk, a pinch of salt and one teaspoonful of baking powder; bake in layers. For the filling, whip one pint of cream, one cup of shredded pineapple—which has been cooked a little—sweeten to taste and spread between the layers just before serving.

Iowa City Press-Citizen, *June 2, 1899*

PINEAPPLE WOW CAKE

Joy McFarland's Pineapple Wow Cake is perfect for a summer potluck, and we loved it in the middle of winter with a fluffy Cool Whip-buttermilk topping.

3 cups cake flour
2½ teaspoons baking powder
½ cup butter or margarine
1¾ cups sugar
1 teaspoon vanilla
2 eggs
1¼ cups milk
1 20-ounce can crushed pineapple, drained, divided

Preheat oven to 350°F. Combine flour and baking powder; set aside. Beat butter 30 seconds; add sugar and vanilla. Beat in eggs. Add dry ingredients alternately with milk. Fold in ½ cup of pineapple, reserving remaining pineapple for topping. Pour into two greased and floured 8- or 9-inch pans. Bake 30 to 35 minutes. Cool 10 minutes; remove from pans. Add topping. Makes approximately to 12–16 servings.

TOPPING
1 3.4-ounce package instant vanilla pudding mix
1 cup buttermilk
Reserved pineapple
½ cup coconut
1 small container frozen nondairy whipped topping

Combine pudding mix and buttermilk; fold in pineapple, coconut, and whipped topping. Cherries, nuts, and additional coconut may be added, if desired.

Joy McFarland, Tingley
First Place, 1992 Cakes, Other Than Named

Butters & Preserves

Preserves have always been a huge part of Iowa State Fair Food Competitions. These fruit jelly and plain lemon jelly recipes from Mrs. Jessie Young of Des Moines made it into *The Home Queen, Chicago World's Fair Souvenir Cook Book*. They are followed by modern-day State Fair butter and preserve winners that continue the tradition.

> **Fruit Jelly.**
> Use recipe for lemon jelly, putting in candied cherries and sour grapes, splitting the grapes lengthwise and removing the seeds.
>
> *Mrs. Jessie Young* — Des Moines, Iowa.
>
> **Plain Lemon Jelly.**
> Soak 1 box gelatine in cold water till it softens, add 6 lemons, 2 large coffee-cups sugar, boiling water; strain and pour into a mold, slice 1 lemon very thin, add to the jelly, set on ice to cool.

MODERN STATE FAIR FRUIT BUTTER AND PRESERVE WINNERS:

PEACH BUTTER

2 quarts peach pulp, from approximately 18 medium fully ripe peaches
4 cups sugar

To prepare pulp, wash, pit, peel and chop peaches. Cook pulp until soft, adding only enough water to prevent sticking. Press through food mill. Measure 2 quarts pulp; stir in sugar. On low heat, cook until thick, about 30 minutes. Stir frequently to prevent sticking. Ladle into hot, sterilized jars leaving ¼ inch headspace. Adjust lids. Process in boiling water bath 10 minutes. Yield: 4 pints.

Cindy Anderson, Grimes
First Place, 1987 preserves and butters, Peach.

APRICOT BUTTER

10 cups apricots
½ cup water
5⅓ cups sugar
1 tablespoon grated orange peel
1½ teaspoons cinnamon
1 teaspoon grated fresh ginger
2 tablespoons frozen orange juice concentrate, thawed

Wash, pit, and slice apricots. Combine apricots and water in heavy saucepan and cook until soft. Press through sieve. Measure pulp and to each cup add ⅔ cup sugar. Stir in concentrate, peel, and spices. Cook until thick, about 10 to 15 minutes, stirring frequently. Ladle undo hot, sterilized jars. Put caps on, screw bands tight, and process in boiling water bath 10 minutes. Yield: Eight 8-oz. jars.

Judy Arnold, Indianola
First Place, 1987 preserves and butters, Apricot

RHUBARB JELLY

For Louise Piper, making this rhubarb jelly is her annual rite of spring. Her recipe is a five-time blue ribbon winner and was chosen as the Best Jelly of the Fair in 1991.

4 pounds fresh rhubarb
7 cups sugar
2 3-oz. packets liquid pectin

Pick approximately 4 pounds of the strawberry variety of rhubarb in May or early June. Wash, cut, and then grind the raw rhubarb. Allow the juice to run through layers of cheesecloth or a piece of white cloth. You need 3½ cups of the rhubarb juice. Place in a large, heavy kettle with 7 cups of sugar and stir well. Over high heat, stir and bring to a full rolling boil. Now add 2 foil packets of liquid pectin. Return to a full rolling boil for 1 minute. Skim off the foam. Ladle the jelly into hot, sterilized half-pint jars, leaving ¼ inch of headspace. Put lids on jars and process in a boiling water bath for 10 minutes. Yield: approximately 8 half-pint jars.

Louise Piper, Garner
First, Place, 1991 Best of Fair Jelly

PICCALILLI AND CHOW CHOW

Piccalilli and Chow Chow were popular late summer pickling recipes for anyone with a kitchen garden. There are many opinions on how to make these. Recipes differ by region, and there is a lot of overlap in what vegetables go into Piccalilli and Chow Chow. Here are examples of how Super Exhibitors Mrs. L. Knapp and Miss Cellie Keene would have made their winning jars in the late 1880s.

How to Make Piccalilli

Combine 1 peck green tomatoes, ½ peck onions, 1 cauliflower, 1 peck small cucumbers. Slice vegetables. Leave in salt and water for 24 hours, then put in kettle with a handful of scraped horseradish, 1 ounce turmeric, 1 ounce cloves (whole), 1 ounce cinnamon, 1 pound white mustard seed, 1 pound English mustard. Place in kettle in layers and cover with cold vinegar. Boil 15 minutes, constantly stirring.

–*Iowa City Press-Citizen,* October 4, 1899

How to Make Chow Chow

Mince half a peck of green tomatoes, half a peck of small onions, one peck of tiny cucumbers, and six green peppers; mince the seeds; to these add three medium-sized heads of cauliflower, broken in small pieces. Sprinkle salt over all and let them stand for 24 hours. At the end of this time drain well and cover with vinegar. Put 3 heads of celery cut in small pieces, one cupful of grated horseradish, half a pound of ground mustard, half a pound of mustard seed, 2 ounces of ground black pepper, 2 ounces of brown sugar, half an ounce of ground cloves and half an ounce of turmeric into enough cider vinegar to cover. Boil for 15 minutes; pour over pickles. Put in glass jars and keep for a month before using. It improves with age.

–*Davenport Weekly Republican,* August 27, 1887

THE EARLY 1900s

CELEBRATING 20TH-CENTURY COOKS AND WINNING THE WAR WITH FOOD

RECIPES

1900 SIGNATURE RECIPE CARDS
Chicken Pie and Sauce, *Mrs. D. E. Perkins* **37**
Fig Cake, *Mrs. E. W. Carrington* **37**
Spice Cakes, *Miss Nettie B. Smith* **37**
Bird's Nest, *Mrs. Fenton Groves* **37**
Chocolate Cake, *Miss Nettie A. Wyman* **40**

BREADS
Cinnamon Coffee Rolls, *Des Moines Tribune Wartime Cooking School* **49**
Corn Bread with Rye Flour, *"Food Will Win the War"* **49**
Oatmeal Bread, *"Food Will Win the War"* **49**
Raisin Buns Bettina, *Louise Bennett Weaver and Helen Cowles LeCron* **50**
Bran Bread, *Beulah Schenk* **51**

CAKES
Chocolate Cake, *Karen Schafer* **40**
Angel Food Cake, *Patty Rogers* **41**
Coconut Cake, *Crisco* **44**
Marble Cake, *Crisco* **45**
Fairy Cupcakes, *1917* **46**
Sunshine Cake, *Crisco* **47**
Honey Glazed Buttermilk Coffee Cake, *Marjorie Rodgers* **48**

CANDY
Divinity Cream Candies, *Evelyn Birkby* **51**

CELEBRATING 20TH-CENTURY COOKS

Falcon Flour Company celebrated the new era with a series of recipe cards signed by the women who created them. These culinary gems appeared weekly in the *The Des Moines Register* and inspired everything from Sunday dinners to county and State Fair cake exhibits. Elegant signatures of everyday cooks like Mrs. Fenton Groves and Miss Nettie B. Smith set them apart. Recipes still lacked precise instructions, but this began to change. The first two editions of *Fannie Farmer's The Boston Cooking School Cook Book* in 1896 and 1906 set the bar for recipes that were more in keeping with what modern-day cooks expect.

Railway expansion in the late nineteenth and early twentieth centuries made things like rotary egg beaters and Fannie Farmer's standardized measuring cups more widely available. Mail-order catalog companies had to earn the trust of homemakers from cities to farms. Home cooks and State Fair exhibitors were eager to show off newfound culinary skills with more-sophisticated recipes and kitchen gadgets. Prettier cake pans and uniform tins replaced patty pans, griddle rings, and teacups. Game-changing ingredients like nuts, chocolate, canned pineapple—along with a revolutionary invention called Crisco—were commonplace after 1911.

Recipes entered at the Iowa State Fair reflected these culinary advances. By 1914, the Pantry and Kitchen Department boasted 55 cake competitions with $3 and $2 prizes in most classes, in addition to a growing list of breads, butters, jellies, pickles, and preserves.

Winning recipes in 1916 included the bright flavors of Mrs. Jesse Alexander's Sunshine Cake and the light texture of Mrs. Ethel B. Baird's Fairy Loaf Cake.

With home and kitchen innovations from gas stoves to electricity, the department was poised for long-term expansion, but everything changed the following spring.

EARLY 1900s

In the early 1900s, the Iowa State Fair and the Pantry and Kitchen Department saw a gradual expansion. The 1900 premium list featured 30 different cake contests, including turn-of-the-century favorites like fruitcake, coconut, jelly, and mountain cake, not to mention the towering triumph of "lucky" angel food cake and increasingly popular chocolate cakes.

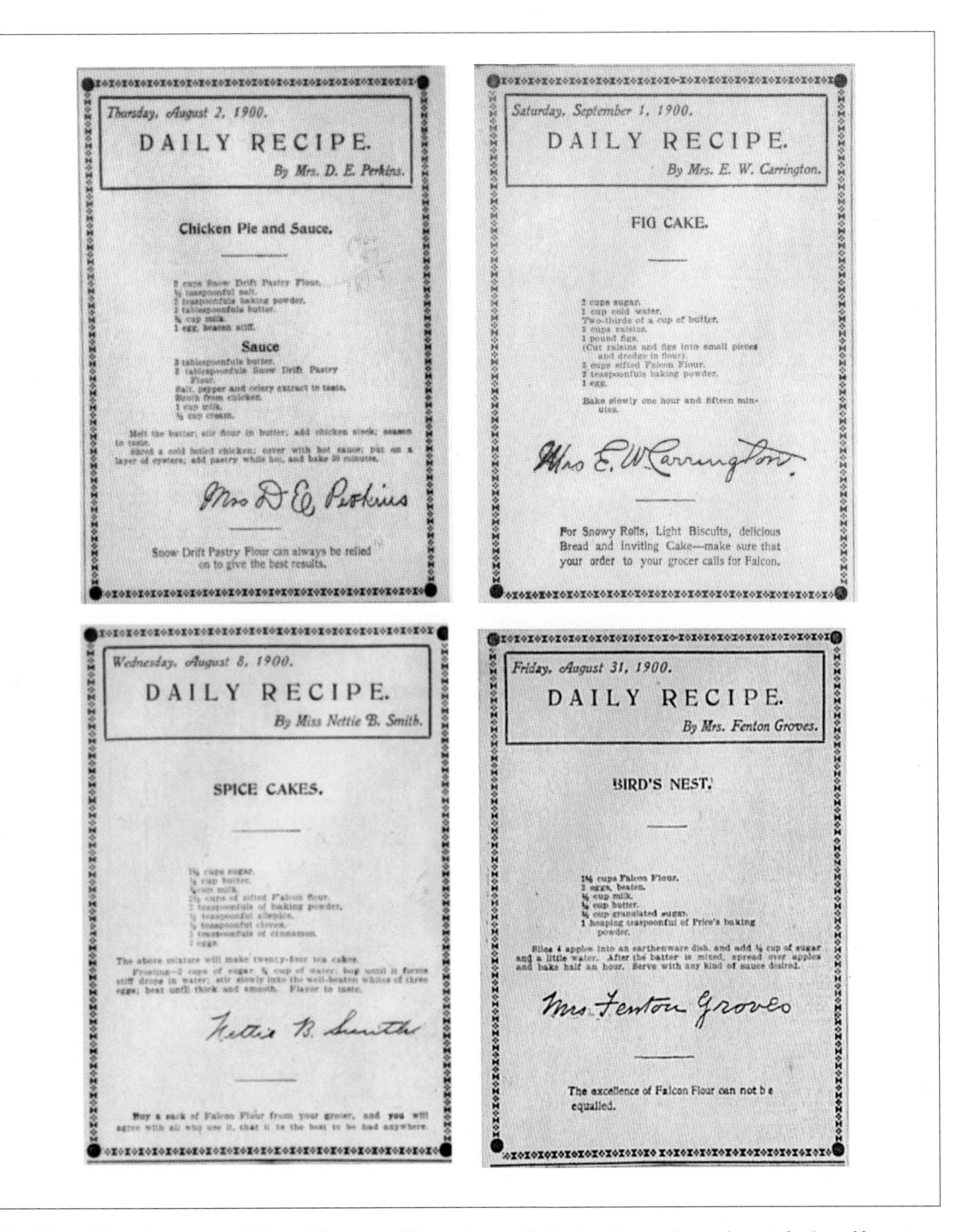

The Falcon Flour Company celebrated the turn of the century with its signature series recipe cards signed by some of Iowa's celebrated bakers. Recipes were simple, with few instructions and no specific oven temperatures. Bakers of the day were skilled at moderating their woodstoves by opening or closing the oven door. Like a sixth sense, they knew how long their recipes needed to bake, but more specific recipes soon followed. The Des Moines Register ran more than 50 recipe cards.

THE EARLY 1900s

"FOOD WILL WIN THE WAR!"

On April 6, 1917, the United States entered World War I. American soldiers joined Allied forces overseas. Millions on the home front supported the troops by saving food and supplies. Iowa native Herbert Hoover led the charge as the newly appointed head of the Food Administration under President Woodrow Wilson. Hoover's declaration that "Food Will Win the War!" began an unprecedented food conservation program across all 48 states. Wheat, sugar, and other commodities were rationed. Regular flour was replaced by conservation flour blended with less wheat and more rye, corn, and other grains. The Iowa State Fair marched on with dramatic changes in the Pantry and Kitchen Division.

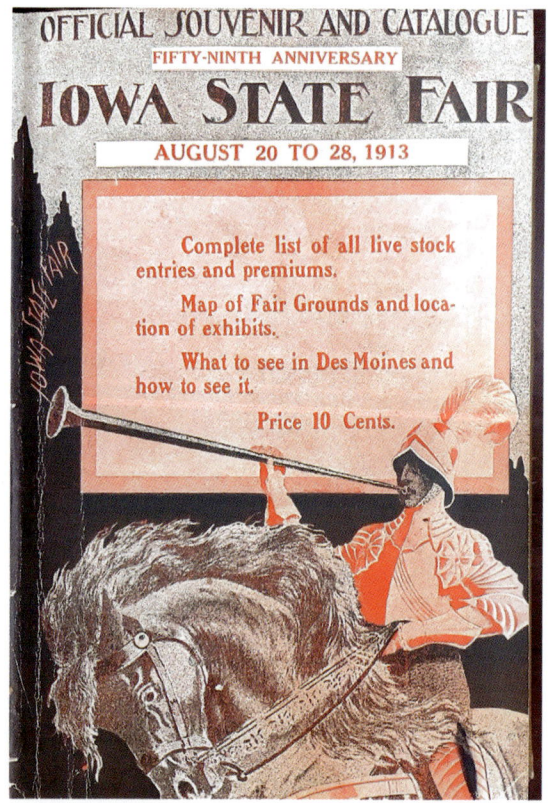

"NO MORE SKYSCRAPER LAYER CAKES"

In 1918, the Iowa State Fair Board banned all food exhibits made wholly of wheat flour and those requiring large amounts of sugar and other rationed ingredients. Popular cakes of the day, like burnt sugar, chocolate, English walnut, and pineapple, were dashed from premium lists along with all frostings. Homemade candies didn't make it through the gates. Bakers had to follow strict guidelines if they wanted to compete. At least one-third of the flour in any recipe had to be other than wheat. Instead, the Pantry and Kitchen Division offered prizes for a full lineup of war breads, cakes, and cookies.

Homemakers rose to the challenge. On the bright side, it gave Iowa State Fair exhibitors an opportunity to show off their creativity with different flours, fats, and natural sweeteners, many of which are echoed in today's healthful recipes.

WARTIME CONSERVATION COOKING SCHOOL

The Des Moines Register and *Tribune* offered a free Wartime Cooking School with recipes, classes, and incentives for women to send in their best conservation recipes. Electric irons, toasters, and sacks of Pillsbury conservation flour were some of the prizes awarded each week. By State Fair time, food competitors had a list of war recipes, including Cinnamon Coffee Rolls, Graham and Barley Gems, Raisin Buns Bettina, and Boston Brown Bread.

After the war, the *Register* and *Tribune's* free cooking school helped homemakers return to normal meal planning while economizing in the kitchen.

1919: VICTORY AT THE FAIR

The State Fair celebrated victory after World War I with a new attendance record of over 400,000 and soaring profits of $60,000–$70,000 in 1919. Food competitions were as sweet as ever with premiums worth $846. Wheat flour and sugar were back on the menu with eight bread competitions; 39 different cakes, including 20 layer cakes; and 14 contests for cookies and doughnuts. Baskets of cookies and fancy cakes graced display tables along with plates of chocolate and divinity creams. Taffy and chocolate fudge rounded out the candies. Premiums ranged from $10 for first-place yeast breads and $3 for winning cakes to $1 for third- to fifth-place awards in many contests. As today, food preservation was a major focus with 147 different contests.

After a resounding success in 1919, Iowa State Fair culinary competitions continued a gradual climb into the 1920s, accelerated by the arrival of a new Pantry and Kitchen superintendent, Beulah Schenk.

THE EARLY 1900s
STORIES AND RECIPES

Cakes

CHOCOLATE CAKE—1900 and Today

Homemade chocolate cakes gained popularity in the early 1900s as different types of chocolate and cocoa became more widely available. Miss Nettie A. Wyman shared her best chocolate cake recipe in 1900 as part of Falcon Flour Company's signature recipe series. Since then, chocolate cake has earned countless blue ribbons and devoted fans. More than a century after Nettie's classic, Karen Schafer won twice with her versatile, deep chocolate layer cake. Her use of lard echoes recipes of yesteryear, and the cake is also a winner with Karen's butter-shortening substitute.

1 cup lard (substitute ½ cup softened butter plus ½ cup vegetable shortening)
1½ cups sugar
3 large eggs, slightly beaten
1 teaspoon vanilla
2 cups all-purpose flour
½ cup unsweetened cocoa powder
1 teaspoon baking soda
1 cup cold strong coffee
1 tablespoon cider vinegar

Preheat oven to 375°F. Grease and flour two 9-inch round cake pans. Cream together lard and sugar with electric mixer until smooth and creamy. Add eggs and vanilla; beat well. Sift together flour and cocoa. Add baking soda to coffee; stir well. Add liquid mixture alternately with dry ingredients, beginning and ending with flour mixture. Beat together until well blended. Stir in vinegar. Pour into prepared cake pans. Bake for 30 to 35 minutes or until toothpick inserted into centers of cake comes out clean. Cool on racks 10 minutes; remove from baking pans and cool. Frost cakes.

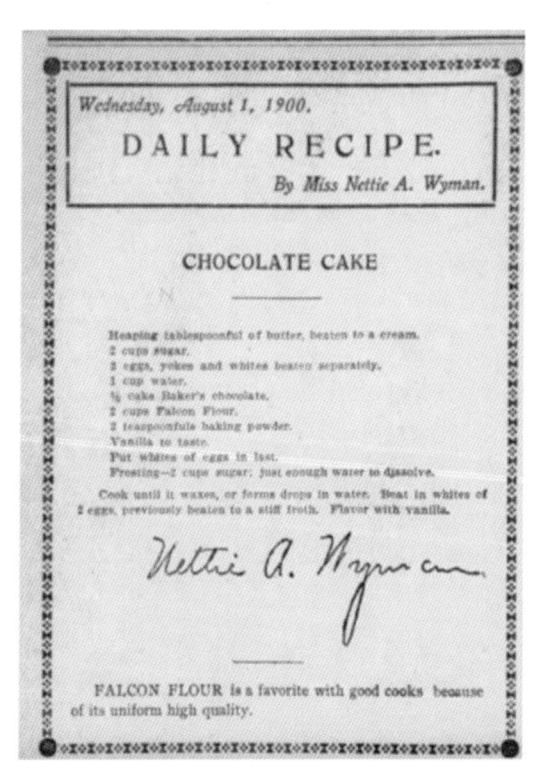

CHOCOLATE FUDGE ICING

1 pound powdered sugar
¾ cup unsweetened cocoa powder
⅛ teaspoon salt
1 cup unsalted butter, softened
1 cup marshmallow crème
¼ cup boiling water
1 teaspoon vanilla
1 teaspoon chocolate extract

In mixing bowl sift together powdered sugar, cocoa, and salt. Add butter; beat at medium speed with mixer until combined. Add marshmallow crème; beat until smooth. Add water, vanilla, and chocolate extract and beat until mixture reaches the desired spreading consistency. Store in airtight container in refrigerator until ready to use.

Karen Schafer, Brighton
First Place, 2008 Make It with Lard — Cakes Other Than Named
First Place, 2009 Smile in Every Aisle Cakes — Chocolate

1908: A LUCKY ANGEL FOOD CAKE WINS FIRST PRIZE

Many angel food cake recipes call for an even dozen egg whites. In 1908, Mrs. Ruth Mason of Danville took first place at the Fair with "the sugar and sweetness of 13 eggs and air." Over 100 years later, this updated winner brought Patty Rogers good luck in the form of a blue silk ribbon. We're not sure if Mrs. Mason decorated her cake, but we think she would have loved Patty's frosting.

"the sugar and sweetness of 13 eggs and air"

ANGEL FOOD CAKE

1¼ cups cake flour
1½ cups plus 6 tablespoons granulated sugar, divided
2 cups egg whites
1¾ teaspoons cream of tartar
¼ teaspoon salt
1½ teaspoons vanilla
½ teaspoon almond extract

Preheat oven to 375°F. Sift flour with ¾ cup plus 3 tablespoons of the sugar four times; set aside. In separate bowl, beat egg whites with cream of tartar, salt, vanilla, and almond extract until soft peaks form. Add remaining sugar, 2 tablespoons at a time. Continue beating until egg whites hold a stiff peak. Sift about one-fourth of the flour-sugar mixture over the egg whites; fold in. Fold in remaining flour mixture by fourths, making certain mixture is well blended with the egg whites. Pour into an ungreased 10-inch tube pan, turning the pan gradually to distribute batter evenly. Cut through batter with spatula to remove air pockets. Bake 40 minutes or until cake is golden brown. Invert cake onto a glass bottle. Cool at least 1 hour before removing from pan.

FROSTING

¼ cup butter, melted
2 cups sifted powdered sugar
2 to 4 tablespoons heavy cream
1½ teaspoons vanilla

Combine all ingredients; beat with an electric mixer until smooth and easy to spread. Gently spread over top and sides of cake. Serves 12–14.

Patty Rogers, Des Moines

First Place, 2019 Homemade Angel Food Cake

Valentine and Mary Jane Arbuckle

MEMORIES OF A 1909 FOOD STAND

At Fair time, food stands are everywhere. The menu of foods on a stick is endless, but back in the early 1900s, Fairgoers brought picnics. Food stands were far fewer in number. Barb Bare of Des Moines shares a family memory of her grandparents, Valentine and Mary Jane Arbuckle, who ran a food stand at the 1909 State Fair.

Valentine worked on the railroad in Valley Junction, and the couple also operated a small grocery store on Main Street. With a newborn and a toddler in tow, they set up their stand at the Fair. The baby mostly slept in her basket, but the adventurous three-year-old, Muriel, kept running off. Fair policeman had to bring her back to the booth on the Grand Concourse.

Crisco hadn't been invented yet, but Mary Jane made pies from scratch, along with breakfasts, sandwiches, soups, and coffee. At night, the exhausted young family slept on the floor of the stand.

After the Fair, Valentine was transferred to Udell in Southern Iowa, where the railroad was expanding—and would soon be bringing more modern kitchen supplies to Iowa farmwives.

1911: AN ABSOLUTELY NEW PRODUCT CALLED CRISCO

In 1911, a scientific discovery called Crisco forever changed the culinary landscape. Procter & Gamble created the future billion-dollar baking sensation when an attempt to make hard soap from fats resulted in the first pure shortening of its kind. The name came from Crisco's original ingredient, crystallized cottonseed oil. It came in a tin with a white wrapper. Once print ads, and later radio advertising hit, it flew off the shelves. There were no food labeling laws, and P&G made the first all-vegetable shortening sound almost as healthful as vegetables from the garden. The company gave away thousands of cookbooks that featured Crisco in recipes from asparagus soup to coconut ("cocoanut") and marble cakes, which were popular contests at the Fair.

This magic ingredient became a pantry staple, but Iowa farm wives, with access to the freshest butter and purest lard, were harder to convince than the average cook. Crisco ads in Iowa newspapers tried hard to convince these "old-fashioned cooks," stating that the "only good reason why a woman should use lard ... is because she has not heard of Crisco."

Today Iowa State Fair bakers use a variety of fats in their pie pastries, from Crisco and butter to pure lard and vegetable oil. As veteran pie judges will tell you, the best pie crust recipe to enter is the one that works best for you. Experiment with our blue ribbon winners, and you may find a new favorite.

BAKING BLUE RIBBONS

Use Crisco in Cocoanut Cake and see why

Crisco makes cake that has never been equaled with the ordinary shortening.

Butter is nearly one-fifth water. Crisco is all shortening.

Use Crisco in making white cake; use exactly as you would butter, only add salt. You will find your cake is finer grained, *better flavored*, equal to Angel Food in whiteness.

Use Crisco and find out for yourself its better results for all cooking wherever you now use butter or lard; its absolute cleanliness, its health value, its economy. You will see why experienced chefs prefer it—why the leading New York cooking school considers Crisco of the greatest benefit of any food product discovered in recent years.

Sold in 25c packages by all grocers.

The Procter & Gamble Co.

Press and Sun Bulletin, *Binghamton, New York, December 1, 1911*

Convincing the Old-fashioned Cook

At first she says that she and her family are satisfied with the shortening she always has used. It *is* pretty hard to improve upon her pie crust and cake.

But someone induces her to *try*

CRISCO
For Frying—For Shortening For Cake Making

Perhaps it is her daughter who has used it at Domestic Science School, or a neighbor who has obtained excellent results.

After the first trial, the old-fashioned cook slowly but surely comes to use Crisco for all cooking. She has become a Crisco enthusiast. She has found these advantages:

Frying. There is no smoke nor odor. Fried foods are free from the taste of grease. Now they are tasty and crisp and digestible. The same Crisco can be used to fry fish, onions, doughnuts, etc., merely by straining out the food particles after each frying.

Shortening. Crisco gives pastry a new flakiness and digestibility.

Cake Making. Crisco gives richness at smaller cost. It brings cake making back to popularity.

The Daily Gate City and Constitution-Democrat, *(Keokuk), May 10, 1916*

An Absolutely New Product
for Frying, for Shortening and for General Cooking

A scientific discovery that will affect every kitchen in America

Crisco is a new and heretofore unknown product; an absolutely wholesome and delicious cooking material, made under hygienic conditions from edible vegetable oils by a process controlled exclusively by ourselves. It is in no sense a compound or mixture of oils and fats.

All the points in favor of Crisco have been tested by the leading chefs and domestic science teachers. The following claims seem unbelievable but they are now known facts in domestic science schools and in hotel kitchens, where modern, progressive cooking is a business or science.

Crisco makes the best pastry

Until Crisco was discovered, butter was the standard for good pastry.

Butter is nearly one-fifth water. Crisco is 100% shortening.

To-day, Crisco gives a crisper pie crust, a richer shortcake, or cream roll, than butter.

You do not have to do any experimenting with Crisco. Use it just as you would butter, except add salt.

Crisco fries in half the time without smoking

Butter smokes and burns at 329°. Lard at 400°.

You can heat Crisco very much hotter than lard and it will not smoke. You heat Crisco hot enough to cook the outside of food *instantly*, so that a crust forms and prevents grease from soaking in.

This is the secret of the crispness of foods cooked in Crisco. They are a uniform golden brown and without any burnt black specks—the most appetizing fried foods you have ever eaten.

Crisco absorbs no odors

You can use the same Crisco for fish, onions, then potatoes—without the slightest odor or flavor being carried from one to the other.

This does not seem possible? Try it yourself and see. You will find it a decided economy.

Three more new features of Crisco

Watch for our following announcements. They explain many more new features of Crisco.

When you have read them, you will agree with the food authorities that Crisco is the ideal product for cooking—one that American housekeepers have always needed and one which they will be quick to appreciate.

The Procter & Gamble Co.

News-Journal, *(Mansfield, Ohio), October 3, 1911*

Crisco ads in Iowa newspapers tried hard to convince these "old-fashioned cooks," stating that the "only good reason why a woman should use lard ... is because she has not heard of Crisco."

THE EARLY 1900s

COCONUT CAKE

Coconut Cake has been a winner at the Fair for more than a century. This version combines the best of Crisco recipes from yesterday and today. White frosting and fluffy coconut make this showstopper an elegant centerpiece for any occasion.

1¼ cups sugar
1 cup Crisco
5 eggs
1 teaspoon coconut extract
2¼ cups flour
1½ teaspoons baking powder
½ teaspoon salt
1 cup buttermilk
1 cup shredded coconut

Preheat oven to 350°F. Grease a 10-inch tube pan well; set aside. Combine sugar and shortening; blend well at medium speed. Add eggs, 1 at a time, beating slightly after each addition. Blend in coconut extract. Combine flour, baking powder, and salt in separate bowl; add alternately with buttermilk to shortening mixture. Beat at low speed after each addition until well blended. Add coconut; mix until evenly incorporated. Spoon batter into prepared pan. Bake 40–45 minutes until toothpick inserted in center comes out clean and cake is golden. Cool in pan 10 minutes; turn out onto wire rack. Frost when completely cooled.

FROSTING
1 cup Crisco
½ teaspoon vanilla extract
1 teaspoon coconut extract
½ teaspoon salt
5 cups powdered sugar
5–6 tablespoons milk
1–2 cups shredded coconut to spread over cake

Blend Crisco until smooth; add extracts and salt. Carefully blend in powdered sugar, 1 cup at a time, alternating with tablespoons of milk, until frosting is smooth and creamy. Frost cake. Sprinkle with coconut, pressing gently into frosting.

Makes approximately 12 servings.

The Story of Crisco cookbook, 1913, Procter & Gamble Company

Crisco's marble cake features molasses and spice that give the chocolate part of the batter a distinctive spiced flavor—like vanilla, chocolate, and spice cake all in one. According to State Fair cake champ Brian Keul, it has a wonderful cinnamon-molasses aroma while it bakes. Brian added a classic vanilla cream frosting and dusted it with black and silver sprinkles for a State Fair presentation. We think you will love it on its own as a snack cake or with your favorite chocolate or vanilla frosting for special occasions.

CRISCO MARBLE CAKE

1 cup Crisco
2 cups sugar
4 eggs, separated
3½ cups flour
1 teaspoon salt
3 teaspoons baking powder
1 cup milk
1 teaspoon powdered cinnamon
½ teaspoon nutmeg
½ teaspoon allspice
2 tablespoons molasses
2 tablespoons melted chocolate

Preheat oven to 350°F. Grease two 9-inch round cake pans. Cream Crisco; slowly add sugar, egg yolks beaten until thick, flour, salt, baking powder, and milk. Beat egg whites until stiff peaks form and carefully fold into batter. To one-third of the mixture add spices, molasses, and melted chocolate. Drop batters into cake pans, alternating a spoonful of each mixture, and draw a knife through once or twice to swirl the colors. Bake for 45–50 minutes, until cakes are golden brown.

Approximately 12–14 servings.

The Story of Crisco cookbook, 1913, Procter & Gamble Company

1916: SUNSHINE AND FAIRIES TAKE THE CAKE

In 1916, Mrs. Ethel B. Baird of Des Moines won first prize in the Fairy Cakes class, which had become a regular contest. Fairy Cakes are an early ancestor to modern-day cupcakes. Bakeries and grocers in the late 1800s and early 1900s advertised them as "a newly discovered jewel of the cuisine," perfect for weddings, afternoon teas, and special occasions. They offered flavors such as violet, fruit, and the magical fairy's breath. Before muffin tins were widely available, these cakes were baked in individual cups, patty pans, or in thin layers to be cut into fairy-size servings while warm from the oven. During World War I, these lighter, smaller desserts were festive while conserving butter, sugar, and eggs. Instead of heavy frostings, fairy cakes are often topped with a simple glaze or decorated with fruit, edible flowers, or other colorful garnishes. Here is a Fairy Cake recipe from the early 1900s, updated for cupcakes. The evaporated milk makes these light, fluffy, and moist.

FAIRY CUPCAKES

½ cup margarine or butter, softened
1 cup sugar
2 eggs, beaten
⅔ cup evaporated milk
⅓ cup water
½ teaspoon almond or vanilla extract
2 cups flour
3 teaspoons baking powder
½ teaspoon salt
Edible flowers or fruit for garnish

Preheat oven to 350° F. Grease muffin pan or line with paper cupcake liners. Cream butter and sugar; add beaten eggs and mix well. Mix evaporated milk, water, and extract in small bowl; set aside. Sift dry ingredients into a separate bowl and add alternately with wet. Pour into prepared pan. Bake for 20–25 minutes or until tops are light golden and cupcakes spring back when gently touched. Cool completely. Drizzle with glaze. Once glaze is dry, garnish with edible flowers or fruit, if desired. Makes 12 cupcakes.

GLAZE
1 cup powdered sugar
2–3 tablespoons milk, cream, or orange juice
½ teaspoon vanilla

Mix ingredients well, adding liquid gradually until glaze reaches desired consistency. Drizzle over cupcakes.

Adapted from The Journal and Tribune, *Knoxville, Tennessee. December 23, 1917*

SUNSHINE CAKE

Sunshine Cake is a festive dessert that earned high honors for Mrs. Jesse Alexander of Indianola in 1916. She was a winning baker during the 1910s and beyond. Crisco's 1916 recipe may have inspired her first-place bake. Here is an updated version from Crisco's *A Calendar of Dinners* cookbook. "A culinary triumph in which Crisco gives tasty results."

2½ cups cake flour
3½ teaspoons baking powder
1 teaspoon salt
⅔ cup Crisco
1½ cups sugar
3 eggs, beaten
1¼ cups milk
½ teaspoon vanilla extract
½ teaspoon lemon extract
⅓ to ½ cup orange marmalade or apricot jam for filling
Powdered sugar and citrus peel and slices for garnish

Preheat oven to 350°F. Grease two 9-inch round cake pans and line bottoms with parchment paper. Combine cake flour, baking powder, and salt in medium bowl; set aside. Cream Crisco and add sugar gradually, creaming after each addition. Beat in eggs and mix well. Add flour mixture alternately with milk; mix well. Beat in extracts. Pour batter into prepared pans. Bake for 20–25 minutes until tops are golden. Rest cakes in pans for about 5 minutes. Turn out onto wire rack and remove parchment to cool completely. When ready to serve, invert one cake on platter, top side down. Spread with preserves, which may drip down the sides. Top with second cake, top side up. Sprinkle with powdered sugar and garnish with citrus peel and slices or other fresh fruit if desired. Serves approximately 12.

Adapted from *A Calendar of Dinners* cookbook, 1916, Procter & Gamble Company

HONEY-GLAZED BUTTERMILK COFFEE CAKE

Anna B. Frost won first place for her coffeecake in 1916 before wartime rations were put in place. Nearly a century later, Marjorie Rodgers of Indianola won with this buttermilk coffeecake that is sweetened with honey instead of sugar and uses oatmeal and ground pecans to cut down on flour. Topped off with caramelized pecans, like an upside-down cake, this is a winner for then and now.

1 cup plus 2 tablespoons honey, divided
⅓ cup plus ¼ cup melted butter, divided
2 teaspoons grated lemon zest
4 teaspoons lemon juice
1 cup chopped pecans, divided
1½ cups regular rolled oats
1 cup all-purpose flour
1 teaspoon baking powder
¾ teaspoon baking soda
½ teaspoon salt
2 eggs, lightly beaten
⅔ cup buttermilk
1½ teaspoons vanilla

Preheat oven to 350°F. In a small bowl combine the 2 tablespoons honey, ⅓ cup melted butter, lemon zest, and lemon juice. Stir in ½ cup pecans. Pour into generously greased 9-inch round cake pan. Spread evenly; set aside. Place oats in blender or food processor and process until finely ground. Transfer to a large bowl. Stir in flour, remaining pecans, baking powder, baking soda, and salt. Make a well in center of flour mixture. In a medium bowl combine eggs, buttermilk, remaining honey, remaining melted butter, and vanilla. Add egg mixture to well in flour mixture. Stir until moistened; batter should be lumpy. Pour batter over honey-pecan mixture in pan, spreading evenly. Bake 25 to 30 minutes. Immediately invert cake onto serving plate. Spoon any honey mixture remaining in pan onto cake. Approximately 8 servings.

Marjorie Rodgers, Indianola
First Place, 2014 Foods Made with Honey—Honey Coffee Cake

Breads

1918: WARTIME CONSERVATION

Here on the home front during World War I, Iowa housewives found ways to conserve sugar, butter, and flour while still making their families' favorites, like cinnamon rolls, bran bread, and gems. White flour was replaced by conservation flour and other grains. Sweeteners like honey, molasses, and syrups were used instead of white sugar.

Here are examples of recipes from World War I.

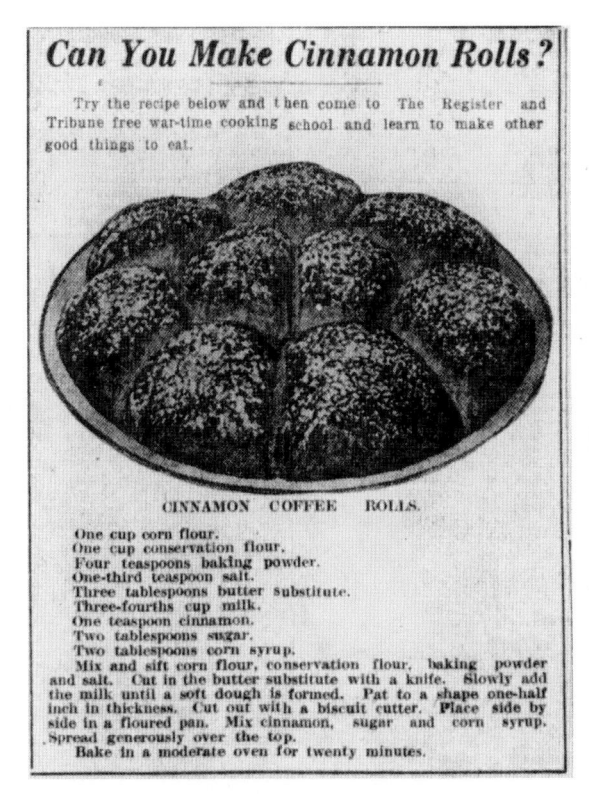

The Muscatine Journal, *March 27, 1918*

©The Des Moines Tribune
– USA TODAY NETWORK, *1918.*
Free Wartime Cooking School.

©The Des Moines Tribune
– USA TODAY NETWORK, *1918*

THE EARLY 1900s   49

RAISIN BUNS BETTINA

Barley, fine corn flour, and raisins come together for a hearty breakfast treat that is not too sweet and perfect for breakfast toasted and spread with butter and honey.

1 cup barley flour
1 cup corn flour
2 teaspoons baking powder
1 teaspoon baking soda
1 teaspoon salt
¾ cup raisins
1 egg well beaten
1 cup buttermilk
¼ cup corn syrup
¼ cup honey
1 tablespoon vegetable oil

Preheat oven to 350°F. Mix and sift the barley flour, corn flour, baking powder, baking soda, and salt. Stir raisins into dry ingredients to evenly distribute. Add the egg, buttermilk, corn syrup, honey, and oil. Beat vigorously for 2 minutes. Fill bun or muffin pans half full. Bake 18–20 minutes, until tops are golden and sides are deep golden brown. Serve hot or cold. Makes 12 muffins or 6 large buns, baked in a hamburger bun tin.

Recipe adapted from Louise Bennett Weaver and Helen Cowles LeCron, food writers at The Des Moines Register, *October 16, 1918.*

BRAN BREAD

Before Beulah Schenk took charge of the Iowa State Fair Culinary Department in 1924, she wrote "The Housewife's Corner" column for the *Audubon County Journal*. Beulah offered tips on housekeeping, raising kids, and recipes, including this World War I Bran Bread. It is tempting to add sugar and spices, but molasses carries the day in this simple, unsweetened loaf. It is perfect plain, but feel free to slather with butter and a drizzle of honey while still warm from the oven or toasted the next day.

1¾ cups bran
¾ teaspoon salt
3 teaspoons baking powder
1 egg
3 tablespoons molasses
1 cup milk
2 tablespoons vegetable oil
1 cup flour

Preheat oven to 350°F. Grease a 9x5-inch loaf pan. Pulse All-Bran cereal to form a coarse meal. Mix bran, salt, and baking powder. In separate dish, beat egg, molasses, milk, and vegetable oil. Add egg mixture to bran mixture and stir to combine. Add enough flour to make a batter that will drop from a spoon, about 1 cup. Beat well. Turn into bread pan and bake about 35 minutes, or until a toothpick inserted near center comes out clean. Bread will be a deep golden brown and edges well-baked. In this 1917 recipe, Beulah suggested to bake in gems if desired. Makes 1 loaf.

Beulah Schenk, recipe adapted from Audubon County Journal, Extra. *December 6, 1917.*

Candy

1919

Sugar was back in style after World War I with celebration treats like Divinity Cream Candies. This delicate candy can be made with many different flavor combinations. Here is a great recipe to start with by former Iowa State Fair food judge, radio host, columnist, and cookbook author Evelyn Birkby.

DIVINITY CREAM CANDIES

½ cup water
½ cup corn syrup
2 cups sugar
2 egg whites
½ teaspoon vanilla

Combine water, corn syrup, and sugar. Cook, stirring to dissolve sugar. Continue boiling over moderate heat without stirring until brittle when a little of it is dropped in cold water (280°F on a candy thermometer). Beat egg whites until stiff, then continue beating while drizzling in the hot syrup. Add flavoring. When mixture holds its shape, drop onto waxed paper in little mounds. Allow candies to sit at room temperature until dry to the touch and no longer sticky.

Makes approximately 40 candies.

Evelyn Birkby, Up a Country Lane Cookbook, *University of Iowa Press, 1993*

THE EARLY 1900s

1920s – 1930s

IOWA'S RISE TO THE TOP

RECIPES

BREADS
Caraway Rye Bread, *Sharon Lesan* **60**
Date Nut Yeast Bread, *inspired by Mrs. Jake Galloway* **62**
Nut Quick Bread, *Mrs. A. A. Johnson* **62**
Date Pecan Quick Bread, *Marjorie Burkgren* **63**
Cornmeal Buns, *Joyce Larson* **63**

MUFFINS & DOUGHNUTS
Apple Crunch Muffins, *Kitchen-Klatter* **65**
Oatmeal Date Muffins, *Kitchen-Klatter* **66**
Quick Bake Cinnamon Doughnuts, *Mrs. Elliott Smith* **67**

CAKES
Election Day Cake, *inspired by Beulah Schenk* **68**
Almond Cake Roll with Raspberry Sauce, *Kathleen Tinley* **70**
Pear Walnut Upside Down Cake, *Cassandra Hyatt* **71**
Lemon Layer Cake, *Jessica Denner* **72**
Dark Fruit Cake, *Mrs. A. A. Johnson* **73**
Applesauce Cake, *Monica Wittry* **74**

COOKIES
Lemon Ice Box Cookies, *Mellie Moser* **76**
Coconut Cookies, *Mellie Moser* **77**

CANDY
Penuche, *Phyllis Person* **78**

1920s–1930s
IOWA'S RISE TO THE TOP

Ruth Law

Opening day of the 1920 Iowa State Fair set new records with more than 49,000 in attendance. Crowds at the Grandstand cheered the best pyrotechnic pageant in the Midwest, and aviatrix ace Ruth Law looped above the racetrack in a trail of colored fire.

BEULAH SCHENK: CULINARY SUPERWOMAN

While Ruth Law set records in aviation, Iowa State Fair food competitors raised the bar to new heights of their own. The Pantry and Kitchen Division blossomed into the Culinary Department. Mrs. Beulah Schenk of Des Moines became supervisor in 1924. Within a few years, she took over as superintendent and reorganized the department. During her 18-year tenure, culinary contests moved from the first floor of the Horticulture Building to a larger space in the Education Building. Glass display cases brimmed with prizewinning exhibits. Food judges tasted and critiqued a wave of entries from across the state. Exhibitors held an annual picnic, where the lunch baskets were legendary and recipe swapping must have lasted into the afternoon. With Beulah in charge, baking contests changed with the times, while food preservation and other traditional favorites expanded.

Beulah competed in the Culinary Division before she ran it. Her Election Day Cake earned her one more first-place ribbon at the 1923 Iowa State Fair. Mrs. Jesse Alexander of Indianola was the cake champion that year.

DEPARTMENT HEAD

MRS. BEULAH SCHENK.

Photos ©The Des Moines Register – USA TODAY NETWORK

54   BAKING BLUE RIBBONS

She joined the ranks of Super Exhibitors, winning virtually every cake category with 18 blue ribbons, including vintage favorites like bride's cake, almond layer, pineapple, and citron. Longtime competitor Mrs. A. A. Johnson of Gladbrook earned top premiums for whole grain bread and rye, along with several quick breads and cakes. Mrs. J. A. Peters of Ankeny baked the best white bread.

LATE 1920s: FANCY CAKES AND MORE SPACE

A debut fancy cake contest took the art of cake decorating to a new level in 1927. Helta McFarland of Conrad won with an elegant dessert shaped like a log with a fondant swan on top. Showstopping cakes like this are still a favorite State Fair food exhibit.

> *"All day yesterday women with entries in the food contests sat outside the glass partitions and watched the judges work. Their eyes followed every move the judges made, and they needed no announcement when the names of winners were released."*
>
> –The Des Moines Register, *August 30, 1927*

A new culinary space was built inside the Agriculture Building in 1926 to accommodate the growth. It was expected to house the contests for another decade but had to be enlarged in 1927 and again in 1928 due to the rapid rise in food exhibits.

1923: Miles and Miles of Cakes and Cookies

> *"If put in a row, side by side, all the cookies and cakes promised for the Culinary Department at the 1923 Iowa State Fair would extend miles and miles. You simply can't miss them!"*
>
> Des Moines Register, *August 15, 1923*

1930s Iowa State Fair

EDUCATING IOWA'S HOME COOKS

Beulah Schenk's extensive home economics training came through in everything she did for the Fair. The focus on educating Iowa's home cooks set a course for success that continues today.

Judging entries did not end with first-, second-, and third-place ribbons. A uniform scoring system emphasized criteria such as flavor, texture, and appearance. Exhibitors received scorecards with checkmarks and handwritten tips to improve their recipes and techniques at home. As more women entered, the standard of excellence improved. Gone were the days of judging breads and cakes on looks alone.

"Every loaf must look as good as it tastes and taste as good as it looks. A loaf that isn't better than mother used to make doesn't stand a chance, and fancy decorations will not win a prize for a cake that is hard in the center," said 1928 culinary judge Mrs. Grace Ellis of Sac City.

A few recipes that made the grade included Applesauce Loaf Cake and Gingerbread made by Mrs. Dora Person of Runnells, English Walnut Cake by Mrs. Otis W. Henry of Indianola, Fig Cake from Mrs. A. H. Ketchum of Des Moines, and Penuche Candy Squares from Mrs. J. Galloway of Beaman.

1930s

Culinary premiums topped $1,100 in 1930, with more than 200 contests in addition to awards from sponsors. New classes for whole grains and other health-focused foods were added.

By 1932, the Iowa State Fair Culinary Department rose to #1 in the nation. Despite the Great Depression, Iowa's food entries increased from a few hundred in the 1920s to over 4,000 in the 1930s, outpacing other state fairs by 1,000 or more. Everyone wanted to know the secret to Iowa's success. State Fair directors contacted Beulah for advice on organizing their culinary departments with the best judging and scoring practices so that bakers across the nation could benefit.

"Every loaf must look as good as it tastes and taste as good as it looks."

– Mrs. Grace Ellis, Culinary Judge, 1928 Iowa State Fair

BAKING BLUE RIBBONS

The Diamond Jubilee and a Giant Baby Called "Mine"

Des Moines, Special:
Iowa boys and girls are buying this baby elephant for their very own, with thousands of youngsters all over the state contributing nickels and dimes for the purchase of the baby pachyderm from the Indian jungles. The elephant is now on its way to Iowa and will make its first public appearance in a giant boys and girls' parade on Children's Day, August 23, at the Diamond Jubilee Iowa State Fair. Every boy and girl who helped to purchase the elephant is expected to participate in the parade, and the one submitting the best name for the animal will have the honor of riding it at the head of the parade.

The Nashua Reporter, *July 31, 1929*

At the 1929 Iowa State Fair thousands of kids cheered the arrival of their very own baby elephant, which they named "Mine." The 1,160-pound pachyderm kicked off the 75th Anniversary Diamond Jubilee and brought joy to many at the beginning of the Great Depression.

BEULAH BEYOND THE FAIR

When Beulah Schenk wasn't making the Culinary Department #1 for generations to come, she applied her talents throughout the community and beyond. She married Casper Schenk, a prominent Des Moines lawyer, in 1911 and raised their family of three children. As the kids grew, so did Beulah's accomplishments.

She became the *Des Moines Tribune* food editor in 1928. Her motto, according to the newspaper, was "Happy-Efficient-Livable-Progressive Homes."

Beulah wrote a popular book for housewives, *The House That Runs Itself*, with coauthor Gladys Denny Shultz, published in 1930. Reviewers noted that this little book gave housewives and mothers hands-on advice on how to lessen the burden and find more enjoyment in taking care of a home and family. Beulah was a popular speaker and home economics consultant. She offered expertise on topics such as child-rearing, meal planning, and how to design kitchen- and home-based workspaces. She encouraged women to make their homes as efficient as possible so that they would have more time for hobbies, civic engagement—and entering the Fair.

1932 STATE FAIR SIDELIGHTS

A popular place at the Fair this year is the writing desk in the lobby of the Administration Building. There you may write all the folks at home on stationery with the State Fair letterhead, proving that here you are.

A hush fell over the Fairgrounds shortly after 4 p.m. Saturday. The streets and tents were deserted. The stillness increased until almost a pin could be heard on its traditional drop. Not a barker barked. Even the Chamber of Commerce booth was deserted. Why?— *The big train smash!*

WONDER BAKERS AND THEIR RECIPES

As the Culinary Department rose to the top, baking companies took notice. Brands like Omar Wonder Flour and Gold Medal featured Iowa State Fair champions in print ads across the state. "Wonder Bakers" like Mellie Moser of Dallas Center, Carol Wiggins of Prairie City, Mrs. J. Galloway of Beaman, and others were pictured with testimonials of their blue ribbon totals. They gained local celebrity status and elevated the hard work and creativity of home cooks.

Advertisements and contest sponsorships added prize money during difficult economic times. Several hundred dollars might be awarded in a single cake contest, versus the typical range of $5, $3, or $2 in official State Fair premiums.

Prize money is tantalizing, but Iowa's home cooks through the generations would tell you that silk ribbons, shared recipes, and friendships are much longer-lasting.

The recipe section highlights a few of Iowa's Wonder Bakers along with vintage recipes inspired by winning entries of the 1920s and 1930s.

Image from The House That Runs Itself, *by Beulah Schenk and Gladys Denny Shultz, 1930.*

58   BAKING BLUE RIBBONS

Wonder Bakers

Wonder Bakers, clockwise from top right: Mrs. J. A. Peters of Ankeny, Mrs. V. S. Hanft of Columbus Junction, Mrs. Bertha Wiggins of Prairie City, and Mrs. Agnes Dwyer (judge) congratulating Mrs. Mellie Moser of Dallas Center. —The Daily Times Davenport, Iowa, August 31, 1934

1920s–1930s

1920s – 1930s
STORIES AND RECIPES

Breads

Mrs. A. A. Johnson began exhibiting at the Iowa State Fair in 1914 and was still winning ribbons in the 1930s. In 1931, she submitted the largest number of culinary entries with 100 exhibits across all classes. Over the years, her baked goods and preserves earned prizes in everything from doughnuts, breads, and cakes to jams and butters. Three of Mrs. Johnson's winning recipes were rye bread, nut bread, and fruit cake. This is an updated rye bread recipe that won first place in 2019, followed by Mrs. Johnson's original quick nut bread and original dark fruit cake in the cakes section.

CARAWAY RYE BREAD

1½ packages active dry yeast
¼ cup warm water (110°F–115°F)
¾ cup boiling water
1 tablespoon shortening
¼ cup dark molasses

1½ teaspoons salt
4 teaspoons caraway seeds
1⅜ cups rye flour, divided
1⅜ cups bread flour, divided

In a small bowl soften yeast in warm water. In a pan with boiling water, add shortening, molasses, salt, and caraway seeds; let cool. Add yeast to cooled mixture. Add 1 cup of the rye flour and 1 cup of the bread flour; beat well. Stir in remaining rye flour and enough remaining bread flour to make a firm dough. Turn out onto a lightly floured surface; knead well. Place in greased bowl and turn once to grease top. Cover and let rise until doubled in bulk, about 1 hour. Punch down dough; form into a round loaf. Cover; let rise until doubled in bulk.

Preheat oven to 375°F while dough is rising. Bake for 30 to 40 minutes or until done or internal temperature reaches approximately 205°F. Makes 1 loaf.

Sharon Lesan, Ankeny
First Place, 2019 King Arthur Flour Bread–Caraway Rye Bread
Second place overall, King Arthur Flour Bread

Wonder Bakers: Center, Mrs. J. Galloway (Beaman) Top row from left: Mrs. L. O Gaston (Madrid); Mrs. Leroy Bane (Bondurant); Mrs. C. F. Peitzman (Grimes). Bottom row: Mrs. N. E. Johnson (Des Moines); Mrs. W. H. Paynter (Colfax). The Muscatine Journal and News-Tribune, *October 11, 1933.*

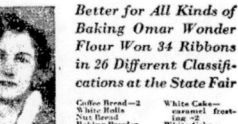

DATE NUT BREAD—TWO WAYS TO WIN

Mrs. Jake Galloway of Beaman earned many blue ribbons for her cakes, breads, and rolls throughout the 1920s, 1930s, and beyond. She had lots of practice, baking several times a week for her four boys. Her date nut quick bread and yeast bread versions were both favorites at the Galloway dinner table and at the Fair. The recipes on the following pages are two modern winners, one from the 1990s and the other an updated version inspired by Mrs. Galloway.

DATE NUT YEAST BREAD

1 package active dry yeast
¼ cup water
½ cup sugar
2 teaspoons salt
¼ cup shortening
2 cups scalded milk
6½ to 7 cups sifted flour, divided
1 cup chopped dates
1 cup chopped walnuts

Soften the yeast in warm water (about 110°F). Add sugar, salt, and shortening to milk and cool mixture to lukewarm. Add 2 cups flour and mix well. Add softened yeast mixture to this; mix well. Stir in dates and walnuts. Add flour to make a moderately stiff dough. Turn out onto a lightly floured surface and knead until dough is smooth and satiny, 5 to 8 minutes. Shape into a ball and place in a greased bowl. Turn dough to grease top. Cover and let rise in a warm place until doubled in bulk, about 1½ to 2 hours. Punch down. Divide into 2 equal balls of dough. Let rest 10 minutes. Shape each one into a loaf and place in 2 greased 9x5-inch loaf pans. Let rise until dough doubles, about 1 hour. During the second rise, preheat oven to 375°F.

Bake for about 40 minutes. Brush with butter while still warm, if desired. Makes 2 loaves.

Recipe inspired by Mrs. Galloway and adapted from Better Homes & Gardens New Cookbook. *Meredith Publishing Company, 1953.*

NUT QUICK BREAD

Mrs. A. A. Johnson's recipe for Nut Bread won first place at the Iowa State Fair for eight years during the 1920s and 1930s. An updated version follows this vintage recipe.

1 egg
1 cup milk
2½ cups flour
1½ cups sugar
2½ teaspoons baking powder
¾ cup chopped nutmeats

Preheat oven to 350°F. Beat egg well. Combine with milk. Sift dry ingredients together into a large bowl. Add milk and egg mixture to dry ingredients. Mix in nuts. Beat until batter is smooth. Pour into greased 9x5-inch pan. Let stand 15 minutes, then bake for about 45 minutes. Makes 1 loaf.

Mrs. A. A. Johnson, Gladbrook
First Place Quick Bread, 1920s–1930s, multiple years

DATE PECAN QUICK BREAD

This updated nut bread with dates comes from Marjorie Burkgren, who first entered State Fair baking competitions in the early 1990s. She earned many awards for cinnamon rolls and other recipes. Marjorie inspired her daughter, Marta Burkgren, and grandchildren, Meredith and Tim, to continue the tradition. Marjorie's signature quick bread is a family favorite.

1 cup chopped dates
1 cup boiling water
1 egg, beaten
1 cup sugar
2 tablespoons butter or margarine
½ teaspoon salt
2 cups all-purpose flour
1 teaspoon baking powder
½ cup chopped pecans

Preheat oven to 350°F. Combine dates and boiling water; set aside until cool. In large bowl combine egg, sugar, butter, and salt. In separate bowl combine flour, baking powder, pecans, and dates with liquid; add egg mixture. Gently mix until moistened. Pour into two greased 8x4-inch loaf pans; let rest 10 minutes. Bake until toothpick inserted in centers comes out clean (45 to 55 minutes). Let rest in pans 15 minutes; remove and cool completely. Makes 2 loaves.

Marjorie Burkgren, Dayton
First Place, 1999 Quick Breads, Dried Fruit

CORNMEAL BUNS

Cornmeal breads have long been a staple of the Iowa State Fair food competitions. Many Wonder Bakers in the 1920s and 1930s earned premiums with different twists on traditional corn bread recipes. Here is a classic cornmeal bun by Joyce Larson that was a big winner in 2018.

1/3 cup cornmeal
½ cup honey
1 teaspoon salt
½ cup melted butter-flavored shortening
2 cups milk
1 package active dry yeast
¼ cup warm potato water (110°–115°F)
2 eggs, beaten
4 cups bread flour

Combine cornmeal, honey, salt, shortening, and milk in top of double boiler. Cook until thickened and cool to lukewarm. Dissolve yeast in warm potato water; let double in size. When cornmeal mixture is lukewarm, add yeast mixture and beaten eggs. Fold in just enough flour to make soft dough. Turn out onto lightly floured surface; knead until smooth. Form into 24 buns. Let rise until light. Place on greased baking sheets; bake for 18 to 20 minutes until golden brown.

Makes 2 dozen buns.

Joyce Larson, New Market
First Place, 2018 King Arthur Flour Yeast Rolls–Non-Sweet Yeast Rolls Other Than Named
Second Place Overall, 2018 King Arthur Flour Yeast Rolls

Muffins & Doughnuts

KITCHEN-KLATTER

Mrs. Leanna Field Driftmier was Iowa's First Lady of recipes and all things domestic for many generations. She began hosting her *Kitchen-Klatter Club and Radio Show* in 1926. Leanna was to radio listeners and housewives across the country what Beulah Schenk was to *Des Moines Register* readers and home cooks. She was a trusted source for recipes to take to the State Fair, or anywhere. Leanna shared thousands of recipes from her listeners through the radio, *Kitchen-Klatter Magazine*, and later the *Kitchen-Klatter Cookbook*, where we found delightful muffins to start your day.

The Evening Journal, *Wilmington, DE, February 4, 1928*

> The Kitchen Klatter Club comes to order each week with a membership of 15,000 and a visiting list of many more thousands. With that Mrs. Leanna Field Driftmier opens another of her series of weekly household meetings over station KFNF at Shenandoah, Ia., for which she has become famous. She's been at it for two years, and has gained almost as great a following as her famous brother Henry, owner of KFNF. Yet, this busy woman is mother of seven children.
>
> **Mrs. Driftmier**

©*The Des Moines Register* – USA TODAY NETWORK, 1924

64 BAKING BLUE RIBBONS

APPLE CRUNCH MUFFINS

"There is no muffin that tastes quite so good in the fall as an apple muffin. We hope you stir these up for your family. They are also delicious for those drop-in coffee guests."
—Mrs. Leanna Field Driftmier and *Kitchen-Klatter Cookbook* editors.

¼ cup margarine or butter, softened
½ cup sugar
½ cup milk
1 egg, beaten
½ teaspoon vanilla
1½ cups flour
¼ teaspoon salt
2½ teaspoons baking powder
½ teaspoon cinnamon
1 cup diced raw apple

Preheat oven to 350°F. Cream butter and sugar. Add milk, egg, and vanilla. Combine dry ingredients. Add diced apple. Gently mix until apples and dry ingredients are evenly distributed. Place in greased or lined muffin pan and prepare topping.

TOPPING
⅓ cup brown sugar
½ teaspoon cinnamon
½ cup finely chopped nuts

Combine and sprinkle topping over muffins and bake for about 20 minutes.

Makes 10–12 standard muffins.

Leanna Field Driftmier, Kitchen-Klatter Cookbook, *Third Edition, published by The Prairie Press, Inc., 1973*

OATMEAL DATE MUFFINS

This combination of dates and oatmeal is packed with flavor and light on sugar. If you prefer large muffins, we suggest doubling the recipe.

1 cup sifted flour
¼ cup sugar
3 teaspoons baking powder
½ teaspoon salt
3 tablespoons shortening
1 cup quick-cooking rolled oats
½ cup chopped dates
1 egg
1 cup milk
½ teaspoon Kitchen-Klatter butter flavoring (or vanilla)

Preheat oven to 400°F. Sift the dry ingredients into a bowl. Cut in the shortening until the mixture is well blended. Stir in rolled oats and chopped dates. Combine the egg, milk, and flavoring; add to the dry ingredients. Pour batter into well-greased muffin tins or line with paper cups. Bake for about 15–20 minutes. Makes 10–12 standard muffins.

Leanna Field Driftmier, Kitchen-Klatter Cookbook, *Third Edition, published by The Prairie Press, Inc., 1973*

MRS. SMITH'S BAKED DOUGHNUTS, 91 YEARS LATER

Both baked and raised doughnuts have racked up ribbons at the State Fair since at least 1916. These supereasy cinnamon baked doughnuts earned first place in 2019 for Mrs. Elliott Smith of Des Moines, following in the footsteps of Mrs. Lester Smith's 1928 winner.

QUICK BAKE CINNAMON DOUGHNUTS

2 cups all-purpose flour
1½ cups sugar
2 teaspoons baking powder
1 teaspoon ground cinnamon
½ teaspoon ground nutmeg
½ teaspoon kosher salt
1 egg, lightly beaten
1¼ cups whole milk
2 tablespoons unsalted butter, melted
2 teaspoons pure vanilla extract

FOR THE TOPPING:
8 tablespoons (1 stick) unsalted butter
½ cup sugar
1 tablespoon ground cinnamon

Preheat the oven to 350°F. Spray two doughnut pans well. Sift together flour, sugar, baking powder, cinnamon, nutmeg, and salt into a large bowl. In a separate bowl whisk together egg, milk, melted butter, and vanilla. Stir wet mixture into dry ingredients until just combined.

Spoon the batter into doughnut pans, filling each one about three-quarters full. Bake for 12–15 minutes, until a toothpick comes out clean and doughnuts are light golden brown. For mini doughnuts, bake approximately 8 minutes. Allow to cool for 5 minutes, then tap the doughnuts out onto a sheet pan.

For the topping, melt the 8 tablespoons of butter over medium heat. Combine sugar and cinnamon in a small bowl. Dip each doughnut first in butter and then in cinnamon-sugar on one side or both sides. Makes 12 donuts or approximately 36 mini doughnuts.

Mrs. Elliott Smith, Des Moines
First Place, 2019 Quick Breads–Quick Breads Other Than Named

1920s–1930s

Cakes

BEULAH'S ELECTION DAY CAKE
Celebrating Women Who Vote and Bake

Beulah Schenk won a blue ribbon for her Election Day Cake in 1923, the year before she became superintendent of the Culinary Department. This cross between fruit cake and sweet yeast bread was served to voters after casting their ballots in the late 1700s. The Iowa legislature passed the Nineteenth Amendment in 1919, giving women the right to vote. Women across the nation began voting the following year. Beulah was known for supporting women on the domestic front and in organizations throughout the state. This version of her 1923 winner is a unique breadlike cake with dried fruit and nuts floating in every slice. Beulah's recipe was likely baked as a large loaf cake. Our modern-day version works well in a tube pan. Drizzled with a brandy glaze, it is perfect for celebrating the right to vote or any special occasion.

ELECTION DAY CAKE

4½ teaspoons (2 packets) active dry yeast
1 cup warm water (approximately 105°F)
3 cups all-purpose flour, divided
1½ cups of your favorite chopped dried fruits, such as currants, cranberries, golden raisins, apricots, dates, or figs
½ cup pecans, coarsely chopped and toasted
1 heaping tablespoon brown sugar
3 tablespoons brandy or water
1½ teaspoons cinnamon
½ cardamon
½ teaspoon table salt
¾ cup (1½ sticks) unsalted butter, at room temperature
½ cup sugar
3 large eggs, room temperature
1 teaspoon vanilla extract

GLAZE
1 cup powdered sugar
2 tablespoons brandy or milk
½ teaspoon vanilla extract

BAKING BLUE RIBBONS

For the cake: Sprinkle the yeast over warm water in a large bowl. Gently stir and let stand until the yeast has dissolved and mixture begins to bubble, about 1 to 2 minutes. Sift 1½ cups of the flour into the bowl and stir until mostly smooth. Cover and set in a warm place for about 30 minutes. The mixture will expand and should have a loose texture with large bubbles on the surface. Place dried fruit, pecans, brandy or water, and brown sugar in a microwave-safe bowl and heat through for about 30–40 seconds. Stir until the sugar is dissolved; set aside to cool. Sift the remaining 1½ cups flour, cinnamon, cardamon, and salt into a medium bowl. Generously butter a 12-cup tube pan or spray with a vegetable oil and flour baking spray. When the flour-yeast mixture has risen, beat the butter, vanilla, and sugar in a large bowl until light and fluffy. Beat in eggs, one at a time, scraping the sides of the bowl after each addition. Mix thoroughly. Stir in the flour-yeast mixture until combined, then gradually beat in the flour-spice mixture. Add the fruit and nut mixture with any remaining liquid and beat until the fruit is evenly distributed. The dough should be soft, loose, and elastic, like a cross between silky dough and thick batter. Transfer the dough to the prepared pan and cover. Let rise in a warm place until the dough fills the pan a little more than ¾ of the way to the top, approximately 1 hour. Preheat the oven to 375°F about halfway through the rising process. Remove the cover and bake the cake for about 40–45 minutes until golden brown and a cake tester placed in the middle comes out clean. Cool for 30 minutes in the pan, then loosen and turn the cake out onto a wire rack to cool completely.

For the glaze: Stir the powdered sugar with milk (or brandy) and ½ teaspoon vanilla in a small bowl. Add additional liquid, a teaspoon at a time, to achieve a thick glaze. Drizzle over the cake; glaze will drip down the inside and outside and cover most of the cake.

Serves 12–14.

Modern recipe inspired by Culinary Superintendent Beulah Schenk, adapted from multiple sources from the 1950s and 2000s.

ALMOND CAKE ROLL WITH RASPBERRY SAUCE

Mrs. Jesse Alexander of Indianola and others entered winning almond cakes in the 1930s. Eighty years later, Kathleen Tinley of Council Bluffs kept the almond winners on a roll with this swirled confection, complete with mascarpone filling and raspberry sauce.

CAKE
2/3 cup all-purpose flour
½ teaspoon baking powder
1/8 teaspoon salt
4 eggs, separated
¾ cup granulated sugar, divided
1 teaspoon vanilla
¼ teaspoon almond extract
½ cup finely chopped toasted almonds
¾ cup powdered sugar

Preheat oven to 375°F. Butter a 17x12x1-inch baking sheet and line with parchment paper; set aside. Whisk together flour, baking powder, and salt in a small bowl. Beat egg yolks in large mixing bowl. Slowly beat ½ cup of the granulated sugar into egg yolks. Beat until mixture is pale yellow and thickened. Beat in vanilla and almond extract. Fold flour mixture into egg yolks. Wipe clean large mixing bowl and beaters with paper towel dampened with vinegar. Beat egg whites until foamy. Slowly add remaining granulated sugar; beat to soft peaks. Fold egg whites and almonds into egg yolk mixture. Gently spread batter into prepared pan. Bake 12 to 14 minutes, until cake bounces back when lightly touched in the middle. Cool cake in pan 2 minutes. Sift powdered sugar onto kitchen towel spread out on counter. Invert cake onto towel; remove parchment paper. Starting at longer side, roll cake up in towel. Cool rolled up cake on baking rack.

MASCARPONE FILLING
1½ cups mascarpone cheese
1 cup cold heavy cream
2 cups powdered sugar, divided
1 teaspoon vanilla
¼ teaspoon almond extract

Beat mascarpone cheese with whisk attachment in large mixing bowl until smooth. Add cream, ¼ cup of powdered sugar, vanilla, and almond extract. Beat to firm peaks. Unroll cake; spread filling over cooled cake. Roll up cake. Place filled cake seam side down on tray. Slice ends off cake at an angle. Sift remaining powdered sugar over cake and chill. Serve with Raspberry Sauce.

RASPBERRY SAUCE
24 ounces frozen raspberries, thawed
2 teaspoons lemon juice
2/3 cup granulated sugar

Press thawed raspberries through strainer to release 1 cup juice. Heat raspberry juice in small saucepan over medium heat. Bring juice to a boil; reduce to ¼ cup. Puree strained raspberries. Press through strainer to collect 1 cup raspberry puree. Stir together reduced raspberry juice, raspberry puree, sugar, and lemon juice. Serve alongside cake roll slices. Serves approximately 14–16.

Kathleen Tinley, Council Bluffs
First Place, 2019 Hy-Vee Smiles in Every Aisle—Cake Rolls
First Place Overall, 2019 Hy-Vee Smiles in Every Aisle—One-layer cakes and cupcakes

PEAR WALNUT UPSIDE-DOWN CAKE

For this recipe, we fast-forward from winning English walnut loaf and layer cakes from the 1920s to the 2000s where Cassandra Hyatt added pears for a beautiful autumn upside-down cake. The crushed walnuts blend into the flour and the pears shine through the rich caramelized topping.

TOPPING
4 tablespoons unsalted butter, melted
½ packed brown sugar
2 teaspoons cornstarch
⅛ teaspoon salt
3 ripe, but firm Bosc pears

Lightly grease a 9-inch round cake pan and line with parchment paper. Pour butter into pan and swirl to coat. Combine brown sugar, cornstarch, and salt in small bowl. Sprinkle over butter. Peel, halve, and core pears. Cut 5 pear halves into 4 wedges each. Set aside remaining half for other use. Arrange pears in circular pattern in cake pan.

CAKE
1 cup toasted walnuts
½ cup flour
½ teaspoon salt
¼ teaspoon baking powder
⅛ teaspoon baking soda
3 large eggs
1 cup sugar
4 tablespoons unsalted butter, melted
¼ cup vegetable oil

Preheat oven to 300°F. In food processor pulse walnuts, flour, salt, baking powder, and soda until walnuts are finely ground. Transfer to a bowl. Process eggs and sugar until lemon color, about 2 minutes. With processor running, slowly add melted butter and oil until mixed. Add walnut mixture; pulse to combine. Pour batter evenly over pears. Bake until center of cake bounces back, 70 to 80 minutes. Cool cake for 15 minutes. Loosen cake by running knife around edge. Invert cake onto wire rack; remove parchment paper. Let cool 2 hours before serving.

Cassandra Hyatt, Ankeny
First Place, 2019 Hy-Vee Smiles in Every Aisle—Any Fruit Cake Other Than Named Second Place Overall, One Layer Cakes and Cupcakes

LEMON LAYER CAKE

Bright, lemony cakes have graced the winners' table since the early 1900s when Mrs. F. M. Person of Altoona and other bakers brought their best lemon and citron creations. Here Jessica Denner triples the citrus intensity with three layers filled with lemon curd and covered in lemon buttercream.

LEMON CURD FILLING
6 egg yolks
1½ tablespoons grated lemon zest
¼ teaspoon lemon extract
½ cup freshly squeezed lemon juice
¾ cup sugar
½ cup unsalted butter, cut into small pieces

In medium saucepan whisk together egg yolks, zest, lemon extract, lemon juice, and sugar until thoroughly combined. Using a wooden spoon, stir constantly over medium heat. Cook about 20 minutes until thick and bubbly. Remove from heat; add butter, one piece at a time, stirring to incorporate. Refrigerate overnight.

CAKE
1½ cups self-rising flour
1¼ cups all-purpose flour
¾ cup whole milk
¼ cup freshly squeezed lemon juice
2 teaspoons grated lemon zest
1 cup unsalted butter, softened
2 cups sugar
4 eggs, room temperature

Preheat oven to 350°F. Grease and lightly flour three 9-inch round cake pans. Combine flours in a medium bowl; set aside. In separate bowl combine milk, lemon juice, and zest, whisking until smooth; set aside. In a large bowl beat butter on medium speed until smooth. Gradually add sugar; beat until fluffy, about 3 minutes. Add eggs, one at a time, completely incorporating each before adding the next. Add flour blend in four parts, alternating with the milk mixture, beating well after each addition before adding the next. Scrape the bowl and beater, making sure there are no unincorporated ingredients in the bottom of the bowl. Divide batter equally among the prepared pans, smoothing the tops. Bake 20 to 25 minutes, rotating and reversing pans halfway through, or until a toothpick inserted into centers of cake comes out clean. Let cakes cool in pans 10 minutes. Remove from pans; cool completely on a wire rack. When cakes have thoroughly cooled, place one layer on serving plate. Spread one-third of the lemon curd over top; top with second layer. Repeat with curd and then top with third layer.

LEMON BUTTERCREAM
1 cup unsalted butter, softened
8 cups powdered sugar, divided
½ cup freshly squeezed lemon juice
1 teaspoon grated lemon zest

Place butter in large bowl. Add 4 cups of the powdered sugar, the juice, and the zest. Beat until smooth and creamy. Gradually add remaining sugar, one cup at a time, until icing is of spreading consistency. If desired, add a few drops of yellow food coloring and mix thoroughly. Frost the top and sides of cake. Serves 12–14.

Jessica Denner, Polk City
First Place, 2018 Hy-Vee Smiles in Every Aisle—Triple-Layer Lemon Cake

MRS. JOHNSON'S DARK FRUIT CAKE FROM 1934

1 cup brown sugar
½ cup white sugar
½ cup shortening
4 eggs
½ cup sour milk (buttermilk)
¼ teaspoon baking soda
3 cups flour, sifted
2 teaspoons baking powder
1 teaspoon cinnamon
1 teaspoon nutmeg

1 teaspoon allspice
½ teaspoon cloves
1 pound raisins
1 pound currants
1 cup dates
1 cup nuts
1 cup orange, lemon, and citron mixed peel
Blanched almonds
Candied cherries

Preheat oven to 300°F. Cream sugars and shortening very thoroughly. Add well-beaten eggs and continue to beat. Dissolve baking soda in buttermilk. Add to mixture. Sift flour, baking powder, and spices. Add half of flour mixture to fruit and nuts; mix to coat them well. Combine all ingredients; mix thoroughly. Pour into tube pan lined with parchment paper. Bake approximately 2 hours. Mrs. Johnson suggested aging this dark fruit cake for a couple of months before serving. We also enjoyed it served in the first week after baking. Approximately 12 servings.

Mrs. A. A. Johnson, Gladbook
First Place, Fruitcake, 1934

APPLESAUCE CAKE

Apple cakes have come in all shapes and sizes at the Fair since the early 1900s when Iowa was a major U.S. apple producer. This winning recipe by Monica Wittry features a honey-sweetened batter filled with spice and baked in a modern Bundt pan for added moistness and flair—the next generation of Mrs. Dora Person's 1928 Applesauce Cake.

½ cup butter or margarine, softened
¼ cup honey
1 egg
1½ cups plus 3 tablespoons sifted cake flour
1½ teaspoons baking powder
1 teaspoon baking soda
¾ teaspoon cinnamon
¾ teaspoon nutmeg
½ teaspoon salt
½ teaspoon cloves
1 cup unsweetened applesauce

Preheat oven to 325°F. Cream butter and honey until blended; beat in egg. Sift together flour, baking powder, baking soda, cinnamon, nutmeg, salt, and cloves. Gradually add to creamed mixture alternately with applesauce. Pour into greased 6-cup Bundt pan. Bake 55 to 60 minutes or until cake tester indicates done. Cool in pan 10 minutes; remove and cool completely. Prepare frosting. Makes approximately 12 servings.

FROSTING
½ cup powdered sugar
4 teaspoons apple juice
⅓ cup chopped toasted walnuts

Combine powdered sugar and apple juice; beat until smooth. Spread on cake and sprinkle with nuts. To toast walnuts, place in single layer on baking pan. Bake at 325°F 5 to 10 minutes or until toasted.

Monica Wittry, Urbandale
First Place, 1994 Foods Made with Honey, Cakes

Cookies

"Cooking is an adventure that lifts the commonplace routine of meal preparing to the realm of beauty and art"

– Mellie Moser, 1936 Iowa State Fair

MELLIE'S LEMON ICE BOX AND COCONUT COOKIES

Mrs. Mellie Moser of Dallas Center was a champion State Fair baker who won more than 150 prizes from 1926–1936. For Mellie, Fair week was the most exciting time of the year. She rose before sunrise and stayed up late into the night preparing everything from cakes, breads, and cookies to pickles, jams, and canned goods. She was known for her generosity in helping other cooks and for the artistry of her exhibits. Mellie was one of Iowa's Wonder Bakers who appeared in several advertisements for Omar Wonder Flour. As she said in a 1936 *Des Moines Register* interview, "Cooking is as exciting as a mystery story—you never know exactly how it is going to turn out." In addition to managing Moser Farms and cooking for her family, Mellie thrilled at the challenge of culinary competitions.

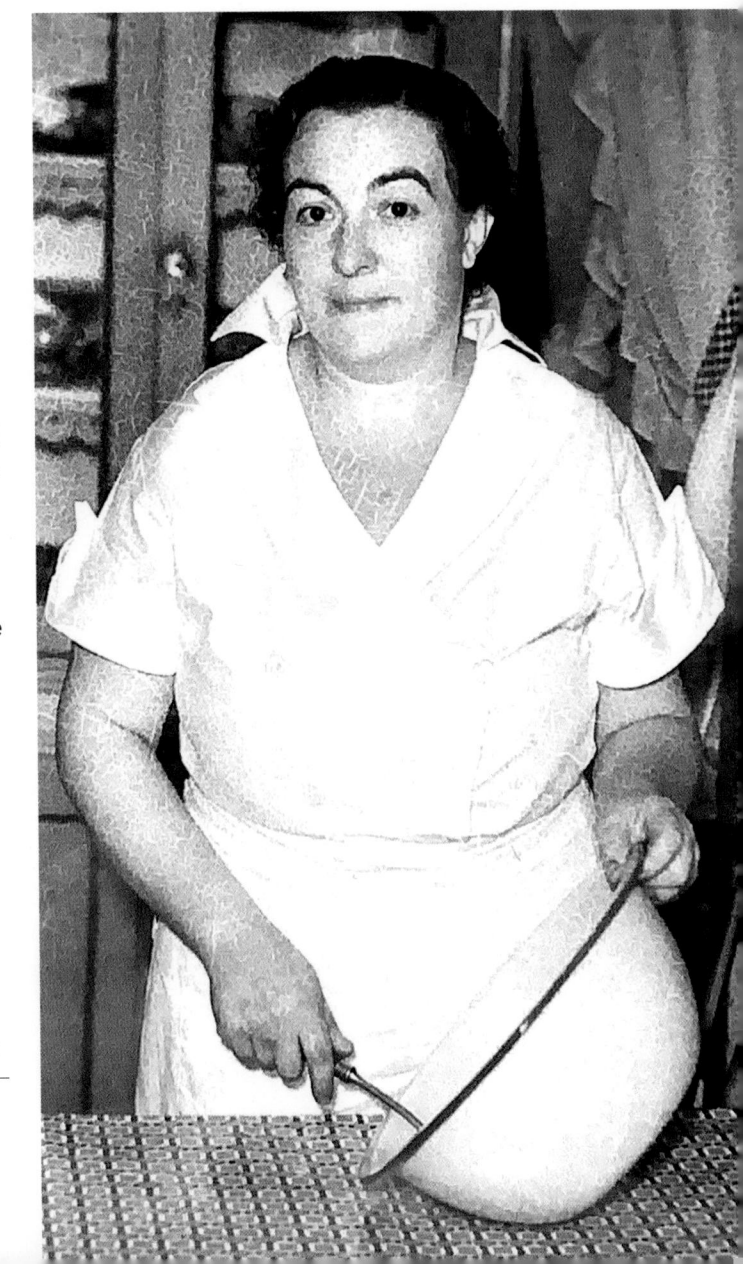

Mellie Moser baking at her farmhouse in Dallas Center.

Mellie Moser's cookies won first place every year she exhibited at the Fair. Lemony ice-box treats like these were her favorite, along with her coconut drop cookies. For the lemon cookies, we've swapped Crisco for lard in her original recipe and added a zippy drizzle to complement Mellie's artistic flair.

LEMON ICE BOX COOKIES

¾ cup butter, room temperature
¾ cup Crisco
3 eggs
1 teaspoon lemon extract
1 cup brown sugar
1 cup white sugar

5 cups flour
1 teaspoon salt
1 teaspoon baking soda
1 teaspoon cinnamon
Zest of 1 lemon
1 cup finely chopped nuts

Blend butter and Crisco until light and thoroughly combined. Scrape down sides of bowl and add eggs and lemon extract, beating until well blended. Blend in sugars and mix well. In a separate bowl sift together flour, salt, baking soda, and cinnamon. Add lemon zest and dry ingredients to butter mixture and blend until fully incorporated. Mix in nuts until evenly distributed. Form soft dough into four logs, each about 6½ inches long and 1¼ inches in diameter. Wrap logs in plastic wrap and place in freezer for at least 2 hours or overnight. When ready to bake, preheat oven to 350°F. Line cookie sheets with parchment or baking mat. Slice dough into rounds, about ¼ inch thick. Bake for 8–10 minutes or until light golden brown. Cool completely and decorate with lemon icing.

LEMON ICING
2 cups powdered sugar
4 tablespoons fresh lemon juice or milk
A few drops vanilla

Combine powdered sugar with lemon juice, one tablespoon at a time, until you have the consistency of a thin frosting. Add vanilla and mix well. Pipe over cooled cookies. Keep any leftover dough in the freezer for cookies anytime. Makes 5–6 dozen.

Mellie Moser, Dallas Center
Adapted recipe for prizewinning Ice Box Cookies, 1934 Iowa State Fair

COCONUT COOKIES

Mellie's recipes made cookies to feed a crowd like this dough, which is sprinkled with shredded coconut and baked into cakelike treats.

1½ cups sugar
1 cup butter, softened
½ teaspoon baking soda
½ cup sour cream
½ teaspoon salt
⅛ teaspoon nutmeg
2 teaspoons baking powder
4½ cups flour, divided
3 eggs, beaten
1 teaspoon coconut extract
½ teaspoon lemon extract
Shredded coconut to sprinkle on cookies before baking

Preheat oven to 350°F. Line cookie sheets with parchment paper or baking mat. Cream sugar and butter until very light. Dissolve baking soda in sour cream; add to sugar-butter mixture. Sift salt, nutmeg, and baking powder with 1 cup flour. Beat thoroughly into sugar-butter mixture. Blend in eggs and extracts. Add remaining flour and mix well. Chill cookie dough for at least 30 minutes. Drop by 2-tablespoon scoops onto prepared baking sheets. Sprinkle generously with coconut and press into dough. Bake 10–12 minutes until golden brown. Makes about 4 dozen.

Mellie Moser, Dallas Center
Updated recipe for First Place cookies, 1934 Iowa State Fair

Candy

Penuche is a 1920s and 1930s treat that often appeared around the holidays. In 1995, it returned to the Fair with this winning Recipe of Yesteryear.

PENUCHE

1½ cups granulated sugar
1 cup packed brown sugar
⅔ cup light cream
2 tablespoons butter
1 tablespoon light corn syrup
1 teaspoon vanilla
½ cup broken pecans

Butter sides of a heavy 2-quart saucepan. Combine sugars, cream, butter, and corn syrup; cook to soft ball stage (234–240ºF). Remove from heat; cool without stirring to lukewarm. Add vanilla and nuts. Beat until mixture becomes very thick and starts to lose its gloss. Spread in a buttered shallow 9x9-inch pan. Score in squares while warm; cut into 1-inch squares when cool and firm. Makes 81 squares or about 50 1¼-inch squares.

Phyllis Person, Runnells
First Place, 1995 Recipes of Yesteryear, Penuche

The Sioux County Index, *Hull Iowa. February 18, 1927*

1920s–1930s

1940s – 1950s
WONDER BAKERS AND CHAMPION JUDGES

RECIPES

BREADS
Lemon Cherry Coffeecake, *updated from Mrs. Francis Falada* **90**
Best Bread in Iowa, *Mrs. Florence Ponder* **92**
Walnut Yeast Bread, *Mrs. Oscar Vik* **92**
Orange Sunshine Rolls, *Joyce Larson* **94**

CAKES
Lady Baltimore Cake, *Terri Treft* **95**
Mandarin Orange Bundt Cake, *Helen Hutchison* **97**
Unbeatable Gingerbread, *Mrs. Jeanette Van Peursem* **99**
Spice Cake, *Mrs. James Dwyer* **100**
Apricot Picnic Cake, *Alvina Mattes* **101**

COOKIES
World War Victory Snaps, *Charles Peebler* **102**
Chocolate Chip Cookies, *Mrs. Charles Estrem* **103**

PRESERVES
Apricot Jam, *Mrs. Jeanette Van Peursem* **104**

"Many women bake in the evening, then ride all night to get into the Fairgrounds by 9 a.m.," superintendent Beulah Schenk told *The Des Moines Register*. She and 12 assistants welcomed them and collected their entries for a full day of contests and culinary education.

BEULAH'S LAST DAY AT THE FAIR

The department had another banner year in 1941, but it was Beulah's last as superintendent. That summer no one knew that the lights of the Fair would go dark for the next four years. It was a moment to savor sweets—and the availability of sugar—with winning desserts like Lady Baltimore Cake. The elegant three-layer confection has been passed down from generation to generation, collecting ribbons along the way.

WORLD WAR II

The Iowa State Fair was canceled from 1942 through 1945 as part of the national World War II Victory effort. The Fairgrounds and fireproof buildings became a supply depot for the Army Air Corps. Exhibitions across the nation were canceled to conserve gasoline and rubber tires along with food ingredients, including sugar, flour, and butter. Much like World War I, food conservation recipes appeared in newspapers nationwide. While the State Fair went dark, many county fairs continued. Iowa bakers might have won blue ribbons with recipes like Victory Snaps that used honey or syrup instead of sugar.

1940s

In 1940, the Iowa State Fair Culinary Department continued its reign as #1 in the nation. More than 3,000 cakes, pies, cookies, breads, and preserves filled the tables during the Fair. Judging took place in the east end of the Educational Building under the Grandstand. Exhibitors lined up at 7 a.m. on opening day.

Iowa State Fair Cancelled

The 1942 Iowa State Fair has been cancelled, in deference to the wishes of the office of Defense Transportation, and to operate with the government's conservation program for the national victory effort.

The Fredericksburg News, July 2, 1942.

1946: IOWA'S CENTENNIAL EXPOSITION

After World War II, the Fair was back and bigger than ever. Fairgoers were eager to celebrate victory, and Iowa's 100th birthday was a perfect party theme. For the first time, attendance surpassed the half-million mark with the largest profit the Fair had seen. Crowds were drawn to impressive displays of the nation's aerial might, which helped gain victory for the American Allied Forces. The G.I. Farm Family contest honored Iowa's outstanding veterans, and Iowa youth displayed fruits and vegetables from victory gardens. America's biggest stock show along with favorites like the rodeo, harness races, and nightly fireworks lifted spirits. Fairgoers honored the pioneers, who founded Iowa in 1846, and looked ahead to brighter days for the state and our nation after the war.

MRS. JAMES DWYER LIFTS UP THE CULINARY DEPARTMENT

The return of the Iowa State Fair set records in many divisions, but the Culinary Department suffered from continued shortages of key ingredients. Mrs. James Dwyer of Des Moines became the new Culinary Department superintendent. She taught homemaking at Callanan Junior High School and judged contests throughout the 1930s and 1940s. She and her team, along with many longtime competitors, brought the department back to life.

Homemakers saved sugar throughout the year to compete at the Fair. Mrs. Dwyer praised them for their dedication. Culinary premiums declined to $779 from previous highs of well over $1,000. The number of entries in the cake division was down from 200 to 30, but the spirit and quality presented by Iowa's home cooks reached new heights. Mrs. Dwyer appointed Miss Louise Anderson of Des Moines to judge the contests.

Centennial culinary exhibits highlighted kitchens from 1846 and 1946, along with pioneer baking contests where women used recipes from their great-grandmothers' generation.

Mrs. James Dwyer of Des Moines was superintendent of the Culinary Department from 1946–1960. ©The Des Moines Register – USA TODAY NETWORK

Miss Louise Anderson was the 1946 Iowa State Fair culinary judge. She was a graduate of Iowa State University and a home economist for the Iowa Power and Light Company. Louise advised homemakers on how to safely prepare and freeze foods as electricity and modern refrigerators and freezers became widely available in rural Iowa.

Back then, the Culinary Department typically had one judge who tasted and evaluated every type of entry, except preserves and canned goods. In addition to breads, cookies, and other entries, Louise judged cakes on general appearance, texture, quality of crumb, flavor, and aroma while Fairgoers watched her every move. In 1947, Louise had help from Mrs. Chester Pratt of Des Moines.

BEST BIRTHDAY CAKE EVER

The centerpiece of the 1946 culinary show was a display of Iowa centennial birthday cakes. Mrs. Robert Walker of Waterloo entered several fancily iced cakes, but her Iowa birthday cake was a work of art that stood out from the rest. It featured wildflowers surrounded by 100 tiny taper candles. Mrs. Walker fashioned the blossoms out of hot taffy and coated them with glucose. A frosting farmer stood at the center of the giant confection with "Iowa" iced on his blue jeans. A basket of fruit on one arm and a basket of corn on the other and a pig at his feet took the display over the top. For the finishing touch, she frosted each candle to soften the color. We can only imagine the spectacle of this incredible cake.

WONDER BAKERS TO THE RESCUE

Many Wonder Bakers from the 1930s and other longtime competitors grew the department after World War II. Mrs. A. A. Johnson of Eldora and Mrs. W. W. Paynter of Colfax were two of the oldest entrants in both age and years of participation. Mrs. Johnson was back with a winning watermelon cake. Mrs. Paynter's molasses cookies took home the blue. Others included Mrs. Barbara Hayne of Des Moines in her 35th year of competition, Mrs. J. E. Soutter of Des Moines (16 years), and Mrs. W. E. Sanders (15 years) with a blue ribbon recipe for Orange Rolls.

Mrs. Alfred (Mary Florence) Ponder, who began competing in 1928, won 35 first-place ribbons out of 45 entries in 1946. She was presented with an electric stove on the national *Vox Pop* radio show in front of 25,000 Fairgoers who packed the amphitheater for the live broadcast. In 1947, this Super Exhibitor was the grand champion of both white and corn breads with 67 entries overall. Her daughters also competed, following in their mom's impressive footsteps.

Mary Florence Ponder of Newton amassed over 1,000 Iowa State Fair ribbons from 1928 to 1946.

BAKING BLUE RIBBONS

1949 Super Exhibitor

Mrs. Glen Atkins of Yale (far right) came to the Fairgrounds with 77 entries in the family car. Mr. and Mrs. Atkins and daughter Joan (far left) unloaded the culinary cargo. Joan, 16, also had several entries and said that they were up at 2:30 a.m. to start the bread.
–*Iowa State Fair, 1949*, ©The Des Moines Register – USA TODAY NETWORK

1949

Total Iowa State Fair premiums reached nearly $149,000 in 1949, with culinary awards back over $1,000 along with sponsored prizes. Bread winners won $5 from the State Fair Board plus another $10 from the sponsor for that same entry.

Mrs. Chester Pratt of Des Moines served as judge, Mrs. James Hall of Des Moines as assistant, along with help from homemaking students from Callanan Junior High School and Roosevelt and North High Schools in Des Moines. Today students from many central Iowa schools volunteer in the Food Department.

Super Exhibitors like Mrs. Glen Atkins continued to give the department a lift with help from the whole family.

1950s: FIRST CULINARY SWEEPSTAKES AND A TIP FOR TENDER WHITE BREAD

In 1952, Mrs. Oscar Vik of Onawa won the first-ever sweepstakes awarded in the State Fair Culinary Department in the bread division. The sweepstakes award was given to the competitor who won the largest amount in premiums across a single division—not just first place, but all winnings combined. Mrs. Vik earned a total of $20 across the bread contests, placing with several yeast breads, quick breads, and fruit bread. The previous year, she was the top winner with more than 40 blue ribbons in canned goods alone. She began exhibiting the year before World War II and continued for many years.

The 1952 reserve sweepstakes went to Mrs. Vik's friend, Mrs. Francis (Anna) Falada, age 30, of Garner. Mrs. Falada's white bread took top honors out of more than 50 entries. She first won the coveted white bread contest in 1941 at the age of 19.

Her secret? Use potato water instead of milk in your favorite yeast bread recipes for longer-lasting loaves with the best texture and softness.

CAKE MIXES AT THE FAIR?

In the early 1950s, cakes made from boxed mixes were allowed at the Iowa State Fair, but only the homemade frostings covering them were judged. Even so, the Duncan Hines brand proudly advertised that "All Award-Winning Frostings at the Iowa State Fair Won with Duncan Hines Cake Mix Cakes!" Print ads for both flour and cake mix featured champion bakers, including sisters Anna Falada and Agnes Simper of Garner.

Second Place Wins

In 1953, Mrs. W. L. (Jeanette) Van Peursem of Mitchellville won the sweepstakes award in the bread division. She earned a ribbon in virtually every contest she entered, but none of them were blue. Her top premium total came from earning seven second place awards and one third.

7 red ribbons and 1 third + 1 giant sweepstakes ribbon + the most prize money = one terrific year at the Fair!

Jeanette went on to become the superintendent of the Culinary Department in 1961.

Bread Sweepstakes Winner, Jeanette Van Peursem. ©The Des Moines Tribune – USA TODAY NETWORK

BAKING BLUE RIBBONS

NO ONE DOES FOOD JUDGING LIKE THE IOWA STATE FAIR

As food editor for *The Des Moines Register* in the 1940s and 1950s, Wilma Phillips Stewart often judged State Fair food competitions. Many Fairgoers envy the food judge who gets to taste all those perfect cakes, cookies, pies, and breads, but "if they knew what a rugged task it is, they wouldn't envy her a bit," said Mrs. Stewart in 1953.

For Wilma, being a State Fair culinary judge meant getting up early and skipping breakfast for a cup of black coffee. She reported to the Culinary Department in a spotless white judge's dress. Her day began with breads and other less sweet entries. She sliced the loaves and eliminated any with air pockets, uneven bakes, or colors. When it came down to the final loaves still on the table, it was often a better texture or more appealing aroma that put the winner in the spotlight.

So Much More Than Your Score

"One especially nice thing about the score cards is this: If you are really and truly interested in improving your products, a quick check on the back of your score card will tell you the things to do. And if you are a wee bit puzzled about the scoring, you can always find some cooking expert around who can give you the answers."

—Wilma Phillips Stewart, The Des Moines Register food editor 1938–1955.

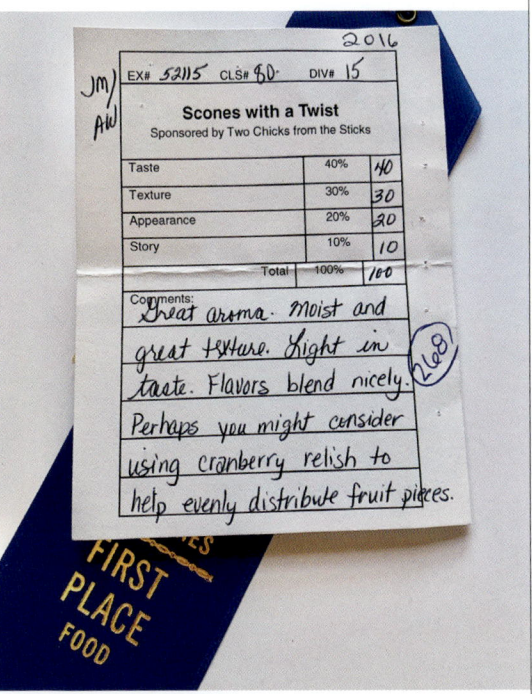

Score cards list the Exhibitor's number. They also include the Division number, which is the contest category, such as Machine Shed Pies, and the Class number, which is the specific contest, such as Lemon Meringue Pie.

1940s–1950s

State Fair Champion Judges

Mrs. Chester Pratt, culinary judge in the late 1940s, wearing the official white judge's uniform and badge.

As the sole judge of the 1949 Culinary Department, Mrs. Chester Pratt of Des Moines sampled every entry, except preserves and canned goods. Assistants helped organize foods and get them to the correct contests, but the judge did the tasting. Like Louise Anderson, Wilma Phillips Stewart, and others, Mrs. Pratt took small bites of at at least 200 cakes, 200 cookies, 75 batches of candy, 25 loaves of white bread, not to mention a large number of quick breads, coffee cakes, cinnamon rolls, popcorn balls, and more during the run of the Fair. "My taste for pastries is more than satisfied during the Fair, and I find myself craving meat and potatoes and fruit," she said in a *Des Moines Register* interview. During the Fair, Mrs. Pratt judged from 9 a.m. to 5 p.m. Friday through Tuesday with Sunday off.

PASS THE DINNER ROLLS
WILMA'S CHECKLIST FOR WINNING ROLLS

- Dough should feel soft and spring back to the touch.
- Rolls must be uniform in shape and size.
- Golden-brown crust.
- Creamy white interior.
- Even grain and texture.
- Not heavy or dense when broken apart—never cut with a knife.
- Balanced taste, not too salty or sweet, and no hint of yeast or flour.
- "A toasted nut flavor with a mouthwatering taste that asks for more."

—Wilma Phillips Stewart on how to judge dinner rolls. The Des Moines Register, August 22, 1948

CLEANSING THE JUDGE'S PALATE

The first few hours of food judging weren't so bad, but after a while it can become difficult to determine which of the excellent cakes or breads is truly the best.

When this happened, Wilma Phillips Stewart gave her taste buds a rest with ice water and lemon juice. Lunch breaks and short naps also helped when possible. Her recommended snack for judges was iced coffee or tea with bland cheese or salty crackers. Watermelon and cantaloupe refreshed the palate. In those days, judges had to sample every entry and speak to the audience in addition to writing comments on the back of each score card.

Any food judge would be exhausted after testing more than 200 entries. As Wilma said, "Food judging is not an enviable job, but still a lot of fun. You meet so many nice people. All women like to swap recipes and ideas, and there's no better place to do it than at the

Iowa State Fair. Get acquainted with your food judge—she's a homemaker who enjoys cooking, just like you and me."

Today there are many judges across different food divisions and contests. They are paired with writers who jot down their comments and advice for the exhibitors to take home at the end of the Fair.

WHY ALL THE NUMBERS, STICKERS, AND TAGS?

Keeping track of thousands of food entries is no easy task. One year, two exhibitors both claimed that they had entered the winning dinner rolls. After much confusion, the first-place baker proved that she had earned the blue ribbon because she had stuck her thumb into the bottom of each one to test it. Sure enough, those perfect rolls all had indentations in the bottom, and the Thumbprint Lady took home the silk.

To this day, every food entry must include a sticker on the bottom of the dish with the exhibitor's number, in addition to entry tags and recipes attached. Food Department exhibitors make their entries online at least a month before the Fair. Stickers, tags, and entry forms are mailed with plenty of time to prepare. In August, when contestants arrive at the Elwell Family Food Center, assistants check each item for proper identification before it is entered into competition. Exhibitors receive a number that stays with them every year that they enter so that the judges cannot identify who prepared the entries. Once judging is complete, the tags are opened to reveal the names of winners, which are announced to the audience along with comments on why they won and tips to improve.

Miss Anna Simper won the white bread award in 1941 at age 19. After she married Francis Falada, she went on to win numerous awards after World War II, including the golden ribbon pin from Fleischmann's Yeast Company in 1959. ©The Des Moines Register – USA TODAY NETWORK, *1946*

1959: ONE GOLEN RIBBON AT THE FAIR

Mrs. Francis (Anna) Falada won the only gold and diamond ribbon pin ever awarded at the Iowa State Fair by the Fleischmann's Yeast Company for her cinnamon rolls. Anna began baking at the age of eight when her big sister, Agnes, taught her. The two culinary artists from Garner amassed more than 1,000 ribbons between the North Iowa and Iowa State Fairs. They were featured in numerous advertisements. Both had impressive competitive baking careers, but Anna surpassed her sister in awards.

When Anna won the golden ribbon in 1959, Agnes could not have been prouder. "I taught her how to bake, but now she is much better than I," she said in a *Mason City Globe-Gazette* interview.

We wish we had Anna's and Agnes' recipe cards, but we begin the 1940s and 1950s recipe section with a Lemon Cherry Coffeecake, inspired by the original Fleischmann's Yeast print ads that celebrated Anna's achievement.

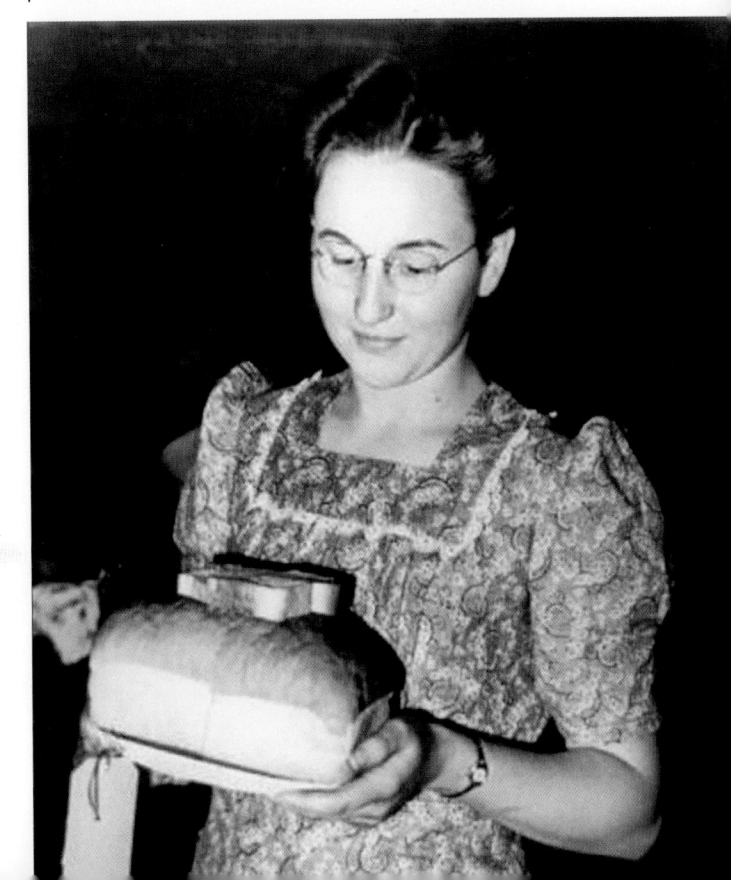

1940s – 1950s
STORIES AND RECIPES

Breads

LEMON CHERRY COFFEECAKE
3½ cups flour
⅓ cup granulated sugar
½ teaspoon salt
Zest of 1 lemon
¼ cup shortening or butter, softened
1¼ cups warm water (110°–115°F)
1 packet active dry yeast (2¼ teaspoons)
1 large egg, lightly beaten
1 large egg white, lightly beaten
½ cup lightly sweetened dried lemon peel, chopped

Whisk flour, sugar, salt, zest, and butter (or shortening) in a large bowl; set aside. Pour water into separate mixing bowl; stir in yeast. Let stand 3 to 5 minutes until bubbly. Add egg, egg white and ½ of flour mixture to yeast mixture and mix on medium speed for about 2 minutes. Gradually add remaining flour mixture and lemon peel. Mix with wooden spoon or dough hook until smooth. Dough will be sticky. Scrape from sides of bowl. Cover and let rise in a warm place until doubled, about 45 minutes to 1 hour. Prepare topping.

LEMON CHERRY TOPPING
⅓ cup sugar
3 tablespoons flour
3 tablespoons butter
½ teaspoon cinnamon
⅓ cup lightly sweetened dried lemon peel, chopped
⅓ cup dried cherries, chopped
⅓ cup pecans, chopped

Add sugar, flour, butter, and cinnamon to a bowl. Using a pastry blender, cut in butter until evenly distributed. Toss in remaining ingredients and stir until all are coated with flour mixture. Set aside until ready to use.

When dough has risen, stir with a wooden spoon for about 20 strokes. Dough will be thick and elastic, like a cross between batter and light bread dough. Generously grease a 9x13-inch pan or 2 round 8- or 9-inch cake pans. Place dough in prepared pan(s). Prepare egg wash and brush over top; sprinkle topping evenly over egg wash. Press lightly into dough, almost to the bottom of pan(s), with your fingertip or a butter knife, making indentations to release air pockets. Cover pan(s); let rise again until doubled, 30–45 minutes. Preheat oven to 375°F. Bake approximately 30 minutes until well-browned. Tent at 20 minutes if browning too fast. If using cake pans, rest for about 5 minutes, then release and cool on a wire rack. When completely cool, drizzle with white glaze, if desired. Approximately 16 servings.

EGG WASH
Beat together 1 egg yolk and 1 teaspoon water.

WHITE GLAZE
1 cup powdered sugar
1–3 tablespoons orange juice

Place powdered sugar in small bowl. Gradually stir in orange juice to achieve desired consistency. Drizzle over coffee cake.

Updated recipe inspired by Cheery Cherry Coffeecake in Fleischmann's Yeast print ads featuring Mrs. Anna Falada, 1959.

BEST BREAD IN IOWA

For 25 years running, until she passed away in 1949, Mrs. Alfred (Mary Florence) Ponder won many ribbons in the Culinary Department. She and her family loved camping at the Fair, and Mary Florence loved watching each day of food judging and catching up with her friends. She was named the overall food winner at the 1946 State Centennial Fair. Mary Florence was so proud of that honor, her family put it on her tombstone: "Centennial Winner 1946 Iowa State Fair."

This is her winning bread recipe, which she called Best Bread in Iowa.

1 tablespoon sugar
1 tablespoon shortening
  (Mary Florence used lard)
1½ teaspoons salt
1 cup boiling water
1 cup scalded milk
2 packets active dry yeast
6–7 cups flour

Put sugar, shortening, and salt in a bowl and pour hot liquids over them; stir to blend and cool. Mix yeast in an additional ¼ cup lukewarm water and stir into the cooled mixture. Gradually add flour and stir until smooth. Turn dough onto a floured surface and knead until mixture feels elastic. Return to bowl, cover, and let stand for 2½ hours in a warm place. Turn out and knead. Shape dough into 2 loaves and place in greased 9x5-inch loaf pans. Let stand for an hour or until dough has doubled in size. Preheat oven to 375°F. Bake approximately 40–50 minutes; cool. Makes 2 loaves.

Mary Florence Ponder, Newton
First Place, 1946 White Bread

MRS. VIK'S WALNUT BREAD

Mrs. Oscar Vik of Onawa won the first Iowa State Fair sweepstakes award for bread. One slice of this yeast nut bread, and you'll know why. Her recipe has the right amount of sweetness to complement the walnut flavor. Mrs. Vik added the champion's touch by braiding her bread after slathering the rolled dough with butter and cinnamon sugar for a beautiful bake, inside and out.

1 cup milk, scalded and cooled
1 tablespoon sugar
1 packet (¼ ounce) dry yeast
3 cups sifted flour
⅓ cup sugar
2 tablespoons melted butter
1 egg white, beaten
½ teaspoon salt

¾ cup finely chopped walnuts, lightly toasted for added flavor
2–3 tablespoons melted butter
¼ cup cinnamon-sugar mixture

Stir yeast and 1 tablespoon sugar into lukewarm milk and allow to rest for about 10 minutes. Add flour, ⅓ cup sugar, 2 tablespoons melted butter, egg white, and salt and mix thoroughly.

Knead by hand or mixer until a smooth dough forms. Cover and let rise in a warm place for approximately 1½ hours, until dough is roughly doubled in bulk. Turn dough out onto a lightly floured surface. Knead in the chopped walnuts. Continue to knead until evenly distributed and dough retains a soft, silky texture.

Roll dough into a rectangle. Brush with melted butter. Sprinkle with cinnamon and sugar mixture. Roll dough up lengthwise and cut into three long equal sections, leaving the top of the dough intact. Braid from the top and pinch ends to seal loaf, tucking ends under. Place in a well-greased 9x5-inch bread pan. Cover and let rise for an hour until the loaf has crowned over the pan about an inch. Preheat oven to 350°F near the end of the second proofing. Bake for 35–40 minutes. Check bread at 20 minutes and tent with foil to avoid overbrowning. Remove from oven and cool 5 minutes before turning out onto a rack to cool. Brush with melted butter and additional cinnamon sugar while loaf is warm, if desired. Makes 1 loaf.

Mrs. Oscar Vik, Onawa.
First Place, Nut Bread, adapted recipe from 1951 Iowa State Fair.

1940s–1950s   93

ORANGE SUNSHINE ROLLS

Another winning entry at the 1946 Centennial State Fair was Mrs. W. E. Sanders' orange rolls. We couldn't find her recipe, but we wanted to share Joyce Larson's winning orange roll recipe, which is refrigerated overnight and ready to bake the next morning for brunch.

ROLLS
¼ cup warm potato water (110° F–115°F)
1 cup granulated sugar, divided
1 package dry yeast
2¾ to 3 cups flour
1 teaspoon salt
2 large eggs
2 tablespoons melted butter
½ cup cold sour cream
⅓ cup softened butter

Combine potato water, 1 teaspoon of the sugar, and yeast. Let sit until foamy. Mix sifted flour, salt, and remaining sugar in a large bowl. Add beaten eggs, melted butter, and sour cream. Add yeast mixture. Turn out onto floured bread board. Knead until smooth. Place in a warm buttered bowl. Butter top of dough. Cover with plastic wrap and chill overnight. The next morning, roll into a rectangle. Spread with softened butter. Spread filling over softened butter. Roll up; slice into 12 to 18 rolls. Place rolls in pan; Let rise until light. Bake in 350°F oven for 18 to 20 minutes. Glaze warm rolls.

FILLING
¼ cup orange marmalade
¼ teaspoon orange flavoring
½ cup sugar
¾ cup toasted coconut flakes
2 tablespoons orange zest

Combine all ingredients and mix well.

GLAZE
¾ cup sugar
½ cup sour cream
¼ cup softened butter
2 teaspoons fresh orange juice
1 tablespoon orange-flavored liqueur

Combine ingredients except liqueur in a heavy saucepan. Heat until boiling; boil 3 minutes. Cool and add liqueur.

Joyce Larson, New Market
First Place, 2018 King Arthur Yeast Rolls–Refrigerated Rolls
First Place Overall, 2018 King Arthur Flour Yeast Rolls

Cakes

HER ROYAL HIGHNESS: LADY BALTIMORE CAKE

Leading up to the 1941 Fair, *Des Moines Register* food editor, Wilma Phillips Stewart, offered her Lady Baltimore Cake recipe that was handed down from her mother. As Wilma said, "No innovation in cake recipes will ever take the place of that royal hand-me-down from Grandmother's cookbook."

Wilma was right. Just ask Terri Treft of Sioux City, who won the Lady Baltimore Cake contest in 2021 with her recipe that is similar to Wilma's heirloom version. Terri has won many cake contests. She researched vintage recipes and added her own twist with peach preserves between each layer for presentation and flavor.

The contest was sponsored by Leisa Ely in honor of her mother, Marjorie Rodgers, a longtime State Fair food exhibitor who retired from competition and could not attend the Fair. After the contest, Terri met Leisa and gave her the cake to take home to Marjorie.

LADY BALTIMORE CAKE

¾ cup unsalted butter, softened
2 cups sugar
3 cups cake flour
3 teaspoons baking powder
½ teaspoon salt
½ cup water
½ cup milk
1½ teaspoons almond extract
6 egg whites

Preheat oven to 350°F. Line bottoms of three 9-inch cake pans with parchment paper and coat with nonstick cooking spray. Cream butter and sugar until light and fluffy. Sift cake flour, baking powder, and salt and set aside. Combine milk, water, and almond extract. Add small amounts of flour mixture to creamed butter mixture, alternating with the milk mixture, and beat until smooth after each addition. Beat egg whites until stiff peaks form and gently fold into batter.

Pour into prepared pans and bake for 20–25 minutes. Allow to cool completely, then divide filling evenly between each layer. Frost sides and top of the assembled cake.

1940s–1950s

FILLING
16-ounce jar peach preserves
¾ cup chopped pecans
2 cups of 7-Minute Frosting, divided

Mix the preserves and pecans together and set aside while making the frosting.

Add 1 cup of frosting to the preserves and pecans.

7-MINUTE FROSTING
2 egg whites
1½ cups sugar
⅓ cup cold water
1 teaspoon corn syrup
1 teaspoon vanilla extract

Combine egg whites, sugar, water, and corn syrup in the top of a double boiler with a few inches of water in the bottom. Mix thoroughly. Place double boiler over low heat and beat constantly with an electric mixer until frosting holds a peak, about 7–10 minutes. Remove from heat and add vanilla. Beat until thick enough to spread.

Makes 1 three-layer cake. Serves 14–16.

Terri Treft, Sioux City
First Place, Lady Baltimore Cake, 2021

MANDARIN ORANGE BUNDT CAKE

In honor of the Bundt pan, invented by H. David Dalquist in 1950, we wanted to include a fantastic Bundt cake recipe in this section. Bundt cake contests did not arrive at the Fair until later, but we couldn't wait for this bright, citrusy winner from youth exhibitor Helen Hutchison, who won the overall prize in the Junior Division in 2018. She is a creative scratch baker, like her mom, Eileen Gannon. This cake gets an extra kick with orange juice glaze drizzled with vanilla or chocolate icing for added flavor. Helen says this cake is one of her all-time favorites. "One of my passions is making things, so that's why I like baking," said Helen. "I get to be creative and eat it too! So baking is really better than art."

2 cups all-purpose flour
1 teaspoon baking soda
¾ teaspoon salt
½ teaspoon baking powder
1¾ cups granulated sugar, divided
¾ cup (1½ sticks) unsalted butter, softened
2 eggs, room temperature
1 cup sour cream, room temperature
4 tablespoons orange liqueur, divided
1 teaspoon pure vanilla extract
2 (11-ounce) cans mandarin oranges, drained well and coarsely chopped
Zest of 1 orange, finely chopped
½ cup orange juice, for glaze

Helen Hutchison (10) with her mom, Eileen Gannon, in 2018, holding Mini-Mandarin Orange Bundt Cakes with vanilla icing.

Preheat oven to 350F. Grease and flour a 10-cup or 12-cup Bundt pan (see note on page 98 for tips on preparing the pan). In a bowl sift together flour, baking soda, salt, and baking powder.

In a stand mixer fitted with a flat beater, beat 1¼ cups of the sugar and butter until light and fluffy. Beat in eggs one at a time. Add sour cream, 1 tablespoon of the liqueur, and vanilla; beat for 2 minutes more. Add the sifted dry ingredients, beating on low speed until just combined. With a rubber spatula, gently stir in mandarin oranges and orange zest by hand. Spoon into the prepared pan, smoothing with spatula. Bake for 45 to 50 minutes or until a toothpick inserted near center comes out with a few moist crumbs still clinging. Do not overbake.

Transfer cake in the pan to a wire rack; let cool 10 minutes. Loosen the cake by jiggling it side to side until it moves slightly. Place a piece of parchment paper over a wire rack. Invert cake onto the parchment paper (which will catch any drips from the glaze).

Meanwhile, to make the glaze, in a small saucepan combine orange juice, the remaining ½ cup sugar, and the remaining 3 tablespoons orange liqueur. Bring to a boil, stirring constantly. Cook until sugar has dissolved. While the cake is still warm, poke holes in the cake with a toothpick. Use a pastry brush to cover the cake with glaze, applying a fourth of the glaze at a time and letting it soak into the cake between additions. Allow the cake to cool completely.

To serve, place the cake on a large platter. Drizzle with vanilla or chocolate icing, if using. Cut into slices. Store covered at room temperature. Serves 12-16.

Tip: To prepare the pan (including the center), use a pastry brush and softened butter and coat the entire interior surface of the pan. Add 2 tablespoons of flour and turn the pan in all directions so the flour coats the butter completely. Tap out excess flour over a sink or trash can.

VANILLA ICING (optional)
½ cup powdered sugar
2 tablespoons butter, melted
¼ teaspoon vanilla
2 teaspoons hot water

Mix together powdered sugar, butter, and vanilla. Stir in water, one teaspoon at a time, until consistency of thick syrup. Drizzle over cake.

CHOCOLATE ICING (optional)
8 ounces (1¼ cups) semisweet chocolate chips
½ cup heavy cream

Place the chocolate chips in a large bowl. Heat the cream in a microwav-safe bowl for 1½ minutes on high in the microwave. Pour hot cream over chocolate and stir with a whisk until smooth. Drizzle over cake.

Helen Hutchison, Des Moines
First Place, 2018 Junior Casey's Favorite Creations—One Layer Cake from Scratch Overall Winner

Mandarin Orange Bundt Cake with chocolate icing.

MRS. VAN PEURSEM'S UNBEATABLE GINGERBREAD

Mrs. Jeanette Van Peursem was a perennial winner before she became the Culinary Department superintendent in 1961. Her amazing Gingerbread recipe was featured in print ads in the early 1950s.

½ cup butter
½ cup sugar
1 egg
2½ cups flour
1½ teaspoons baking soda
½ teaspoon salt
1 teaspoon cinnamon
1 teaspoon ginger
½ teaspoon cloves
1 cup molasses
1 cup hot water

Preheat oven to 350°F. Melt butter and let cool. In a large bowl add sugar and egg to butter and beat well. Sift flour, baking soda, salt, and spices together. Combine molasses with hot water. Add alternately with flour to first mixture. Pour into greased 9x9-inch pan. Bake for about 35–40 minutes or until cake is deep brown. Serve with whipped cream, if desired. Serves 9–12.

Mrs. Jeanette Van Peursem, Mitchellville
1951 Blue Ribbon Winner

1940s–1950s 99

Cake Insurance

Mrs. Tucker's The ONLY SHORTENING That's TRIPLE GUARANTEED!

Culinary superintendent Mrs. James Dwyer became a spokeswoman for Mrs. Tucker's shortening in the 1950s. Mrs. Tucker's stood apart from Crisco by guaranteeing that it would make your cake better than ever before. If you were not satisfied, Mrs. Tucker's would give you your money back, plus payment for your ingredients and a dollar for your baking time. "That's cake insurance any woman would like to have when she bakes, and I can certainly recommend Mrs. Tucker's shortening for anyone to try!" said Mrs. Dwyer in the ads, which included her winning spice cake recipe.

MRS. DWYER'S SPICE CAKE

½ cup Mrs. Tucker's shortening
1 cup brown sugar
1 egg
1 teaspoon vanilla
1¾ cups sifted cake flour
1 teaspoon baking soda
1 teaspoon cinnamon
½ teaspoon nutmeg
¼ teaspoon cloves
1 cup sour milk (buttermilk)
½ cup chopped nutmeats
1 cup raisins

Preheat oven to 375°F. Grease two 8-inch round cake pans with shortening and dust with flour. Cream together shortening and brown sugar. Beat in egg and vanilla. Sift together cake flour, baking soda, and spices. Gradually add flour mixture to egg mixture, alternating with buttermilk. Gently stir in chopped nuts and raisins. Bake for 25 minutes until golden brown.

Makes 2 cakes, which may be layered with frosting or dusted with powdered sugar and served as snack cakes. Serves 12–16.

Mrs. James Dwyer, State Fair winner, before she became Culinary Department superintendent.
Adapted from The Courier, *Waterloo, Iowa. December 15, 1953.*

APRICOT PICNIC CAKE

New aluminum cake pans with lids were all the rage in 1955. Now cakes could be baked, stored, and safely transported in the same pan. No need for plastic wrap, which became popular for home use in the 1950s. This Apricot Picnic Cake from *Des Moines Register* food editor Alvina Mattes is still the perfect treat to make and take for a picnic at the Fair.

CAKE
- 1¼ cups very finely snipped dried apricots
- 1 cup water
- ½ cup butter
- 1 cup sugar
- 1 egg
- 1¾ cups sifted flour
- 1 teaspoon baking soda
- ½ teaspoon salt
- 1½ teaspoons baking powder
- ½ teaspoon cinnamon
- 2 tablespoons lemon juice
- ⅔ cup evaporated milk

Preheat oven to 350° F. Grease a 9x9-inch baking pan. Place apricots and water in a small saucepan and bring to a boil. Cover and simmer 15 minutes, until apricots have absorbed most of the liquid. Remove from heat, mash to a pulp, and cool. Cream butter, then gradually add sugar and cream together until mixture is light and fluffy. Add egg and mix well. Sift flour with baking soda, salt, baking powder, and cinnamon. Stir lemon juice into evaporated milk. Add sifted dry ingredients to creamed mixture, alternating with soured evaporated milk, beginning and ending with dry ingredients. Add apricot pulp to batter, mixing it in evenly. Spread batter in prepared baking pan. Bake 45–50 minutes, until inserted toothpick comes out clean. Finish with broiled frosting. Cool in pan.

BROILED FROSTING
- ⅓ cup sliced blanched almonds, plus more for garnish
- 3 tablespoons butter
- ½ cup brown sugar
- 2 tablespoons evaporated milk or cream

Spread almonds in shallow baking pan and brown lightly in the oven. Melt butter. Stir in brown sugar, evaporated milk or cream, and toasted almonds. Spread on cake and place 3 to 4 inches under broiler for 2 or 3 minutes, until mixture is bubbly. Watch closely to avoid burning. Sprinkle additional almonds over cake for serving.

Adapted from recipe by Alvina Mattes, Des Moines Register *Food Editor, 1959.*

Cookies

WORLD WAR II VICTORY SNAPS

These classic cookies are perfect with coffee and even better the next day when the spices are at their peak.

½ cup butter
½ cup maple syrup or honey
¼ cup molasses
2 eggs
2½ cups flour
2 teaspoons baking powder
½ teaspoon salt
1½ teaspoons ginger
1 teaspoon cinnamon

Cream butter with syrup or honey and molasses. Beat in eggs. Mix flour and dry ingredients together. Add flour mixture to egg mixture until thoroughly combined. Shape cookie dough into a thin log and refrigerate for at least 2 hours, or overnight.

Preheat oven to 350°F when ready to bake. Grease cookie sheets or cover with parchment or baking mat. Cut into rounds, about ¼ inch thick. Bake for 8–10 minutes until cookies are golden brown. Cool for a few minutes on baking sheets; remove to wire racks to cool completely. Makes approximately 3 dozen cookies.

Adapted from the 1942 recipe by Charles Peebler of the Northwestern Bell Telephone Company.

MRS. ESTREM'S CHOCOLATE CHIP COOKIES

Mrs. Charles Estrem baked the best chocolate chip cookies at the 1948 Iowa State Fair. Her recipe, which appeared in Iowa Dairy Industry Commission print ads, would still win blue ribbons today. Some chocolate chip cookie connoisseurs might consider these petite cookies, which is a perfect size for lunch boxes and afternoon snacks.

6 tablespoons sugar
6 tablespoons brown sugar
½ cup butter
1 egg, beaten
½ teaspoon baking soda
½ teaspoon salt
1⅓ cups flour
½ cups chopped walnuts
½ teaspoon vanilla
6 ounces chocolate bits (or chocolate chips, regular or mini)

Preheat oven to 375°F. Grease baking sheets or cover with parchment paper or baking mat. Cream butter with sugars. Add the beaten egg and the baking soda moistened with a few drops of hot water. Sift the flour and salt together into the mixture. Add vanilla and fold in chopped nuts and chocolate chips. Drop on prepared baking sheets by rounded teaspoons and bake 8–10 minutes. Makes 3 dozen.

Mrs. Charles Estrem, Story County
First Place, 1948

The chocolate chip was born in 1939 when Ruth Wakefield, who ran the Toll House restaurant in Whitman, Massachusetts, added broken pieces of Nestle Semi-Sweet chocolate to her batter. She expected the chocolate to melt. Instead, the semi-sweet bits held their shape and softened to a creamy texture—and the chocolate chip cookie was born. Ruth's 'Toll House Crunch Cookie' recipe was published in a Boston newspaper, and her invention became the most popular cookie of all time. It would be impossible to calculate how many ribbons have been won for variations of this recipe at Fairs across the country, beginning in the 1940s.

1940s–1950s

Preserves

APRICOT GOLDEN GLOW: A GEM OF A JAM

Future culinary superintendent Mrs. Jeanette Van Peursem of Mitchellville won more than 50 prizes in the Iowa State Fair Culinary Department using beet sugar. She appeared in promotions for the product across Iowa. During canning season, she used at least 100 pounds of beet sugar and put up about 1,000 jars of fruits, jams, jellies, and relishes. In addition, she froze about 50 quarts of strawberries. Here is her prized recipe for apricot jam.

APRICOT JAM

2½ pounds ripe apricots (20 to 30 medium size)
3½ cups sugar
1 medium unpeeled orange, finely sliced
1 cup diced pineapple
¼ teaspoon salt

Wash and pit apricots, put through food chopper using finest blade or cut into small pieces. Combine apricots and sugar in preserving kettle and boil 15 minutes, stirring occasionally. Add finely sliced orange, pineapple, and salt; cook slowly until thick, about 45 minutes longer, stirring occasionally. Pour into hot sterilized fruit jars or jelly glasses; seal or cover with paraffin at once. Makes about 3 pints or 6 8-oz. jars.

Jeanette Van Peursem's winning jam recipe, 1950.

Edgar amd Slyvia Jacobs, 1952 Iowa State Fair

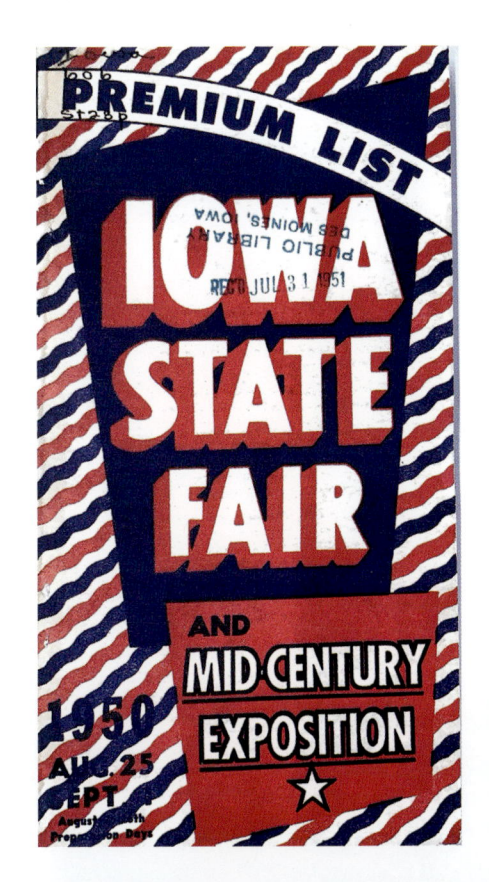

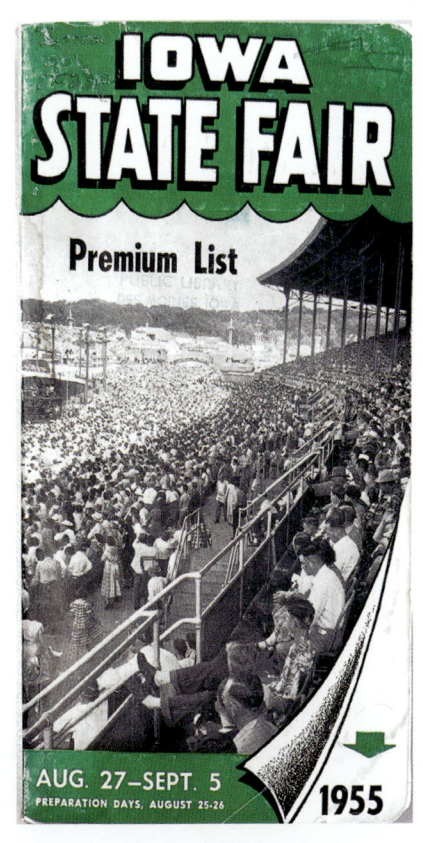

1960s – 1970s
COOKOUT KINGS TO WATERGATE CAKE

RECIPES

BREADS
Corn Bread with Honey, *Mildred Phillips* **116**
Christmas Braid, *Fern Harmon* **118**
Golden Wheat Batter Bread, *Lola Zimmerman* **118**
Kolaches, *Duffy Lyon* **119**

SALADS
Swiss Turkey Salad, Milk Made Magic, *Jeanette Feller* **120**
Watergate Salad **127**

MAIN DISHES & GRILLING
Pork Ribs Seasoning and Old-School Barbecue Sauce, Cookout Kings, *Bob Friesen* **121**
Daddy's Drumsticks, Cookout Kings, *James Lein* **122**
Beef Ribs BBQ Sauce, Cookout Kings, *William R. McGee* **123**
Asian Pork Burgers, Cookout Kings, *Kris Scheppler* **124**
Fruit-Stuffed Pork Chops, Cookout Kings, *Carlene Staade and Ruth Hamilton* **125**
Bacon-Wrapped BBQ Chicken, Cookout Kings, *Mike Anderson* **125**
Bubble Pizza, Milk Made Magic, *Beau Biekert* **126**

CAKES
Watergate Cake **126**
Carrot Cake, *Ruby Groen* **128**
Rhubarb Bundt Cake, *Mrs. Rex Kleckner* **129**

PIES
Key Lime Pie, *Jackie Garnett* **130**
Orange Crunch Pumpkin Pie, *Robert Davis* **132**
Rhubarb Cream Pie, *Jeanette Van Peursem* **134**
North 40 Berry Pie, *Dianna Zaiger Sheehy* **136**

COOKIES
Refrigerator Pyramid Cookies, *Laura Raichle* **137**
Orange Drop Cookies, *Sherri Ihle* **138**
Pineapple Layer Bars, *Robin Tarbell* **138**

DESSERTS
Fruit Clouds, Milk Made Magic, *Tricia Mathiason* **139**

1960s

By 1960, the Fair was on a roll with new innovations and a modern approach. Norma "Duffy" Lyon took over as the butter cow sculptor, the third person and the first woman to do so, on a run that would continue for 45 years. There were free acts on the Plaza Stage (now the Anne and Bill Riley Stage), and major exhibits stayed open until 9 p.m.

Kenneth Fulk was named manager of the Fair in 1962. For the first time, in 1963 Grand Avenue was closed to traffic and became the Fair's Grand Concourse. Sixty-plus high school bands paraded down the street to celebrate. It became the Fair's Main Street and giant walkway. The Clearfield Lions began offering shuttle buses between the Fairgrounds and the Campgrounds in 1964. The first State Fair Queen pageant was held, and the Cookout Kings showed off their grilling prowess on the Grand Concourse.

1961: STAR BAKER-SEAMSTRESS BECOMES CULINARY AND TEXTILE SUPERINTENDENT

Mrs. W. L. (Jeanette) Van Peursem of Mitchellville became the superintendent of the Culinary Department in 1961. Jeanette

CULINARY DEPARTMENT
East End Educational Building and Grandstand

MRS. W. L. VAN PEURSEM
Mitchellville
Superintendent, Culinary and Textile Departments

was born in the Netherlands and came to Iowa when she was 5 years old. Growing up with 10 siblings, she joined 4-H and learned a lot about cooking and sewing. She is the only lady superintendent who oversaw two departments at the same time for 21 years. She had been the Textile Superintendent since 1953 and continued to run both departments through the 1981 State Fair.

Jeanette first entered the culinary contests in 1946 when the Fair reopened after World War II. Alongside veteran exhibitors, she helped rebuild the department by baking and preserving her

108   BAKING BLUE RIBBONS

way to nearly 250 prizes in her first six years. She appeared in print ads for products, including Fleischmann's Yeast and Iowa butter and beet sugar. During the late 1940s, she also dominated the Textile Department. In 1948 she earned 47 sewing and needlework awards and had 60 baking and canning entries. She won the 1953 Culinary sweepstakes award for bread and reserve sweepstakes in spiced foods while running the Textile Department. It must have been busy awarding the prizes in Textiles and collecting them in the Culinary Department. Imagine long days at the Fair followed by late-night baking and rising early to have her yeast coffee cake ready to enter—not to mention her famous Rhubarb Cream Pie. Luckily, the two departments shared space under the east end of the Grandstand, so she did not have far to go.

Iowans love a centennial celebration, and 1961 saw big crowds for the 100th anniversary of the Civil War. There were 250 culinary contests, including throw-back recipes of the 1860s like mince meat pies, dried apples, old-fashioned rolled sugar cookies, dried noodles, and sauerkraut. On the modern side, tried-and-true breads, cookies, cakes, and preserves earned a total of $1,670 in premiums. Jeanette also oversaw an impressive display of original Civil War memorabilia in Textiles.

1963: FROSTING ARTISTS AND CARDBOARD CAKES

Cake artists around the state cheered the return of cake decorating in 1963. Mrs. Van Peursem and her team made it easier by not requiring the designs to be on real cakes. Since these were judged on looks alone, the base could be made from a cake mix, plastic, or cardboard. First-place premiums were $6 in each of four classes: anniversary cake, cake for any occasion, cupcakes, and cookies. For candymakers, she added peanut brittle, white fudge, and mints to popular contests like chocolate fudge, divinity creams, penuche, and popcorn balls. First-place winners received $3.

1964: COOKOUT KINGS

For many years, the State Fair Pantry and then Culinary Department was for women, but in 1964 there was a new contest that only allowed men. Since then, the Cookout Kings have ruled the Grand Concourse with spatulas, spicy marinades, and smokin'-hot grills. Over the decades, more than a thousand county grilling champions have vied for the state title in Des Moines. In 1989, Ms. Gail Goehring of Osceola became Iowa's first Cookout Queen.

Today the Farm Bureau's Cookout Contest is still the hottest competition of summer. The event celebrates backyard barbecues and the hard work of Iowa livestock farmers. Contestants unload their grills and smokers

Bob Henriksen, 1985 Cookout King.
©The Des Moines Register – USA TODAY NETWORK

early. Fairgoers follow the sweet and savory smells to the grilling area, where they meet local celebrities, learn the best grilling techniques, and sample spicy meats and other specialties. State Fair queens and governors have crowned the winners. We've gathered a few favorites in the recipe section, beginning with Bob Friesen's first "old school" barbecue blend from 1964, along with gourmet grillers from across the state and through the decades.

BEST COOKIE OF THE FAIR

Each year hundreds of cookies are entered at the Fair, but only one gets to be the Best of the Fair. Beginning in the mid-1960s, the Archway Cookie Company sponsored State Fair contests throughout the country in search of the ultimate cookie. For generations, Iowa bakers have won $100 savings bonds and bragging rights. In 1969, Mrs. Ahmund Ihle of Slater won the Iowa prize and then clinched the national championship at the 1970 Archway Homestyle Cookie Bake-Off. In addition to her $1,000 savings bond, Archway added her frosted chocolate drop cookie to its brand and distributed them far and wide. Other Iowa winners who have gone on to the national contests include Mildred Phillips, whose peanut butter cookie was featured on *Good Morning America* and in newspapers and magazines.

THE INS AND OUTS OF CULINARY CONTESTS

One challenging job of the culinary superintendent is deciding which contests to add and which to retire. This depends on family and corporate sponsorships as well as food trends.

In the early 1960s, the Sioux Honey Association began a new division with eight honey-sweetened contests, including cakes, candy, pickles, and other baked goods. The sweepstakes winner took home 24 1-pound jars of the golden liquid. Luckily, honey does not expire when properly stored. The all-natural sweetener is still a key ingredient in State Fair food competitions today.

The Porkettes, Iowa Pork Producers Association Auxiliary, brought back the lard division in 1965 after a long absence. Many pie bakers favor lard for their pastry. Back then they competed for $100 in premiums using lard in brownies, cookies, rolls, spice and chocolate cakes, biscuits, pie crust, as well as home-rendered lard. These old-time contests with special ingredients and vintage bakes continue their popularity among sponsors and contestants.

During the late 1960s, contests for hamburger buns, gingerbread boys, frosted marble cakes, and birthday cakes were added. Several conserves, chutney, and pickles were out. Jeanette noticed that Iowa homemakers were baking more entries and canning a bit less. Today, hundreds of jams, jellies, and preserves fill the glass display cases like jewels at the Elwell Family Food Center. One benefit for exhibitors is the convenience of making their entries months in advance to enter in August.

In the early 1970s, cooked rhubarb was out, and corn cob jelly was in, along with orange drop cookies. Traditional pies were added, like two-crust raisin, lemon meringue, and custard. Jeanette prided herself on keeping up with the trends and spending the culinary premiums budget wisely.

1960s AND TODAY: CONTESTS ON THE SPOT

Fairgoers love live competitions, whether bird calling, cow chip tossing, or racing toward a finish line, but things like baking bread take too long. In 1968 Jeanette and the Culinary Department came up with on-the-spot contests for decorating cakes, cookies, and arranging edible centerpieces. Space was limited to the first three to six entrants who brought their own supplies. They had 30 minutes to finish in front of a live audience. This idea gave way to some of the most fun food events of today, like the Mystery Sack competition in which entrants make dishes on a hot plate in front of Fairgoers with whatever ingredients they find in their grocery bag. Cookie and cake decorating events are a fan favorite for both kids and adults.

Emerson Triplett (age 3) enjoys kids' cookie decorating at the 2021 Iowa State Fair, a tradition started in the 1960s.

Madeline Davis (center), winner of the 2021 Mystery Sack contest, and others unpack their ingredients before the timer starts.

1960s–1970s 111

Buttery Bovines Attract Long Lines of Visitors

You know the saying "Everything's better with butter." This is certainly true at the Iowa State Fair Food Competitions. It is impossible to know how many pounds of butter walk through the doors of the Elwell Family Food Center hidden inside some of the best baked goods in the country. The butter may not be seen, but it is certainly tasted.

The most famous butter takes center stage inside a chilled case in the John Deere Agriculture Building. Visitors queue up for pictures of the world's most famous cow and admire the other butter sculptures on display each year.

Beginning in 1960, Norma "Duffy" Lyon of Toledo, Iowa, was the State Fair butter sculptor. For 45 years she created one of the six major dairy breeds—Jersey, Ayrshire, Holstein, Guernsey, Brown Swiss, and Milking Shorthorn. Her other sculptures ran the gamut from Elvis Presley and Garth Brooks to Smokey Bear, the Peanuts Gang, and the figures from *The Last Supper*. She said her favorite was Grant Wood's *American Gothic*, pitchfork and all.

1961: "Duffy" Lyon with her second solo butter cow.

Duffy was the third person, and the first female, to sculpt butter at the Iowa State Fair. J. E. Wallace, who was from Florida, sculpted the first butter cow in 1911, and Earl Frank Dutta of Illinois followed him. Duffy's original plan was to become a veterinarian, but Iowa State University (then College) did not accept women into its program. She took the pre-vet classes anyway and began her sculpting career with a horse made of snow in a campuswide competition. Her work caught the eye of Christian Petersen, a world-renowned sculptor who was an artist-in-residence at ISU. He invited Duffy to apprentice with him, and the rest, as they say, is history.

Sarah Pratt of West Des Moines apprenticed with Duffy for 14 years before taking over in 2006. Besides cows, she has created Superman, Laura Ingalls Wilder from *Little House on the Prairie*, the Muppets from *Sesame Street*, and an antique tractor, among other intricate pieces.

BAKING BLUE RIBBONS

Robert Davis of Des Moines holds his two winning pie entries at the 1977 State Fair. He had not baked a pie in 20 years. ©The Des Moines Register – USA TODAY NETWORK, 1977

1960s AND 1970s SUPER EXHIBITORS

The Culinary Department continued a gradual upward trend with more than 1,300 entries from about 115 exhibitors across 17 different divisions and 184 individual classes in 1967. This averaged to about 11 entries per competitor, but Super Exhibitors of the era kept their pace. Mrs. Jeanette Van Peursem pointed out that some women entered every class with as many as 100 exhibits total. As she said in a *Des Moines Tribune* interview, "These are Iowa home cooks who love variety and are always trying, testing, and entering new things. The ribbons mean more than the premiums," with the top bread winners receiving $6 for first place and $4 for second.

In the 1960s and '70s a few men entered the ranks of Super Exhibitors, like open class pie champ, Ron Sheaffer of Des Moines, and Robert Davis, also of Des Moines, whose Orange Crunch Pumpkin Pie stood out from the rest at the 1977 Fair.

One of Iowa's favorite pie ladies, Dianna Zaiger Sheehy, entered her first State Fair contest in 1977. Her peach ribbon winner was the beginning of a pie-baking journey that took her from her farm in Audubon to New York City and Los Angeles. Dianna's trail of championship recipes includes her signature North 40 Berry Pie.

Other exhibitors who dominated the 1960s and '70s State Fair Culinary Contests include Fern Harmon and her daughter, Lola Zimmerman; Mildred Phillips and her daughter, Olive Jean Tarbell, and granddaughter, Robin Tarbell-Thomas. Blanche Park, Ruby Groen, Laura Raichle, and Sherri Ihle were also among the perennial winners of the era. Find some of their winning entries in the recipe section.

State Fair Themes of the '60s and '70s

In 1965, the Fair focused on themes of Iowa's history, with Heritage Fairs covering explorers, pioneers, the Gay Nineties, and the Roaring '20s. In the 1970s decade, the fairs had themes on Mexico, Canada, Hawaii, and the Discoverers, such as Christopher Columbus and his country of origin, Spain. In 1976 the Spirit of Iowa Fair celebrated the nation's bicentennial. Other themes were New Horizons, Take a Closer Look, and Get in Touch with Iowa.

Grandstand shows, with groups such as Iowa's own Andy Williams, the Beach Boys, Bay City Rollers, and Kansas, drew big crowds in the Grandstand, along with tractor pulls.

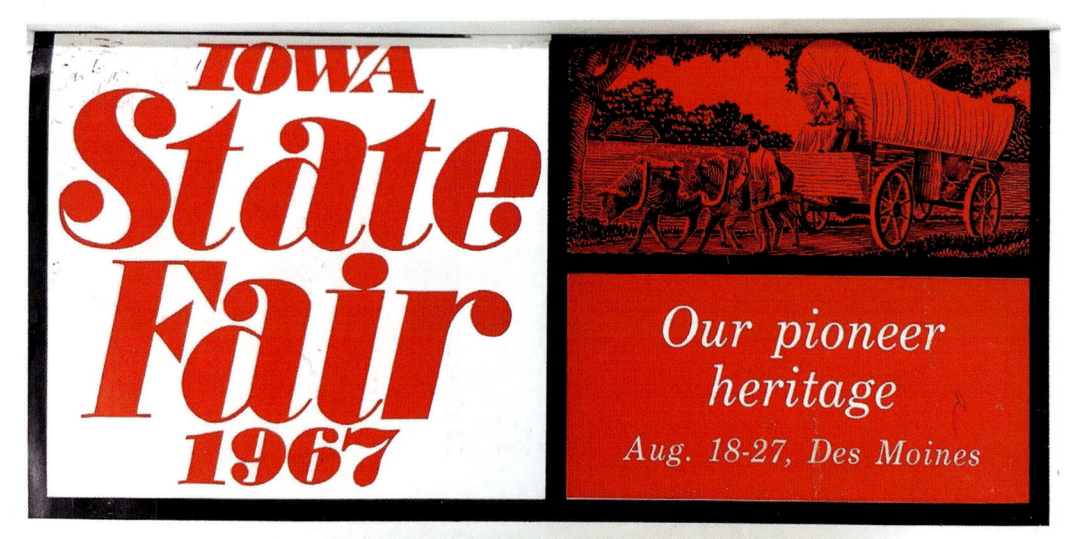

1970: MILK MADE MAGIC

The American Dairy Association launched the statewide Milk Made Magic contests in 1970. Like the Cookout Kings, these grass-roots events drew thousands of home cooks leading up to the championships at the State Fair in Des Moines.

Marilyn Martinez of Johnston, a former home economist with the Dairy Council of Iowa, helped launch the program along with Mary Reagan and Helen Burns of Des Moines. Marilyn directed the contest for the first five years and served on the selection committee that chose which recipes advanced to the sweepstakes round. "There generally were six contestants in each of the categories, including Quick and Easy Main Dishes, Sweet Treats, Salads, Yeast Breads, and Hors d'oeuvres," she said. "The finals took place in the Homemakers Theater in the Maytag Center."

Iowa Farm Bureau took over the contests in 1975. Milk Made Magic championships continued at the State Fair into the mid-1990s. For many years, a free brochure with the top recipes was available in front of the butter cow display. These were an invaluable resource for all things dairy with one of a kind creations like Fruit Clouds, Swiss Turkey Salad, and Bubble Pizza. Today, several counties continue local Milk Made Magic events, mostly through 4-H programs.

BAKING BLUE RIBBONS

POISED FOR GROWTH

The Culinary Department gradually expanded with new contests and trends in the 1970s. Exciting opportunities and a new home for the department paved the way for explosive growth in the 1980s and '90s.

Milk Made Magic Recipes, 1990

1960s–1970s

1960s – 1970s
STORIES AND RECIPES

Breads

CORN BREAD WITH HONEY

1 cup flour
4 teaspoons baking powder
¾ teaspoon salt
1 cup yellow corn meal
⅔ cup honey
¼ cup softened shortening
2 eggs, beaten
1 cup milk

Preheat oven to 400°F. Sift together flour, baking powder, and salt. Stir in corn meal. Add honey, shortening, eggs, and milk. Beat 1 minute or until all ingredients are moistened. Pour batter into a greased 9x9-inch pan. Bake for 25 minutes or until top is golden brown. Approximately 12 servings.

Take Mildred's advice and "Serve with lots of butter!"

Mildred Phillips, Centerville
First Place, 1978, Corn Bread

Mrs. Mildred Phillips' prizewinning cornbread with honey at the Iowa State Fair. ©The Des Moines Register – USA TODAY NETWORK, *1978*

A FAMILY AFFAIR

"It's the only time of year we're together with all of our cooking buddies"

– Fern Harmon of Granger, 1979.

Fern Harmon of Granger and her daughter, Lola Zimmerman of West Des Moines, often went head-to-head in friendly competition. Fern was a champion State Fair bread baker who won many sweepstakes awards for cinnamon rolls, whole wheat breads, fancy tea rings, and other baked goods during the 1960s, '70s, and '80s. Lola enjoyed baking bread but specialized in cakes. The two often entered identical bread recipes to see who would win and how their end products were often quite different. "One year I'll win first, and the next Lola will win first, and I'll win second," Fern said in a 1979 *Des Moines Register* interview. "We meet a lot of friends, and in a way, I guess you could call the Iowa State Fair a homecoming. It's the only time of year we're together with all of our cooking buddies."

Fern's white rolls had a standing audience on Sunday nights when family gathered at the farm for supper and homemade ice cream for dessert. "Mom would hurry home from church to start her rolls for that night," says Lola, whose three daughters grew up with homemade bread. In their eyes, it was a really big treat to have Wonder Bread, like their friends.

Fern's good taste lives on in her Christmas Braid, a Swedish tea ring, for which she won several blue ribbons.

Lola Zimmerman (left) and her mom, Fern Harmon.
©The Des Moines Register – USA TODAY NETWORK, *1979*

CHRISTMAS BRAID

3½ to 3¾ cups all-purpose flour, divided
¼ cup sugar
1 teaspoon salt
1 package active dry yeast
¾ cup milk
¼ cup water
¼ cup shortening or lard
1 egg
¼ cup chopped mixed candied fruit

In large mixing bowl combine 2 cups flour, sugar, salt, and yeast. In small saucepan heat milk, water, and shortening until very warm (120°F–130°F). Add egg and milk mixture to flour mixture. Beat well with mixer.

By hand or dough hook, if using a stand mixer, mix in 1 to 1½ cups flour and the candied fruit to form a stiff dough. Turn out onto a floured surface and knead until smooth, about 5 minutes. Place in greased bowl; cover. Let rise in warm place until double in size, about 1½ hours. Deflate dough by pushing down on it.

Shape dough into 3 equal long, narrow lengths of dough (about 14 inches long). Braid the three strands and tuck the edges under at each end. (Dough may also be shaped into rolls, tea ring, or wreath.) Place braid on greased baking sheet. Let rise in warm place until double in size, about 25–30 minutes. During this time, preheat oven to 350°F. Bake for about 25–30 minutes until top is deep golden brown. Tent after about 15 minutes if the top is getting too dark. Cool. Drizzle with powdered sugar icing and, if desired, decorate with additional candied cherries. Makes 1 large braid or approximately 2 dozen rolls.

ICING: stir together 1 cup powdered sugar with 1 to 2 tablespoons milk until smooth enough to drizzle over the top of cooled braid.

Fern Harmon, Granger
First Place, 1983

GOLDEN WHEAT BATTER BREAD

1 package yeast
1¼ cups warm water
2 tablespoons honey, brown sugar, or molasses
1 cup whole wheat flour, divided
2 cups white flour, divided
2 teaspoons salt
2 tablespoons soft shortening

Dissolve yeast in warm water in mixer bowl. Add honey, half of whole wheat and white flours, salt, and shortening. Beat for two minutes at medium speed or 300 strokes by hand. Blend in remaining flour until smooth. Scrape batter from sides of bowl. Cover with cloth and let rise in warm place until double in bulk, about 30 minutes. Stir down batter by beating 25 strokes. Spread batter evenly in greased 9x5-inch loaf pan. Allow to rise until batter is 1 inch above edge of pan, about 40 minutes. Preheat oven to 375°F. Bake for 45-50 minutes, until top is deep golden brown. Makes 1 loaf.

Lola Zimmerman, West Des Moines
Prize-winning bread, 1979

DUFFY LYON'S KOLACHES

Traditional Kolaches are small round Czech pastries made of a yeast dough and centered with fruit or soft cheese fillings. Butter sculptor Duffy Lyon was not known for her cooking, but her butter cows and kolaches were enjoyed by many.

KOLACHES
1 pint milk, scalded
2 eggs, beaten
½ cup sugar
2 packages dry yeast
1 teaspoon salt
½ cup shortening or butter, softened (Duffy used lard)
About 6½ cups flour

FILLINGS:

Prune Filling (Most typical filling): Cook 1 pound of prunes until well done. Pit and mash them. Add ⅓ cup applesauce (more to stretch) and add sugar and cinnamon to taste.

Cherry Filling (Lyon family favorite): Thicken or sweeten to taste canned or fresh cherries.

Apricot Filling: Cook until apricots can be mashed; sweeten to taste.

Ground Cherry Filling: Like apricot; and lemon juice may be added for more tartness.

Poppyseed Filling:
1½ cups ground poppyseeds
¾ cup sugar
2 rounded tablespoons flour
About 1 cup milk
Combine ingredients. Cook until thick, stirring constantly.

Cool milk; add eggs, sugar, yeast, and salt. Let yeast work until mixture is bubbly. Add butter and mix until smooth. Gradually add flour and stir until mixed in. Knead, or use dough hook, until dough is soft and smooth. Cover and let rise in a warm place for about 1 hour, or refrigerate overnight, until double in size. When dough has risen, punch down and knead briefly; cover and rise in a warm place for another hour, until nearly double in bulk. Cut into portions to make dough balls and press down lightly to form circles about 2½–3 inches in diameter. Cover and let rise for another 45 minutes. Spread centers open with your fingers or the back of an oiled spoon to form indentations in the centers. Place 1–2 teaspoons of filling that is cool or at room temperature. When ready to bake, preheat oven to 375°F. Bake 12–15 minutes until golden brown. Makes about 3 dozen.

Adapted Duffy Lyon Family Recipe

Salads

SWISS TURKEY SALAD

12 ounces (2½ cups) smoked turkey breast
¼ pound (1 cup) Swiss cheese
1 cup red seedless grapes, halved
¾ cup toasted slivered almonds

DRESSING
⅓ cup mayonnaise
⅓ cup sour cream or yogurt
1 tablespoon milk

Cut turkey and cheese into strips. Cut grapes into halves. Combine all salad ingredients in a medium bowl. For dressing, combine ingredients into a small bowl. Pour over salad mixture. Refrigerate until serving time. Makes 4 to 6 servings.

Jeanette Feller, Council Bluffs
First Place, Salads, Milk Made Magic, 1990

WATERGATE SALAD: Please see page 127.

THANK YOU to all of the team members who work behind the scenes to make the Iowa State Fair Food Department the best in the nation.

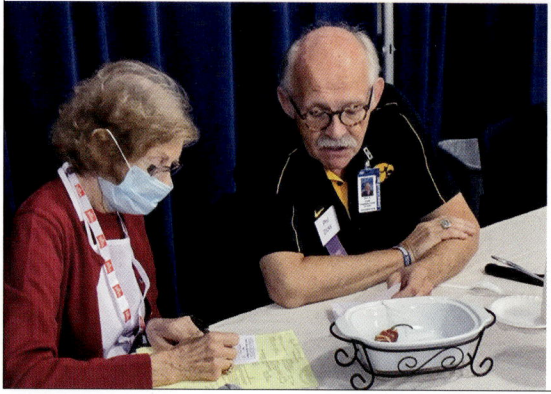

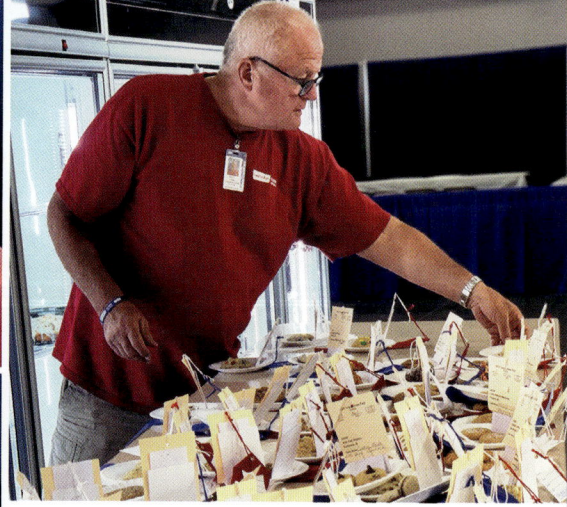

Upper left: Mary Lou Robb. Right: Kurt Larsen. Lower Left: Mary Ann Wegrzyn and Phil Dicks.

Main Dishes & Grilling

GRILLING WITH THE COOKOUT KINGS

Bob Friesen was the first Iowa State Fair Cookout King Champion in 1964. He smoked and grilled his way to the crown with one of his custom-made grills, which he built from a 55-gallon drum. In 2008, at age 78, he returned to the Grand Concourse in the past champions division, along with seven previous Cookout Kings and Queens and 60 contestants. Bob was one of the pioneers of Iowa outdoor cooking contests and brought years of experience to his first State Fair event. His classic recipe for loin back pork ribs makes an easy backyard barbecue.

PORK RIBS SEASONING

Loin back pork ribs for 6
Salt and pepper to taste
1 teaspoon onion salt
1 teaspoon garlic salt

OLD-SCHOOL BARBECUE SAUCE

19 ounces Kraft's Original Sauce
1 teaspoon freshly ground black pepper
½ teaspoon garlic powder
1 teaspoon celery seed
Pinch of ground hot pepper seeds or
   2–3 drops of Tabasco sauce

Combine seasonings and rub over meat. Blend barbeque sauce ingredients for basting meat. Makes about 2½ cups for 6 servings of meat.

Bob Friesen, Johnston
First Place, 1964 Cookout Kings

Cookout King Bob Friesen. ©The Des Moines Register – USA TODAY NETWORK, 2008

"I think I've done everything on the grill except bake a cake."

– Bob Friesen, 1964, First Iowa State Fair Cookout King

DADDY'S DRUMSTICKS ORANGE BARBECUE SAUCE

Governor Robert Ray crowned James Lein of Arlington Iowa's Cookout King in 1970. James shared his recipe for Daddy's Drumsticks coated in a savory-sweet orange barbecue sauce. We tested it 50 years later with rave reviews on a combination of drumsticks and thighs.

ORANGE BARBECUE SAUCE

16-oz. can frozen orange juice concentrate
4 teaspoons grated orange peel
⅓ cup Iowa sorghum
½ cup wine vinegar
¼ cup Iowa honey
¾ cup warm water
1 teaspoon prepared mustard
1 teaspoon soy sauce
½ teaspoon salt
½ teaspoon black pepper
Butter or olive oil to coat the chicken prior to grilling and to coat the grilling grate.

Blend all ingredients. Makes about 2¼ cups of barbecue sauce or enough to coat approximately 2 dozen chicken pieces.

James Lein, Arlington
First Place, 1970 Cookout Kings

Governor Ray presents the Cookout King award to James Lein. Sioux City Journal, *August 27, 1970.*

BEEF RIBS BARBECUE SAUCE

In 1978, William R. McGee of Iowa City entered the Fair to meet other grilling enthusiasts. He ended up earning the Cookout King crown out of 43 contestants with his gourmet barbecue sauce. McGee smoked and grilled the beef ribs in a 55-gallon drum that he converted into a covered cooker with a rib rack, much like Bob Friesen in 1964. He cooked the ribs for hours, but his secret sauce is great for everyday grilling. McGee's advice was to make the sauce ahead of time and refrigerate it for several hours or overnight. "The longer it sits, the better it gets," he said in an interview with the *Iowa City Press-Citizen*. Since the sauce is pretty hot, wait to baste the ribs until the last 10 to 15 minutes and then "slop it on real good at the end." McGee had concocted many spicy barbecue sauces, but this was the first time he had written the ingredients down for a contest.

MR. McGEE'S SECRET BARBECUE SAUCE

¼ cup olive oil
1 cup diced onion
1 tablespoon liquid brown sugar
1 tablespoon whole mustard seed
½ teaspoon cayenne powder
1 teaspoon crushed oregano
1 teaspoon chili powder
1 teaspoon black pepper
½ teaspoon salt
½ teaspoon ground cloves
2 bay leaves
2 cloves of garlic, minced
1 cup ketchup
¼ cup water
¼ cup tarragon vinegar
2 tablespoons wine vinegar
2 tablespoons Worcestershire sauce
3 to 4 drops liquid smoke
2 whole dried red peppers
4 or 5 drops hot sauce

Heat oil and cook onions until transparent. Add rest of ingredients and simmer for at least an hour. Mix well. Makes enough sauce for about 6 servings of ribs.

William R. McGee, Iowa City
First Place, 1970 Cookout Kings

William R. McGee. ©Iowa City Press-Citizen – USA TODAY NETWORK, 1978

ASIAN PORK BURGERS

Kris Scheppler of Rockford won the crown in 1984 at age 16 with his one of a kind recipe for Asian Pork Burgers. Take your grilling game to the next level with this twist on the backyard burger. The sauce is also excellent for baked pork and poultry.

BURGERS
2 pounds ground pork
1 cup soft breadcrumbs
⅓ cup finely chopped green onion
⅓ cup finely chopped green pepper
1 6-oz. can water chestnuts, drained and chopped
1 egg
1 teaspoon salt
2 tablespoons dry cooking sherry
2 tablespoons soy sauce
1 small clove garlic, crushed
⅛ teaspoon ginger
8 large hamburger buns
1 cup fresh alfalfa sprouts or garnish of choice

SAUCE
1 cup crushed pineapple, drained
⅔ cup ketchup
4 tablespoons vinegar
4 tablespoons orange marmalade
2 tablespoons prepared mustard

Kris Scheppler (16), Cookout King. ©The Des Moines Register – USA TODAY NETWORK, 1984

For burgers, combine ground pork with next 10 ingredients; mix well. Shape into 8 equal-size patties. Cover and place in refrigerator. For sauce, combine ingredients in a saucepan over medium heat until marmalade melts. Grill patties until done, spooning sauce over them during the last few minutes. Place on warmed or toasted buns. Spoon any remaining sauce over patties. Cover with sprouts or garnish of choice. Serves 8.

Kris Scheppler, Rockford
First Place, 1984 Cookout Kings

FRUIT-STUFFED PORK CHOPS

Carlene Staade of Garnavillo and Ruth Hamilton of Independence won the Cookout Contest team division in 1992 with these sweet and savory fruit-stuffed pork chops. They recommended garnishing them with applesauce, pineapple rings, or sauerkraut for flavor and flair. This recipe is great on the grill and can be adapted for baked pork chops.

4 double-rib pork chops with pockets cut for stuffing
Salt and black pepper to sprinkle over chops
1 cup small dry bread cubes
½ cup shredded sharp Cheddar cheese
½ cup finely chopped apple
¼ teaspoon sugar or sweetener of choice
⅛ cup butter, melted
⅛ cup orange juice
¼ teaspoon salt
⅛ teaspoon cinnamon
1½ cups pineapple juice for marinating, plus more for basting

Sprinkle salt and pepper over pork chops and rub into meat on both sides. Combine bread cubes, apple, sugar, cheese, butter, orange juice, salt, and cinnamon. Stuff mixture into pockets. Press edges of pockets together. Seal with toothpicks.

Place pork chops in pan with about 1½ cups pineapple juice to marinate pork meat for 6 to 8 hours. Turn every 20 to 30 minutes on each side to coat meat with marinade. Place stuffed pork chops on heated grill and cook for about 40 minutes. Baste with remaining pineapple juice and turn chops every 5 to 10 minutes until pork is evenly cooked through or reaches an internal temperature of about 145°F.

Blue ribbon tip: Turn off the grill (if using a gas grill) when internal temperature reaches about 135° F. Cover with foil while chops rest and continue to cook. Serves 4.

Carlene Staade, Garnavillo, and Ruth Hamilton, Independence
First Place, 1992 Cookout Kings, Team Competition

BACON-WRAPPED BARBECUED CHICKEN

In 2019, Mike Anderson of Madison County took first place in the poultry/combo specialty division with these cheesy bacon-wrapped chicken thighs. The sweet and savory rub complements the bacon and cheese with flavor that any judge will love.

Approximately 12 boneless, skinless chicken thighs
1 slice bacon for each thigh
1 sweet pepper, chopped
Shredded sharp cheddar cheese

SWEET RUB FOR CHICKEN
¼ cup brown sugar
2 teaspoons cracked black pepper
2 teaspoons garlic powder
1 teaspoon ground mustard
1 tablespoon coarse sea salt
2 teaspoons smoked paprika
2 teaspoons onion powder
½ teaspoon cayenne pepper

Generously sprinkle rub on both sides of chicken thighs. Slice a pocket into the center of the thickest section of each thigh. Chop sweet pepper and put inside chicken thighs, along with a generous tablespoon of cheese. Wrap each thigh with a slice of bacon, securing with a toothpick.

Grill thighs until chicken reaches an internal temperature of about 165°F and bacon is brown and crispy. For the last few minutes of cooking, coat chicken with your favorite BBQ sauce, if desired. Makes enough chicken rub for about a dozen chicken pieces.

Mike Anderson, Madison County
First Place, 2019 Cookout Contest, Combo/Specialty

BUBBLE PIZZA

Beau Biekert's Milk Made Magic winner combines the flavors of pizza and lasagna for an easy weeknight dinner.

1 pound ground beef
½ pound ground sweet or spicy sausage
1 medium onion, diced
1 sweet bell pepper, diced
3 cups pizza sauce
2 tubes buttermilk biscuits
1½ cups shredded mozzarella cheese
1½ cups shredded cheddar cheese

Preheat oven to 375°F. Sauté onion and pepper with ground beef and sausage until meat is fully cooked. Drain. Mix in pizza sauce. Quarter the biscuits and mix them with the ground beef mixture. Pour into a greased 13x9-inch pan. Bake for about 20 minutes. Remove from oven and top with the cheeses. Bake an additional 5 minutes. Let stand 5–10 minutes before serving. Makes 12 servings.

Recipe adapted from Beau Biekert, Waverly
First Place, Mini Cooks and Chefs, Quick & Easy Main Dishes 1990, Milk Made Magic

Cakes

1970s: WATERGATE CAKE AND THE RISE OF PISTACHIO PUDDING MIX

Iowa cooks and State Fair food competitors are open to trying new ingredients. Their curiosity has led to some tasty food trends over the years. One example is the rise of Jell-O Brand instant pistachio pudding mix. It began in the mid-1970s and still has a cultlike following today. It came out about the same time as the Watergate scandal, when the name permeated the national conversation. Watergate Cake and Salad got the food trend started. One or both showed up at every potluck, picnic, and family reunion. They worked well for a touch of green for St. Patrick's Day and Christmas. Some sources refer to the cake as Watergate Cake with Coverup Icing. A more sublime story says the recipes may have been concocted by a sous-chef at the Watergate Hotel. The versatile pudding mix found its way into numerous recipes like Pistachio Cream Pie, Pistachio English Toffee Ice Box Cake, Chocolate-Orange Cupcakes with Pistachio Frosting, and the list goes on. Here are the quintessential creations that launched the trend.

WATERGATE CAKE

1 18.5-ounce package yellow cake mix
2 3.4-ounce packages instant pistachio pudding mix
1 cup sour cream
½ cup vegetable oil
4 eggs
½ cup packed brown sugar
½ cup chopped walnuts
1 teaspoon ground cinnamon
¼ cup powdered sugar for dusting or frost with Coverup Frosting

Preheat oven to 350°F. Grease and flour a 9-inch Bundt pan. In a medium bowl stir together cake mix and pudding mix. Add sour cream, oil, and eggs; mix well. Pour half the batter into prepared pan. Combine brown sugar, walnuts, and cinnamon; sprinkle over batter. Cover with remaining batter. Bake 1 hour until cake springs back when lightly touched. Cool in pan 15 minutes before inverting onto a wire rack to cool completely. When cake is cooled, dust with powdered sugar or frost and refrigerate. Makes 12 servings.

COVERUP FROSTING
1 3.4-ounce package Instant Pistachio pudding mix
½ cup milk
8-ounce container whipped topping

Mix pudding mix and milk until thick; fold in whipped topping. Chill frosting until ready to use.

Vintage Watergate Cake Recipe, updated from 1975.

WATERGATE SALAD

1 15½-ounce can crushed pineapple
1 3.4-ounce package pistachio instant pudding mix
1 8-ounce carton whipped topping
½ cup chopped nuts, preferably pecans
3 bananas, diced
1 cup miniature marshmallows
½ cup maraschino cherries, cut in small pieces

Pour pineapple with juice into a bowl. Stir in pudding mix; mix well. Fold in remaining ingredients. Chill until ready to serve. Makes approximately 8 servings.

Watergate recipes adapted from Iowa City Press-Citizen, *August 16 and August 23, 1975.*

RUBY GROEN'S CARROT CAKE

For 25 years, Mrs. George "Ruby" Groen of Spencer had won baking contests at the Clay County Fair. This Carrot Cake was her first entry and first blue ribbon at the state level, which was just the beginning. Ruby entered 31 classes and won at least 21 State Fair ribbons the following year with continued success after that. In 1979, she became the head of her county fair's culinary department. She adapted this prizewinning recipe from a Spencer church cookbook.

CAKE
2 cups flour
1 teaspoon salt
2 teaspoons cinnamon
2 cups sugar
2 teaspoons baking soda
4 eggs
1½ cups vegetable oil
3 cups grated raw carrots
½ cup nuts
2 teaspoons vanilla extract
1 teaspoon maple extract

Preheat oven to 350°F. Sift together flour, salt, cinnamon, sugar, and baking soda. Add the eggs and beat well with mixer. Beat in vegetable oil. Fold in grated carrots, nuts, and flavorings. Pour into 2 well-greased cake pans (8-inch round or square) and bake for approximately 45 minutes. Cool completely. Frost between the stacked layers and swirl frosting over top and sides of cake.

FROSTING
2 egg whites
4 cups powdered sugar
½ cup Crisco
¼ teaspoon salt
1 teaspoon vanilla extract
½ teaspoon maple extract

Beat ingredients together at high speed until very creamy. You may have to add some milk to thin the frosting to a spreadable consistency.

Makes 12 servings.

Ruby Groen, Spencer
First Place, 1976 Iowa State Fair
Recipe adapted from The Des Moines Register, *September 5, 1976*

RHUBARB BUNDT CAKE

Mrs. Rex Kleckner of Howard County won the State Fair Sweepstakes award in the 1975 Milk Made Magic Contest with this Rhubarb Bundt Cake. It earned top honors at the county level before advancing to the State Fair, where Mrs. Kleckner won a blue ribbon and $50.

½ cup butter
½ cup brown sugar
1 cup granulated sugar
1 teaspoon vanilla
1 egg
2½ cups sifted flour
1 teaspoon salt
1 teaspoon baking soda
¼ teaspoon allspice
¼ teaspoon ground cloves
1 cup buttermilk, sour milk, or light cream
1½ cups finely cut rhubarb
1½ cups finely chopped nuts

Preheat oven to 350°F. Cream together the butter, brown sugar, and granulated sugar; add vanilla and egg. Beat well. Sift together flour, salt, baking soda, and spices; add alternately with buttermilk. Stir in finely chopped rhubarb and nuts.

TOPPING
⅓ cup sugar
1 teaspoon cinnamon

Generously grease a Bundt pan. Sprinkle ½ of topping on sides and bottom of pan. Pour in batter; sprinkle remaining topping over batter. Bake 45 minutes or until cake tester inserted near the center of cake comes out clean. Cool 10–15 minutes in pan; turn out on cooling rack and cool completely. Serves 12.

Mrs. Rex Kleckner, Howard County
First Place, Milk Made Magic Sweepstakes, 1975

Pies

Blanche Park of Des Moines won more than 100 prizes and sweepstakes awards for her baking and jellies during the 1950s, '60s, and '70s. "I stopped counting at 75 ribbons eight years ago," she said at her "final" food competition in 1975. At age 83, she retired from competitive baking on a sweet note with two first-place pies—until she came out of retirement for one last pie win at the 1976 State Fair. Blanche had many prize-winning recipes, and Florida Key Lime Pie was one of her favorites. This updated version by Jackie Garnett continued Blanche's winning tradition in 2019.

Blanche Park at the Iowa State Fair Culinary Department. ©The Des Moines Register – USA TODAY NETWORK, 1972

> "I'd take pie over cake any day."
>
> – Blanche Park, 1975 Iowa State Fair

KEY LIME PIE

PIE CRUST
1¼ cups graham cracker crumbs
¼ cup packed golden brown sugar
½ teaspoon kosher salt
¼ cup unsalted butter, melted

Preheat oven to 350°F. Stir together graham cracker crumbs, brown sugar, salt, and melted butter. Press mixture into bottom and up sides of a 9-inch pie pan. Bake until lightly browned, about 10 minutes. Let cool completely.

FILLING
3 large egg yolks
2 14-ounce cans sweetened condensed milk
1 cup key lime juice
1 tablespoon fresh lemon juice
1½ tablespoons finely grated lime zest

In large bowl beat egg yolks until thick, about 3 minutes. Add condensed milk, lime juice, lemon juice, and lime zest. Beat until well blended, about 1 minute. Pour into cooled crust, filling to the brim. Bake at 350°F until center is just set, about 10 to 15 minutes. Cool completely. Chill in refrigerator for 3-6 hours or overnight.

WHIPPED CREAM AND GARNISH
1 tablespoon cold water
½ teaspoon unflavored gelatin
1½ cups heavy cream
5 tablespoons granulated sugar
¾ teaspoon vanilla
Lime peel strips for garnish

In small bowl add the cold water and sprinkle gelatin over it. Let sit 5 minutes. Melt gelatin in microwave 1 minute on the lowest setting, pausing to stir the mixture after 30 seconds. Repeat process until gelatin is completely melted. Set aside to cool. In stand mixer whip cream, sugar, and vanilla until soft peaks form. Pour cooled gelatin into cream; continue whipping until stiff peaks form. Top pie with whipped cream. Garnish with lime strips.

Jackie Garnett, Des Moines
First Place, 2019 Machine Shed Pies – Key Lime
First Place Overall, 2019 Machine Shed Pies – Cream

1977: A BIG WIN ... 30 YEARS LATER

The Cookout Kings weren't the only guys winning prizes at the Iowa State Fair Culinary Competitions in the 1970s. Robert Davis, who was 43 at the time, hadn't baked a pie in 20 years, but still won top honors for both of his entries in 1977. Riding high on his pie-baking prowess, he was back in '78 for another win with his unexpectedly amazing Orange Crunch Pumpkin Pie. Digging a little deeper, we found that Mr. Davis had first tried to enter homemade preserves as a teen in 1948 but was turned away because only women were allowed. Imagine the sweet justice when he returned to the Fair nearly 30 years later and took home 27 ribbons, three sweepstakes, and a reserve sweeps across the jellies, butters, jams, and preserves.

ORANGE CRUNCH PUMPKIN PIE

This orange-infused topping is the perfect complement to pumpkin pie. Our pumpkin purists, and those who thought they didn't like pumpkin pie, all loved it.

PIE CRUST
1 2/3 cups flour
1/2 teaspoon salt
1/2 cup shortening
3–4 tablespoons ice cold water

Preheat oven to 375°F. Blend flour, salt, and shortening with a pastry blender until pea-size crumbs form. Add water, 1 tablespoon at a time, and toss with a fork until pastry begins to hold together in large clumps. Form into a thick disk. Wrap airtight and refrigerate while making the filling and topping.

FILLING
2 eggs, slightly beaten
15-oz. can pumpkin puree
1 cup firmly packed brown sugar
1 teaspoon cinnamon
1/2 teaspoon nutmeg
1/2 teaspoon ginger
1/4 teaspoon ground cloves
1 tablespoon flour
1/2 teaspoon salt
12-oz. can evaporated milk

Blend eggs, pumpkin, brown sugar, and dry ingredients in a large bowl. Add evaporated milk and mix thoroughly. Roll out pie crust to about ⅛-inch thickness and gently ease into a 9-inch pie plate. Crimp edges. Pour filling into lined pie shell. Bake for approximately 30 minutes. Top with Orange Crunch Topping. Continue baking for another 20 to 30 minutes until a table knife inserted near center comes out clean. Makes about 8 slices.

ORANGE CRUNCH TOPPING
1 tablespoon brown sugar
1 tablespoon butter
1 tablespoon flour
½ cup chopped walnuts
2 tablespoons orange zest

Combine topping ingredients and work in butter with a pastry blender until pea-size clumps are evenly distributed. Keep topping chilled until ready to use.

Robert Davis, Des Moines
First Place, 1977
Recipe adapted from The Des Moines Register, *September 6, 1978.*

MRS. VAN PEURSEM'S RHUBARB CREAM PIE

Jeanette Van Peursem helped shape both the Textile and Culinary Departments, beginning as a contestant in 1946 and as the superintendent of both divisions throughout the 1960s and '70s. Times were different then, and her name always appeared as "Mrs. W.L. Van Peursem" in official State Fair premium books and newspaper listings. Her first name remained a mystery to many. But in later years, her name and her legacy of hard work and generosity was shared in local news stories. Jeanette began the tradition of donating extra baked goods from food contests to local pantries and missions—a good deed that continues at the Fair today. One of her best pies combines the tartness of rhubarb with a creamy custard and topped with meringue swirls for a perfect summer match. Even those who claim that they do not like rhubarb will love this.

RHUBARB CREAM PIE
3 cups cut rhubarb
1 cup sugar
2 tablespoons flour
½ cup milk
3 eggs yolks
1 unbaked 9-inch pie shell

MERINGUE
3 egg whites
½ teaspoon vanilla
¼ teaspoon cream of tartar
6 tablespoons sugar

Preheat oven to 425°F. Mix sugar, flour, milk, and egg yolks together. Pour over cut rhubarb and mix well. Pour into pie shell and bake until rhubarb is tender and filling is set, about 50–60 minutes. For meringue, beat egg whites, vanilla, and cream of tartar with an electric mixer until soft peaks form (tips curl). Add sugar, 1 tablespoon at a time, beating on high speed about 4 minutes, until stiff peaks form (tips stand straight). Spread on pie. Bake 10 to 12 minutes. Makes 8 slices.

Jeanette Van Peursem, Superintendent's Signature Recipe
Recipe adapted from the 1986 Iowa State Fair Cookbook

1978: THE PIE LADY

Dianna Zaiger Sheehy of Audubon is one of Iowa's favorite Pie Ladies. She has lived near her family's farm since she was born, but pie baking took her from coast to coast. As she says in her popular State Fair pie seminars, "Pie baking got this old girl off the farm, from underneath a cow, and took me from New York to Los Angeles. It all happened because of the Iowa State Fair. Otherwise, I'd have never gotten to those places, ever."

As a girl Dianna watched her mom, grandmother, and great-aunts make suppers for family gatherings and threshing crews that always included pie. She was fascinated with the rolling pins and how quickly they rolled out the pastry. Nothing was written down, but Dianna created recipes based on everything she learned. At the age of sixteen, her rhubarb pie won the top prize at the local county fair. After several years of winning with a variety of pies, the older ladies started calling her The Pie Lady. People told her she should enter the State Fair. So she drove her peach pie to Des Moines and left it under the Grandstand in the glassed-off judging area. She had to get back to milk the cows. A few days later, an envelope arrived in the mail with a nice white ribbon.

Dianna Zaiger Sheehy, 1980s.

Dianna Zaiger Sheehy entered her first pie at the Fair in 1978. Here she is pictured with her husband, Leo Sheehy, at the 1989 American Pie National Finals in Los Angeles. For many years, Dianna has sponsored her North 40 Pie Contest in Leo's memory.

Since her first State Fair contest in 1978, Dianna has had countless winning pies. She represented Iowa in the Crisco National Pie Baking Championships in Los Angeles in 1989 and the Good Housekeeping Institute Championships in New York City in 1993, where she was a finalist each time. She has won contests in everything from pies and cakes to her famous cinnamon rolls, which netted her two blue ribbons and $4,500 in cash in the 2007 Tone's Cinnamon Roll Contest. In 2008 she retired from competing and become a judge. Dianna has been a part of the State Fair Food Department team ever since. Her pie-baking seminars are one of the most popular events at the Elwell Family Food Center, with live demonstrations and prize-winning samples.

"It all happened because of the Iowa State Fair."

– Dianna Zaiger Sheehy

DIANNA'S NORTH 40 BERRY PIE

CRUST
2 cups all-purpose flour
1 teaspoon salt
¾ cup shortening or ⅔ cup lard
1 egg
3 tablespoons ice-cold water
1 teaspoon vinegar
Milk and sugar for top of pie crust

FILLING
1 cup sugar
2 tablespoons quick-cooking tapioca
1½ tablespoons cornstarch
2¼ cups blackberries
2¼ cups red raspberries
1 tablespoon lemon juice
2 tablespoons butter, cut into cubes

Preheat oven to 400°F. For crust: In a medium mixing bowl stir together flour and salt. Using pastry blender, cut in shortening until pieces are pea size. Combine egg, water, and vinegar. Add 1 tablespoon at a time to flour mixture; gently toss with a fork. Push moistened dough to the side of the bowl and continue adding water until the mixture is evenly moistened and dough sticks together in clumps. Add a little more water if necessary. Divide the dough in half and form each ball into a slightly flattened disk. Wrap and place in refrigerator.

While dough is chilling, make the filling.

In a large bowl stir together the sugar, tapioca, and cornstarch. Stir in berries and lemon juice.

On a lightly floured surface, roll one half of the dough into a 12-inch circle. Transfer pastry to a 9-inch pie plate and ease pastry into plate without stretching it. Fill with berry mixture and dot with butter. Trim pastry to ½ inch beyond rim of dish; reserve extra pastry pieces. Roll second half of pie dough and cut pastry into ½-inch wide strips. Weave strips over filling in a lattice pattern. Press ends of strips into bottom pastry rim. Fold top pastry over bottom pastry; seal and crimp edge. Roll reserved trimmings to ¼-inch thickness; cut into shapes with small cookie cutters. Brush bottoms of shapes lightly with milk. Arrange over pie in a decorative pattern. Brush top of pastry lightly with milk and sprinkle with additional sugar.

Cover edges of pie with foil. Bake for 15 minutes at 400°F. Reduce temperature to 350°F and bake an additional 40 minutes until pastry is golden and filling is bubbly. Remove foil for the last 10 minutes in the oven.

Cool on wire rack. Makes 8 servings.

Dianna Zaiger Sheehy, Audubon
Signature Pie Recipe

Dianna and her son, Luke Zaiger of Harlan, judge the annual North 40 Pie Contest at the 2021 State Fair.

BAKING BLUE RIBBONS

Cookies

REFRIGERATOR PYRAMID COOKIES

In 1975 Mrs. Laura Raichle was new to Iowa and the State Fair. She entered two cakes and thought she was entering too much until she saw "all the grannies with their jars and jars of jelly." In 1976, her husband talked her into entering "almost every contest," which turned out to be great advice. Here is her refrigerator cookie recipe, which earned her a $100 prize for Best of Fair Cookie.

2 cups flour
1½ teaspoons baking powder
½ teaspoon salt
⅔ cup butter
1 cup sugar
1 egg
1 teaspoon vanilla
⅓ cup finely chopped pecans
Red food coloring, optional
¼ cup chopped dried cherries
1 to 2 squares baking chocolate, melted and cooled

Preheat oven to 375°F. Sift together the flour, baking powder, and salt. In a separate bowl cream butter until light and fluffy. Gradually beat in sugar. Add egg and vanilla. Beat in half of the flour mixture, then work the remainder of the flour into the dough by hand or with a dough hook if using a stand mixer. This is the basic dough.

Divide dough into thirds. Add 1 or 2 drops of red food coloring (if desired) and cherries to one third. Add nuts to the next third. Then knead in the chocolate with your hands or dough hook to the last third to maintain the soft consistency of the dough. Divide each batch of colored dough in half. Roll each half to form a log. You now have 6 small logs, two of each color dough. Place a chocolate log next to a cherry log. Place a nut log on top forming a pyramid. Repeat with the remaining three logs. Wrap each dough pyramid in waxed paper. Refrigerate at least 8 hours (overnight works well). Slice into about ⅛-inch rounds or ¼-inch for thicker cookies. Bake at 375°F for about 8–10 minutes. Makes 2 to 3 dozen cookies.

Mrs. Laura Raichle, Des Moines
Best of Fair cookie, 1976.

ORANGE DROP COOKIES

Sherri Ihle of Slater won her first Iowa State Fair baking contest at the age of twelve. In 1977, at 18, she was a veteran baker who had won ribbons every year that she entered. These zippy, orange-frosted rounds are based on a recipe Sherri found in a church cookbook.

1¼ cups sugar
¾ cup Crisco
2 eggs
½ teaspoon salt
1 teaspoon vanilla
Grated rind and juice of 1 orange
1 cup buttermilk
1 teaspoon baking soda
2 teaspoons baking powder
3 cups flour

Preheat oven to 350°F. Cream sugar with shortening. Add remaining ingredients in order given and beat well. Drop by rounded teaspoonfuls onto ungreased baking sheets. Bake until edges are lightly browned, about 8 to 10 minutes. Frost cooled cookies.

FROSTING: Mix 2 cups powdered sugar, 2 tablespoons melted butter, and 2 to 3 tablespoons orange juice.
Makes 4 to 5 dozen cookies.

Sherri Ihle, Slater
First Place, 1977

PINEAPPLE LAYER BARS

Robin Tarbell-Thomas won her first sweepstakes for cookies at the age of 15. The following year, she took first prize again with these pineapple layer bars. Robin has gone on to win countless ribbons at the Iowa State Fair, continuing the dynasty started by her grandmother, Mildred Phillips; her mom, Olive Jean Tarbell; and Robin's daughter, Molly Thomas, who also continues the tradition today. (Please see family story page 174). For these versatile cookies, Robin adapted a recipe for date bars and replaced the fruit with pineapple preserves. She began cooking as a little girl, helping her mother make fudge and cookies.

½ cup shortening or butter
1 cup packed brown sugar
1 teaspoon vanilla
1½ cups sifted flour
1 teaspoon baking soda
½ teaspoon salt
1¾ cups quick-cooking oats
⅔ cup pineapple preserves or your favorite fruit preserves
½ cup chopped nuts
Candied cherries for garnish

BAKING BLUE RIBBONS

Preheat oven to 350°F. Cream shortening, sugar, and vanilla. Sift dry ingredients together; add to oats. Mix with shortening mixture until crumbly. Firmly pat half the mixture into greased 9-inch square pan. Combine preserves and nuts; spread over the base layer. Spread remaining crumbs over the top and pat smooth. Bake for approximately 30 minutes. Cut into bars or squares and top with candied cherries, if desired.

Makes 12 to 16 squares.

Robin Tarbell-Thomas, Centerville
First Place, Cookie Sweepstakes, 1977

Desserts

FRUIT CLOUDS

1 8-oz. package cream cheese, softened
½ cup sugar
1 tablespoon lemon juice
2 teaspoons lemon zest
1 cup heavy cream, whipped
Assorted fruit

Combine cream cheese, sugar, juice, and zest until well blended. Fold in whipped cream. With back of a spoon, shape on wax-paper-lined cookie sheet to form 6–10 shells; freeze. Fill each shell with fruit. Garnish with fresh mint, if desired. Makes 6–10 servings.

Tricia Mathiasen, Harlan
1990 Milk Made Magic, Sweet Treats

1960s–1970s

1980s – 1990s

A MATCH MADE IN FOOD HEAVEN

RECIPES

BREADS & ROLLS
Banana Macadamia Nut Bread, *Krystin Drews* **151**
Yankee Maple Corn Muffins, *Lois Friday* **152**
Applesauce Muffins, *Angela Duke* **152**
Pulled Pork Cinnamon Rolls, *Kelly McCulley* **153**
Soft Pretzels, *Olive Jean Tarbell* **176**
Holiday Fruit Bread, *Molly Thomas* **178**
All-Purpose Yeast Dough, *Ruth Beck* **180**
Pumpkin Bread, *Carol McGarvey* **181**

SALADS
Sweet and Savory Confetti SPAM Salad, *Cheryl Rogers* **155**

SAUCE
Spaghetti Sauce, *Susan Knapp* **156**

MAIN DISHES
Beef Fillets Supreme, *Bette Dryer* **157**
Chorizo Hot Cheese Torte, *Jane Badger* **158**
Turkey Patties with Pears, *Barbara D. Low* **159**
Low-Sodium Stuffed Peppers, *Charles Duke* **160**
Heartland Stew, *Diane Roupe* **160**
Lasagna, *Pat (Hatch) Berry* **161**

CAKES
Coconut Love Cake, *Susie Jones* **163**
Chocolate Praline Layer Cake, *Joy McFarland* **164**
President Bill Clinton's Hope Cheesecake, *JoAnna Lund* **165**

PIES
All-Iowa Rhubarb Pie, *Judy Arnold* **166**
Butterscotch Meringue Pie, *Jamie Buelt* **168**
Stone Fruit Pie, *Chris Montalvo* **169**
Peach Apricot Blueberry Pie, *Louise Piper* **171**
Senator Bob Dole's Double Chocolate Cream Pie, *JoAnna Lund* **172**

RECIPES

COOKIES
Iowa Potato Chip Cookies, *Ileen Wallace,* **172**
Gingerbread Boys, *Eva Horstman* **176**
Best of Fair Peanut Butter Cookies, *Mildred Phillips* **177**
Best of Fair Molasses Cookies, *Olive Jean Tarbell* **178**

CANDIES, SNACKS & DESSERTS
Fruity Tofu Energizer, *Diana Duke* **173**
Classic Vanilla Fudge, *Harold Magg* **173**

1982: "MOVIN' ON UP" WITH A NEW HOME AND FOOD SUPERINTENDENT

The Iowa State Fair Culinary Division transformed into the Food Department in 1982. Like the 1980s theme song "Movin' on Up," the contests were launched into a bigger space with a bright future. Nancy Hopkins of Des Moines became the superintendent. Food contests went from the east end of the Grandstand into the Maytag Family Center. Nancy's background as a registered dietitian and associate food editor for *Better Homes and Gardens* magazine helped grow the department. She focused on corporate sponsorships and the latest culinary trends as well as traditions.

Food displays were redesigned as storefront booths by architecture students at Iowa State University. Bold signs hung above each section, showing off the best in yeast breads, pies, cakes, and cookies, newer categories like healthy creations, and foods with fructose.

In Nancy's first year, contest premiums topped $4,000 with $1,800 in new prizes from major brands. Pillsbury and Tone's took cookie decorating to a new level, hosting 500 kids who each received two cookies and all the frosting and sprinkles to enter their best cookie—and eat the other.

Iowans brought 2,800 food entries in 1983, including 52 types of oatmeal cookies, 34 chocolate chip, and well over 100 pies, all vying for more than $5,000 in prizes. Outside sponsors contributed $3,000 in savings bonds, cash, and other awards. Health food trends continued with contests like salad dressing and low-sodium cooking, as well as new international desserts, a meat-of-Iowa casserole competition, and homemade ice cream, judged by Governor Robert Ray. That year 55,824 ribbons were awarded across the entire Iowa State Fair—that's a lot of silk.

Food Superintendent Nancy Hopkins. ©The Des Moines Register – USA TODAY NETWORK, *1982*

1983: IOWA STATE FAIR COOKBOOKS AND SWEEPSTAKES WINNERS

Under Nancy's leadership, the Food Department launched its first cookbook, *Blue Ribbon Recipes*, in 1983. The selection of first-place entries from the previous Fair highlighted sweepstakes winners in each division. Mrs. Keith (Mildred) Phillips earned the overall Food Department sweepstakes and the bread sweepstakes. She took home 25 blue ribbons, a year's supply of Pillsbury's Best Flour, and a $100 award from Meredith Corporation. Mildred's granddaughter, Robin Tarbell, won the sweepstakes for foods made with honey, finishing ahead of her grandmother who earned the reserve sweeps in that division. Robin baked every winning cookie made with honey and many others in the first State Fair cookbook. Mildred and Robin are two of five winning generations of the Tarbell-Thomas Family. (Find their story on page 174.)

The Food Department continued its ascent with cash premiums nearing $7,000 and many new sponsors and contests when Nancy Hopkins retired from her post in 1985.

A lot was going on at the Fair in the early 1980s. The State Fair Museum opened in 1982. Fair souvenirs, such as T-shirts, hats, and caps, were available for the first time, and Duffy Lyon marked her 25th anniversary as butter sculptor. The premier edition of the Iowa State Fair Cookbook, *Blue Ribbon Recipes*, launched in 1983.

1986: A MATCH MADE IN FOOD HEAVEN

Superintendents at the Iowa State Fair shape their departments in unique ways. Generations of Pantry, Culinary, and Food superintendents have helped make Iowa State Fair food contests the best in the nation. No one has served longer in this area than Arlette Hollister, who worked her magic for 31 years. You might say this was a match made in food heaven—a match that took Arlette by surprise when her husband, Glen, volunteered her for the position in 1986.

144 BAKING BLUE RIBBONS

> *"We use the f-word a lot around here. The 'f' stands for flexibility."*
>
> – Arlette Hollister, Iowa State Fair Food Superintendent, 1986–2016.

She was excited for the job but didn't have a clue as to where to begin, as she said in a 2015 *Des Moines Register* interview. Arlette figured it out quickly. Over the next three decades, she and her team added more competitors, sponsors, prize money, and contests than ever before. She started with 25 food divisions and about $7,000 in premiums. By the end of her 31-year run, the department had 218 divisions, 10,000-plus entries, and a purse worth $76,000. She worked year-round to make the food competitions one of the best experiences at any state fair. Whether you were a corporate sponsor, a first-time contestant, or simply looking for the cookie display, she took the time to answer questions and make everyone feel special.

Arlette brought together a team that many referred to as their "Fair Family." It took 50 to 60 judges, volunteers, and workers with specific jobs and a willingness to pitch in wherever needed. On Sundays before opening day, she gathered the team for a meeting and potluck dinner. This was a time for veteran staff to reconnect and meet new team members before the onslaught of thousands of food entries. Arlette motivated with grace and good humor as she welcomed everyone and explained how the department ran.

"We use the f-word a lot around here," she said, "The 'f' stands for flexibility." Flexibility, creativity, having fun, and never taking "no" for an answer were key ingredients to Arlette's success. If a cash premium wasn't in the budget, she asked for in-kind donations. Contestants walked off with everything from a peck of apples to free weight-loss clinics. There were weekend getaways and microwave ovens, pizza every month for a year, decorated birthday cakes for the whole family—and the list goes on. National sponsors included Crisco, Kraft, Land O' Lakes, Hills Brothers, Keebler, and Nestlé. These added to a growing list of Iowa-based companies, such as Beeler's Meat Co., Hy-Vee, the Iowa Soybean Association, Tone's Spices, and numerous restaurants, associations, bakeries, and family sponsorships.

WINNERS EVERY ONE

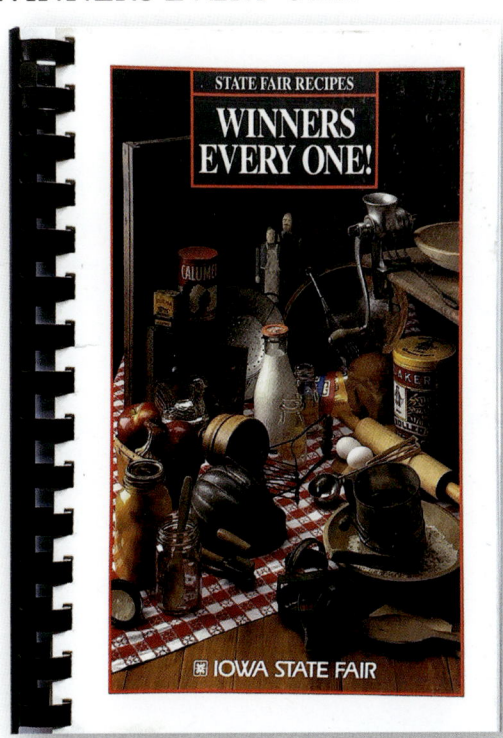

Winners Everyone, Iowa State Fair Recipes, *1986*.

Iowans celebrated the 100th anniversary of the permanent Des Moines Fairgrounds in 1986. In honor of the centennial, Arlette invited past blue ribbon winners to submit Recipes of Yesteryear, which were added to the Iowa

State Fair Cookbook, *Winners Every One*. This collection included blue ribbon recipes from 1985, like Banana Macadamia Nut Bread, and Yankee Maple Corn Muffins as well as vintage recipes like mincemeat pie. Another 100th birthday present for the Fairgrounds was a time capsule that was buried and is set to be opened in 2086.

The biggest new food contest at the Fair in 1986 was the American Pie Celebration, sponsored by Crisco for its 75th Anniversary and *Family Circle* magazine. The hunt for the best pie in the nation began with each state selecting its unique pie flavor. Hawaii chose macadamia nut, Vermont had maple cream, and rhubarb was the perfect choice for Iowa. Judy Arnold of Indianola baked her way to the national championships with a rhubarb filling infused with orange and fresh gingerroot. Her all-expense-paid trip to Nashville, Tennessee, included lots of baking, and lunch with Loretta Lynn at the Grand Old Opry.

CHORIZO TORTE AND TOFU

Like Nancy Hopkins, Arlette added more health-focused contests to attract a new generation of home cooks. Alongside monster cookies and triple-layer cakes, the Food Department hosted a wave of Cooking Lite and Healthy events with low-sodium and low-fat classes. Tofu recipes, roasted stuffed peppers, and breakfast muffins were popular categories. Ethnic and international divisions expanded, including Scandinavian, Asian, Greek, Jewish, and other cuisines. Jane Badger's Chorizo Hot Cheese Torte won the Mexican cook-off.

Arlette and her team ended the decade on a high note with 100 new contests and 10 new divisions in 1989, and the Food Department was just getting started.

1990s

IOWA'S BLUE RIBBON FUN FEST

1991 Program

By 1990, the farm crisis that had plagued rural America during the 1980s ended. The Iowa State Fair set attendance records in both 1989 and 1990, when nearly 874,000 gathered to celebrate Iowa's Blue Ribbon Fun Fest.

BAKING BLUE RIBBONS

Arlette and her team had nearly tripled the Food Department purse, from $7,300 in 1986 to more than $21,000 in 1990. Food entries rose 50% in a single year to 6,000 exhibits, the largest response at that time. Judging began three days before the Fair opened so that events would run smoothly. This was a great opportunity to watch the best State Fair food contests in the nation for free. Dedicated home cooks like Chris Montalvo, Cheryl Rogers, and Pat (Hatch) Berry checked in hundreds of entries. In 1991, Arlette and her team whipped up more new events with national and local sponsors such as Kraft Miracle Whip Salad Dressing, Keebler's Crackers, Tone's Spices, Hormel's Spam, and Crisco. Winners took home more than $24,000 in premiums and awards.

1990: UGLY CAKES

Arlette's plan to get more youth involved exploded in 1990 with the Ugliest Cake Contest. While culinary artists perfected their entries for Dahl's Edible Masterpiece competition, kids across the state piled gummy worms and chocolate dirt onto the ugliest cakes the Fair had ever seen. Instead of rose petals and buttercream, think crushed Oreo gunk and mint jelly goop like eight-year-old Jonathan Eddy of Des Moines, whose supergross creation took top honors. Kids had more than 70 junior contests to enter. For many years, the Fair and Chuck E. Cheese sponsored the Ugly Cake Contest. Since 2016, Bret and Amy Doerring of Newton have sponsored it. The Doerrings give children who enter the contest two tickets to the Giant Slide and $5 in Fair food bucks to make their day at the Fair even more fun.

Jonathan Eddy of Des Moines wins first Ugly Cake Contest. This celebration remains a gold standard of kid contests at the Iowa State Fair. No recipe required, just a list of edible ingredients and a name for your ugly creation! ©The Des Moines Register – USA TODAY NETWORK, 1990

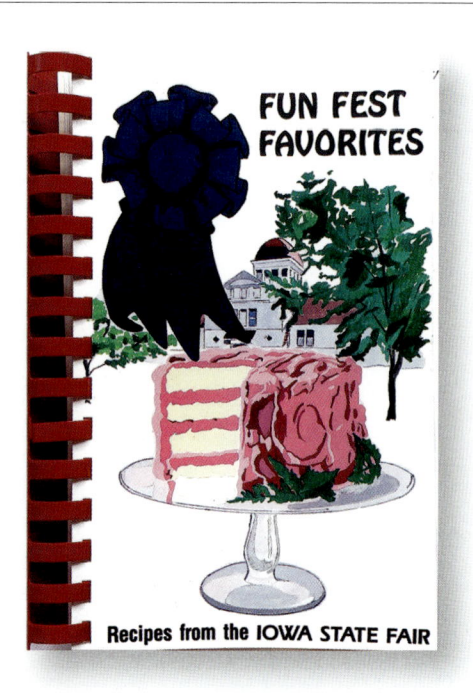

The 1990 *Fun Fest Favorites* Cookbook featured 500 recipes that took home the silks in past years, like Fruity Tofu Energizer, Heartland Stew, and Lasagna. By 1994, Food Department cash and prizes totaled almost $30,000 with 108 divisions and 839 individual classes.

FOOD WINNERS LISTED IN THE DES MOINES REGISTER

With all the food winners during the 1990s, Carol McGarvey, a features reporter at *The Des Moines Register* and contributor to this book, wanted to publish their names in the newspaper. After all, other winners, primarily men in animal- and agriculture-related contests, were listed each day by the farm editor. Carol approached her editors, who said if she wanted to input all those names and towns, go for it.

It wasn't easy. There were no computers at the Fair to transmit the lists. So, instead, Arlette Hollister left them in Carol's home mailbox between 9 and 10 p.m. each night of the Fair. If she couldn't do it, one of her helpers who lived not far from Carol left them in her mailbox and Carol would pick them up and take them to work early the next morning and start typing. She also had help from news assistant Virginia Beery. Carol believes that the contest coverage sold a few extra newspapers and gave credit to winners. Publishing also saved many names, stories, and recipes for posterity.

1996: IOWA'S PIE PRIMARY

Iowa has hosted the first-in-the-nation caucuses since 1972. In 1996, JoAnna Lund of De Witt brought Democrats and Republicans together for the first Pie Primary at the Iowa State Fair. JoAnna contacted both presidential campaigns and created recipes based on the candidates' favorite flavors. She made Hope Cheesecake with lemon, pineapple, Mountain Dew, and pecans for Democrat Bill Clinton and Double Chocolate Cream Pie with a chocolate crumb crust for Republican Bob Dole. JoAnna wrote numerous books and cookbooks, including *Healthy Exchanges*. She was a champion of health-focused recipes and hosted two national PBS TV series, *Help Yourself with JoAnna Lund* and *Cooking Healthy with the Family in Mind*. She made her creamy desserts with low-fat ingredients "guaranteed to help the candidates stay healthy while on the campaign trail," she said in a *Des Moines Register* interview. JoAnna prepared her desserts in front of a live audience at the Maytag Family Food Center. Fairgoers cast their ballots and enjoyed both.

Love at the Fair

Every once in a while, there's a little romance brewing at the Fair. Such was the case when Mike Landers and Heidi Carroll worked one Fair season in the Maytag Family Food Center. Mike was about to be a sophomore at the University of Northern Iowa in Cedar Falls. Heidi was going to be a freshman at UNI. A little romance ensued, but, with working long 12-hour days, there wasn't much courting going on at the Fair. That came in the fall at college.

The rest, as they say, is history. They married on March 15, 1996. Food Superintendent Arlette Hollister attended, and a family friend, Nancy Saltzstein, gave them a brick with their names and wedding date. It's imbedded in the walkway by the Maytag Center. They live in Maple Grove, Minnesota.

1998: THE BIGGEST FOOD PRIZE EVER

In 1998, Mary Johnson of Des Moines won $3,000 in the Tone's cinnamon roll contest out of 141 entries—the largest food prize ever at the Iowa State Fair. Honey Gross of Mitchellville won $1,500 for her second-place rolls, and Mary Sailer of Manning took home $500 for third. Tone's celebrated its 125th anniversary with the event, which is still a marquee of baking contests. The Ankeny-based company sponsored the competition for 15 years. Say the words "cinnamon roll" at the Iowa State Fair, and anyone who bakes or eats these sticky treats knows which event you are talking about. Since the first competition, thousands of Iowa bakers have vied for the prize money and pride in being Iowa's cinnamon roll champ. Incredible rolls have emerged, but one of the most unique was Kelly McCulley's 2010 recipe, which paired the sweetness of sugar and spice with Iowa pork to set a new standard for nontraditional cinnamon rolls.

After Tone's, different sponsors have carried the banner. Though the cash prizes are in the hundreds instead of the thousands, cinnamon roll enthusiasts continue the tradition with gusto.

> ## "We're urging people to enter who have never entered before. It's a fun experience and one meets so many nice people."
>
> – Arlette Hollister, Iowa State Fair Food Superintendent, 1986–2016.

1999: PICKLE POWER

It's one thing to win a blue ribbon at the Iowa State Fair. It's quite something else to have your recipe produced, packed, and shipped to grocery stores around the country. That's what happened to Norita Solt of Bettendorf and to Robin Tarbell-Thomas of Centerville in 1999, after their pickles took top honors in the Fair the year before. The two were taken on a Great American Pickle Tour because the company "relished" their contributions.

Jars of Norita's Sweets, bread and butter pickles, and Gramma's Mellow Dills by Robin Tarbell-Thomas graced the jars of M.A. Gedney's Pickles on supermarket shelves nationwide. The labels featured the Iowa State Fair logo, along with photos of the women.

The backs of the pickle jars featured their quotes. "I love to cook," Solt wrote. "When life gets stressed, my kitchen is my escape and my therapy. I've won quite a few recipe contests over the years, but the first time I entered the Iowa State Fair was 1997. I got so enthused that I entered 70-plus items in 1998—and won 52 ribbons."

Norita waived her royalties from the pickles so that she could remain an amateur food contestant. If she had accepted the money, she would have been considered a professional and ineligible to compete.

For Robin, entering the fair was in her blood. She wrote, "My Gramma Mildred Phillips has won more than 5,000 ribbons. My mom, Olive Jean Tarbell, has won 2,000. So far, I have 2,743. Even my daughter Molly, age 6, has 3."

As Kathie Swift, then marketing director of the Fair, told *The Des Moines Register*, "The Fair and pickles—doesn't that just say it all?"

By the end of the 1990s, the food competitions boasted an annual purse worth more than $65,000, including $24,000 from Tone's. Judges carefully assessed nearly 9,000 entries during their August run through 150 divisions, 880 classes, and 450 pitchers of water. The Iowa State Fair food story was featured in newspapers and magazines like *Gourmet* and *Saveur*.

America's #1 food department had seen two decades of unprecedented growth, with bigger surprises to come in the 21st century.

"When life gets stressed, my kitchen is my escape and my therapy."

– Norita Solt, 1999

---

150   BAKING BLUE RIBBONS

1980s – 1990s
STORIES AND RECIPES

Breads & Rolls

BANANA MACADAMIA NUT BREAD

There are so many great banana bread recipes. Macadamia nuts give this loaf a moist and marvelous texture, which earned Krystin Drews of Des Moines a $75 U.S. Savings Bond in the Chiquita banana bread contest in 1986.

2½ cups cake flour
½ cup sugar
½ cup packed brown sugar
3½ teaspoons baking powder
1 teaspoon salt
1 teaspoon cinnamon
1¼ cups mashed bananas
⅓ cup milk
3 tablespoons vegetable oil
1 egg
1 teaspoon vinegar
¾ cup chopped macadamia nuts

Preheat oven to 350°F. Combine all ingredients except nuts and beat until dry ingredients are just moistened. Stir in nuts. Pour into greased 9x5-inch loaf pan. Bake for 55–65 minutes, until toothpick inserted into the center comes out clean. Cool slightly. Loosen sides of loaf and remove from pan onto a wire rack. Cool completely before slicing. Makes 1 loaf, 8–10 slices.

Krystin Drews, Des Moines
First Place, 1986 Chiquita Banana Bread Contest

YANKEE MAPLE CORN MUFFINS

Many of Lois Friday's recipes appeared in Iowa State Fair cookbooks in the 1980s, like this one, which earned first place and a $50 U.S. Savings Bond in 1985.

2 cups flour
1 cup yellow cornmeal
1 tablespoon baking powder
¾ teaspoon salt
2 eggs

¼ cup packed brown sugar
1 cup milk
½ cup maple syrup
4 tablespoons butter, melted, plus more to brush over baked muffins if desired

Preheat oven to 350°F. Thoroughly mix flour, cornmeal, baking powder, and salt in a large bowl. In a separate bowl beat eggs and brown sugar until smooth. Add milk and maple syrup and whisk together. Pour wet mixture over dry ingredients; add melted butter. Fold with spatula until dry ingredients are just moistened. Scoop batter into greased or lined muffin cups. Bake 25–30 minutes, or until golden brown and firm in the center. Cool for 5 minutes. Brush tops with extra melted butter if desired. Makes 12 muffins.

Lois Friday, Iowa City
First Place, 1985 Quick Breads, Corn Muffins

APPLESAUCE MUFFINS

In the 1980s and beyond, State Fair cooking and baking was a family affair for Diana (Bobbie) Duke of Des Moines and her six children. She and her four oldest kids prepared more than 200 entries for the 1986 Fair with many winners. Everyone started at an early age with recipes like Angela's (age 6) kid-friendly applesauce muffins, Charles' (age 12) Stuffed Peppers (in the Main Dishes section), and Bobbie's Fruity Tofu Energizer (in Candies, Snacks, and Desserts).

1½ cups flour
¼ cup sugar
2 tablespoons baking powder
½ teaspoon cinnamon
¼ teaspoon nutmeg

1 egg or equivalent egg substitute
3 tablespoons safflower oil
½ cup applesauce
¼ cup skim milk
¼ cup water

Preheat oven 400°F. Prepare 12-cup muffin tin. Mix flour, sugar, baking powder, cinnamon, and nutmeg in a bowl. In another bowl beat egg; add oil, applesauce, milk, and water; mix well.

Pour wet mixture over dry ingredients and stir gently, just enough to moisten. Spoon about ¼ cup batter into each muffin cup so it's about ⅔ full. Bake for 15 to 20 minutes. Makes 12 muffins.

The Duke Family. ©The Des Moines Register – USA TODAY NETWORK, *1986*

Angela Duke, Des Moines
First Place, 1985 Youth Quick Breads, Muffins

PULLED PORK CINNAMON ROLLS

The inspiration for Kelly McCulley's standout cinnamon rolls came from her love of all things pork. Her recipe appeared on her blog and in other articles by food enthusiasts who were impressed with her creativity. As she said in her blog, "I'm posting this recipe for free for the world to enjoy!" Well, the world would like to say, "Thank you, Kelly!"

PULLED PORK
1 4- to 5-pound pork butt or shoulder
¼ cup brown sugar
1 tablespoon cinnamon
1 tablespoon kosher salt
½ teaspoon ground black pepper

DOUGH
½ cup 2% milk
½ cup butter
½ cup warm water
1 envelope active dry yeast
¼ cup granulated sugar
1 large egg, plus 2 large egg yolks
1½ teaspoons salt
4 to 4½ cups flour, plus more for dusting workspace
Egg wash (1 egg beaten with 1 tablespoon water)

FILLING
¼ cup butter, softened
½ teaspoon cinnamon
About ¼ cup of your favorite BBQ sauce, plus more for drizzle

Preheat oven to 300°F. Start with roasting the pork. Mix the brown sugar, cinnamon, kosher salt, and black pepper. Coat the outside of the pork roast with this mixture. Place roast in a large roasting pan and roast uncovered at 300°F for 6–8 hours or until the meat is tender and pulls off easily. When done, let roast rest until it cools off a little. Then shred with two forks, discarding fat and gristle. Set pulled pork aside.

FOR THE DOUGH: Heat milk and butter in a small saucepan or in the microwave until butter melts. Remove pan from heat and set aside until the mixture is lukewarm (about 100°F).

In a standing mixer fitted with paddle attachment mix the warm water, yeast, sugar, egg, and yolks at low speed until well mixed. Add the salt, warm milk mixture, and 2 cups of the flour; mix at medium speed until thoroughly blended, about 1 minute. Switch to the dough hook, add another 2 cups of the flour, and knead at medium speed (adding ¼ cup more flour, 1 tablespoon at a time, if necessary) until the dough is smooth, about 10 minutes. Scrape the dough into a large lightly oiled bowl, turn to coat, then cover bowl with plastic wrap. Leave in a warm, draft-free spot until doubled in bulk (1½ to 2 hours). After the dough has doubled, press it down and turn it out onto a lightly floured work surface. Using a rolling pin, shape the dough into a 16x12-inch rectangle with a short side facing you.

FOR THE FILLING: Mix the ¼ cup softened butter with the ½ teaspoon cinnamon and spread over the surface of the dough. Squeeze about ¼ cup BBQ sauce all over butter. Spread a healthy layer of pulled pork over the surface of the dough, leaving a 1-inch open strip on one of the short sides. Roll the dough and when you get to the end, pinch it to seal.

Preheat oven to 350°F. Butter a metal 9x13-inch cake pan. With a sharp serrated knife, evenly cut roll into six equal slices and evenly place them swirl side up in the pan (2 rolls by 3 rolls). Cover with plastic wrap and let rise until puffy and almost doubled (about 1 hour). Gently brush with egg wash before placing in oven.

Bake rolls at 350°F for 40–50 minutes, or until the internal temperature reaches 185°F–190°F on an instant read thermometer. Remove from oven and allow to cool in pan 10–15 minutes. Drizzle with your favorite barbecue sauce and serve. Makes 6 hearty rolls.

Kelly McCulley, Des Moines
First Place, 2010 Tone's Cinnamon Roll Contest, Non-Traditional Cinnamon Rolls

Find Soft Pretzel recipe and All-Purpose Yeast Dough, beginning on page 180.

Salads

WITH A LITTLE HELP FROM HER FRIENDS

For veteran food competitor Cheryl Rogers of Ankeny, the focus is recipes, contests, ribbons, and the buildup of the busy time in August. Before anything makes it to judges' tables, it must pass the first round of neighborhood taste-testers. They know when she texts them or leaves her third garage door open that Cheryl is practicing recipes for the Fair, and they come running with forks in hand.

Cheryl asks for real critiques. "I don't want them to offer rave reviews if they aren't warranted. I want comments for making a dish better for competition." Neighbors know that one time, they may get a fairly balanced meal to judge. The next time, they may get all pies to taste. No one minds. They love it.

With her judging team behind her, Cheryl has won as much as $1,500 in prizes during a single Fair. One of her winning recipes was for Sweet and Savory Confetti SPAM Salad, and it went on to the national Hormel SPAM contest.

Cheryl's Fair adventure also includes a lovely superstition "I have what I call my 'lucky plate.' If I have an entry I feel needs a little extra help, I put it on that plate for the Fair."

So far, the results have been great. What's on that plate almost always wins.

SWEET AND SAVORY CONFETTI SPAM SALAD

1 12-ounce can Bacon SPAM, cut into ½-inch cubes
1 12-ounce can Black Pepper SPAM, cut into ½-inch cubes
½ cup honey mustard salad dressing
½ cup sweet Vidalia onion salad dressing
½ cup diced fresh jalapeño pepper (seeds removed)
½ cup finely diced red sweet pepper
½ cup sliced green onions (both green and white parts)
1 cup cooked sweet corn kernels (fresh or frozen)
2 cups cooked small ring pasta (measure after cooking)
½ cup finely diced celery
2 cups mixed dried fruit bits (mixture I used had black raisins, golden raisins, cranberries, apples, and apricots)
1¼ cups coarsely chopped smoked almonds
Curly parsley for garnish

Preheat a nonstick skillet over medium-high. Working in small batches, cook and stir SPAM cubes until slightly browned on all sides. Transfer to a large bowl and let cool. In a small bowl whisk together the two salad dressings. Set aside. Add all other ingredients except the nuts and parsley to the bowl with SPAM cubes. Stir to combine. When ready to serve, add chopped almonds and pour dressing over salad and stir just enough to evenly coat all ingredients. Transfer to a serving bowl and garnish with curly parsley. Makes 8 main-dish servings or 10 to 12 side-dish servings.

Cheryl Rogers, Ankeny
First Place, 2016 Great American SPAM Cookoff

Sauce

CAMPGROUND COOKS

Most State Fair food contestants prepare their entries in the comfort of their home kitchens with built-in ovens, full spice racks, and favorite kitchen gadgets. It takes a different kind of competitor to enter the Campground Throwdown. These are State Fair campers who prepare their entries on the stoves and ovens of their trailers, campers, and recreational vehicles. Susan Knapp of Van Meter has been an avid campground cook for years across many contests.

She has entered potato salad and pies, including mincemeat, peach, and lemon meringue, among other signature dishes. In 1999 she won the American Beauty Spaghetti contest for sauces, adapting her mother's recipe. "It makes enough to feed an army," she told the *Des Moines Register*. All her entries were made in the kitchen of the trailer she and husband Bill Knapp, Des Moines real estate developer, stay in during the run of the Fair. The couple were State Fair parade marshals in 2007.

Susan, a benefactor of the Iowa State Fair, opened the Susan Knapp Amphitheater in Heritage Village and wrote a children's book, *Bells Goes to the Fair* (McMillen Publishing), with proceeds benefitting the Blue Ribbon Foundation. Her red sauce is a winner, whether you are camping, making lasagna, or serving pasta at home.

SPAGHETTI SAUCE

2 to 3 tablespoons olive oil
4 or 5 cloves garlic, diced
1 large white or yellow onion, chopped
2 green peppers, chopped
1 pound Graziano's medium Italian sausage
2 pounds ground round
3 teaspoons basil
2 teaspoons oregano
2 12-ounce cans whole Italian tomatoes
1 large and 1 small can tomato paste
2 cans condensed tomato soup
2 12-ounce cans tomato sauce
5 to 6 tablespoons brown sugar

Heat oil in large saucepan. Add garlic; stir. Add onions and green peppers; cook 5 to 10 minutes, until soft. Simmer meats until cooked; drain. Add remaining ingredients and simmer 2 to 4 hours on top of stove or in slow cooker. Or, if desired, bake sauce at 325°F for two hours. Makes about 15 servings. (If desired, cut recipe in half. Or serve half and freeze half.)

Susan Terry Knapp, Van Meter
First Place, 1999 American Beauty Spaghetti Sauce

Main Dishes

A LIFETIME IN THE KITCHEN

From 1987 to 2021, Bette Dryer of Des Moines sold her home-grown cookbook series, *A Lifetime in the Kitchen,* at the State Fair. If you ever walked through the north doors at the Elwell Family Food Center during the Fair, you probably saw Bette and her husband, Harry, at their table, welcoming everyone and selling cookbooks. Bette grew up in the South and many of her recipes have a southern flair.

She won hundreds of prizes at the Fair and other cooking contests. She saved the prize money through the years and opened Bette Dryer's Tea Room and Catering in Indianola in 1993 with Harry. She honed her skills as a caterer at Salisbury House and the Rollins Mansion.

Bette wrote 13 cookbooks by hand and Harry, the computer guru, formatted them. "It has been our natural work procedure," he said. They have been married for 58 years.

Bette Dryer, Welcome Home Des Moines *magazine*

In addition to selling cookbooks, the Dryers have sponsored the Fair Delicious food competition. Contestants purchase a food item from any State Fair food vendor and create their recipe using that as the main ingredient. Past winners have used cinnamon rolls, cotton candy, and other items. The cotton candy became the sweetener in a cherry pie.

In 2021, at age 86, Bette retired after she and Harry sold their last six cookbooks. Her most famous recipe for Beef Fillets Supreme is in all her cookbooks. She won the Iowa State Fair Beef Cook-off and three of the five awards given at the National Beef Cook-off in 1987. "It was my moment in the sun," she says.

BEEF FILLETS SUPREME

6 4-ounce beef tenderloin steaks
1 teaspoon lemon pepper
½ teaspoon ground cardamon
3 tablespoons butter
3 tablespoons green onions, sliced diagonally in ½-inch sections
8 small mushrooms, sliced thin
2 tablespoons white wine
1 tablespoon soy sauce
1 teaspoon Dijon-style mustard
Garnish: Lemon, green onion, citrus leaves

Mix lemon pepper and cardamon. Sprinkle over beef fillets. Heat butter in heavy skillet until very hot. Cook fillets 3 to 4 minutes on each side. Remove to heated platter. Add onions and mushrooms; stir-fry for 2 or 3 minutes. Add wine, soy sauce, and mustard, scraping the pan. Heat thoroughly and pour over fillets to serve. Garnish with lemon roses, green onions, and citrus leaves. Makes 6 servings.

CHORIZO HOT CHEESE TORTE

Jane Badger's 1980s Mexican Cook-Off winner makes a great main dish or an impressive appetizer.

1 cup chopped green onions
1 medium green sweet pepper, chopped (about 1 cup)
1 small clove garlic, minced
2 tablespoons butter
1 16-ounce jar hot picante salsa
1 can diced green chiles
1½ cups grated sharp cheddar cheese
1½ cups grated hot pepper Monterey Jack cheese
1 cup oil
6 tortillas
1 pound chorizo (hot Mexican sausage)
Jalapeño pepper slices and chopped green onions for garnish, optional

Preheat oven to 400°F. Sauté onions, green peppers, and garlic in butter in a medium saucepan until soft, about 3 minutes. Add hot salsa and diced green chiles to garlic mixture and simmer for 10 minutes. Combine cheddar and Monterey Jack cheeses in bowl and reserve. Heat oil in large heavy skillet over medium-high heat. Using tongs, dip tortillas in oil, one at a time, turning once. Keep in oil long enough to soften, about 30 seconds. Drain. Cook chorizo in a heavy skillet about 10 minutes. Put 1 tortilla on glass pie plate. Spoon 3 tablespoons chorizo, then 3 tablespoons cheese mixture; top with 4 tablespoons salsa mixture. Repeat layers of tortilla, sausage, cheese, and salsa until all are used. Top last layer with remaining cheese. Bake 5 to 10 minutes or until cheese melts and sauce bubbles. If desired, garnish with jalapeño slices and green onions. Cut in wedges to serve. Serves 4–6.

Jane Badger, Des Moines
First Place, 1989 Mexican Cook-Off

TURKEY PATTIES WITH PEARS

Allspice, pears, and raisins sound like the start to a winning autumn pie or quick bread. They are also uniquely amazing in turkey burgers. Barbara Low's pear-raisin sauce doubles as a compote or the centerpiece of your next charcuterie board. She has also won with creative recipes for microwave main dishes, appetizers, pasta, bread, and a variety of desserts.

1 pound ground turkey
1¼ cups reduced-sodium saltine cracker crumbs
¾ teaspoon allspice
¼ teaspoon salt
¼ teaspoon black pepper
2 egg whites
Nonstick cooking spray
¼ cup raisins (we used golden raisins)
1 cup apple juice
2 tablespoons cornstarch
2 small pears, unpeeled and cut into ½-inch slices

Mix ground turkey, cracker crumbs, allspice, salt, pepper, and egg whites. Shape into 4 patties. Spray a 10-inch skillet with nonstick spray. Cook patties in skillet over medium heat 7 to 8 minutes on each side. Remove from skillet to warm platter; add raisins to skillet. In small bowl mix apple juice and cornstarch until smooth. Stir into skillet; heat to boiling, stirring constantly. Boil and stir 1 minute. Stir in pears; cook until pears are hot. Serve over patties. Makes 4 servings.

Barbara D. Low, Des Moines
First Place, 1998 Let's Cook Turkey – Main Dish

LOW-SODIUM STUFFED PEPPERS

This healthy main dish was one of many winners that Charles Duke, his mom, and siblings entered at the Fair during the 1980s.

8 green or red sweet peppers
1 tablespoon safflower oil
1 medium onion, finely chopped
1 pound lean ground beef
2 tablespoons finely chopped fresh parsley
1 teaspoon basil
¼ cup no-salt-added tomato paste, diluted with ¼ cup water
2 cups cooked rice, cooked without salt
1 cup tomato sauce, or water

Preheat oven to 350°F. Cut tops off peppers and save; discard seeds and white membranes. Put peppers and tops in a steamer and steam about 10 minutes. Meanwhile, make the filling. Heat oil in a skillet and cook onion for a few minutes or until soft. Add meat and cook over medium heat until browned. Drain off any fat. Add seasonings, tomato mixture, and cooked rice. Lightly fill peppers with stuffing. Cover with pepper tops. Place in ovenproof baking pan. Add tomato sauce or water to pan. Bake for about 20 minutes. Serves 4.

Charles Duke (12), Des Moines
First Place, 1986 Low-Sodium Cooking

HEARTLAND STEW

Diane Roupe celebrated cooking in the heartland in her comprehensive cookbook, *The Blue Ribbon Country Cookbook* (Potter, 1998). For many years, she sold her book on the balcony level of the Agriculture Building. She was a frequent exhibitor at the Iowa State Fair and later a food judge.

½ cup flour
1½ teaspoons salt
½ teaspoon black pepper
½ pound beef tenderloin (¾-inch-thick slices)
½ pound pork tenderloin (½-inch-thick slices)
½ pound veal tenderloin (¼-inch-thick slices)
½ cup butter
½ cup minced onion
1 garlic clove, minced
¼ cup water
3½ cups chicken broth
2 tablespoons fresh snipped parsley
1 teaspoon salt
½ teaspoon Worcestershire sauce
½ teaspoon celery salt
⅛ teaspoon black pepper
¼ pound fresh Iowa mushrooms, sliced
¾ cup pearl onions
¾ cup ¼-inch-thick French-cut carrot slices
¾ cup 2-inch-thick French-cut asparagus slices
¾ cup snow peas
¾ cup miniature corn
1 cup half-and-half
¼ cup dry sherry, optional
5 medium potatoes, peeled
1 egg, beaten
⅛ cup milk
2 tablespoons butter
¼ teaspoon salt

Combine flour, 1½ teaspoons salt, and ½ teaspoon pepper. Dredge meat in flour mixture; reserve remaining flour mixture. Cut beef into 1½-inch square pieces, pork into 1-inch square pieces, and veal into 1x1½-inch strips. In skillet brown all meat pieces well in butter; remove meat. In the same pan brown minced onion and garlic until golden brown; add water and deglaze pan. Transfer meat and onion mixture to large saucepan. Add broth, parsley, 1 teaspoon salt, Worcestershire sauce, celery salt, and ⅛ teaspoon black pepper; simmer 15 minutes. Add mushrooms; simmer 15 minutes more. Meanwhile, steam all vegetables except potatoes separately. Add steamed vegetables to meat mixture. Thicken stew with half-and-half and reserved flour mixture. Bring stew to a boil, stirring constantly. Add sherry; stir well: remove from heat. Turn stew into ovenproof casserole. Boil and mash potatoes; beat in egg, milk, butter, and ¼ teaspoon salt. Using pastry bag and No. 8B tip, pipe mashed potatoes on top of stew to garnish. Brown quickly under broiler; serve. Makes 8 to 10 servings.

Diane S. Roupe, West Des Moines
First Place, 1988 Iowa Farm Bureau, Iowa Stews

LASAGNA

Pat (Hatch) Berry has many winning recipes in Iowa State Fair cookbooks, like this Cooking Light and Healthy Lasagna. She later served as a judge and became the Food Department Superintendent beginning with the 2021 State Fair (story, page 192).

1 pound 95%-lean ground beef
1 cup chopped onion
½ teaspoon minced garlic
1 16-ounce can no-salt tomatoes
1 6-ounce can no-salt tomato sauce
2 teaspoons basil
1 teaspoon oregano
⅛ teaspoon ground red pepper

8 ounces lasagna noodles
¼ cup frozen 99%-real egg product, thawed
2 cups low-fat cottage cheese
¾ cup grated Parmesan cheese
1 tablespoon dried parsley flakes
½ teaspoon black pepper
8 ounces mozzarella cheese, sliced

Preheat oven to 375°F. In a large skillet brown beef, onion, and garlic. Drain fat; stir in next 5 ingredients. Cover; simmer 15 minutes, stirring frequently. Cook noodles according to package directions, omitting oil. Mix egg product, cottage cheese, ½ cup of the Parmesan cheese, parsley, and pepper. In 13x9-inch baking dish, layer in order half the noodles, half the cottage cheese mixture, half the mozzarella, and half the meat sauce. Repeat layers; sprinkle with remaining Parmesan. Bake 30 to 35 minutes or until heated thoroughly. Let stand 10 minutes before serving. Makes 12 servings.

Pat (Hatch) Berry, Urbandale
First Place, 1989 Iowa Methodist Nutrition Center—Cooking Lite and Healthy, Casseroles

Cakes

A BRUSH WITH FAME

In 1999, entertaining, decorating, and cooking maven Martha Stewart came to the Iowa State Fair to film some "down-home" segments for her television show.

Few people were more excited than Susie Jones of Waukee. Her relationship with the Fair was long and loving. In the 1960s, she watched the pie judging with her Grandma Charlotte who was an amazing cook and inspiration. "I remember thinking, could there be any better job on Earth than judging pies?" Susie says.

Years later, Susie worked with the Blue Ribbon Foundation's first few Corndog Kickoff events. One of the silent auction items was the chance to judge pies at the Fair. Susie's husband, Jack, made sure he had the highest bid. When Susie arrived to judge, the surprise was even bigger. Martha Stewart was the celebrity guest pie judge.

"As Martha and I visited before the contest, she asked what the winner receives as a prize. I told her a beautiful blue rosette ribbon and ten dollars (the prize money at that time)."

Martha's reaction was, "Ten dollars! Ten dollars? You mean women pour their hearts and souls into making these pies for ten dollars?"

Susie says, "I gathered my thoughts and responded that ten dollars is just ten dollars, but a rosette blue ribbon from the Iowa State Fair is priceless."

Entering fair competitions is part of Susie's story. She was petrified when she first entered, but a veteran winner, Louise Piper, showed Susie around and sat with her during the judging. "It was so special. It's an important part of my life."

Since then, Susie has entered as many as 40 items in a year and spends lots of time perusing recipes, always looking ahead to the next Fair. She kept entering the All-American Apple Pie contest until she finally won that elusive blue ribbon. In cakes, she searched until she came up with this "just right" recipe for her husband's favorite Coconut Cake, modeled after one his mother used to make. It also won a blue ribbon and has held a special place on the cake stand that has held all the favorite cakes in Susie's family for three generations.

Martha Stewart, right, filmed a segment of her show at the 1999 Iowa State Fair and was a celebrity guest judge in the Food Department.

©Quad-City Times, *August 20, 1999*

COCONUT LOVE CAKE

1 cup unsalted butter, room temperature
2 cups sugar
4 egg yolks (save whites for later)
1 teaspoon vanilla
3 cups cake flour

4 teaspoons baking powder
½ teaspoon salt
½ cup cream of coconut
¾ cup buttermilk
1 cup unsweetened shredded coconut

COCONUT FROSTING

1 8-ounce package cream cheese, softened
1 cup butter, room temperature
1 cup Crisco shortening
2 pounds powdered sugar
2 teaspoons vanilla

1 cup sweetened coconut, toasted
4 tablespoons milk
⅓ cup cream of coconut
1 cup coconut, untoasted

Preheat oven to 350°F. For cake, place one oven rack in the bottom third of oven and another in the top third of oven. Grease three 9-inch round cake pans. Line the bottoms with parchment paper and grease the paper and then the pans. In a large mixing bowl cream together butter and sugar until fluffy and resembles whipped cream, about 2 to 3 minutes. Beat in egg yolks and vanilla. Sift together cake flour, baking powder, and salt. Mix cream of coconut and buttermilk. Add dry and wet ingredients alternately into creamed mixture. Beat egg whites until fluffy and fold into batter until just incorporated. Fold in 1 cup coconut. Pour batter into three baking pans. Set two pans on top rack and third pan on lower rack. Stagger the cake pans on racks so that no layer is directly over another and heat can circulate around each pan. Bake 40 minutes or until toothpick inserted in center comes out clean.

For frosting, beat cream cheese, butter, shortening, powdered sugar, vanilla, 1 cup toasted coconut, milk, and cream of coconut together. If desired, reserve a small amount of toasted coconut for garnish. Place half of frosting in a separate bowl and add 1 cup untoasted coconut. Frost top and sides of cake with frosting with untoasted coconut. If desired, garnish edges of cake with toasted coconut. Makes approximately 12 servings.

Susie Jones, Waukee
First Place, Nostalgic Comfort Food—Cakes

SHE TAKES THE CAKE

Joy McFarland of Tingley, a longtime winner at the Iowa State Fair, entered one cake into competition in 1980, back when judging took place under the Grandstand. "I was so scared, but I got a third-place ribbon, and I was hooked."

Fast-forward through the years, and she doesn't know how many ribbons she has won, except for three years—1992, 47 blue ribbons; 1993, 71 blue ribbons; and 1995, 59 blue ribbons. Cakes are her specialty. "Winning ribbons is great, but that's truly never the goal for me," she says. "The importance comes in just doing it." Joy is the third-generation State Fair baker. Her daughter, Landi Livingston of Tingley, is the fourth.

Joy's husband, David, says that moving items to the Fairgrounds is the worst day of his year. Hauling layer cakes 80 miles in the heat, some cakes on ice, in a truck is a real trick.

There was a major blip in Joy's State Fair career in 2016 when she had a stroke. Landi was determined to get her mother back to baking. "We used flash cards and photos, as I had to re-learn many things," Joy says. "The Fair is good for me. I need to do it. Now recipes have to be all written out, and I have to set out all the ingredients and utensils before I start a recipe."

The Fair has been a goal for her recovery, and she has made it work. As David says, "There are three things you don't do. You don't mess with Superman. You don't pull off the mask of the Lone Ranger. And you don't bother Joy while she's baking for the State Fair."

CHOCOLATE PRALINE LAYER CAKE

PRALINE LAYER
½ cup butter
½ cup whipping cream
1 cup brown sugar
½ tablespoon butterscotch schnapps
1 cup chopped pecans

CAKE
½ cup cocoa powder
½ cup boiling water
2 tablespoons butterscotch schnapps
½ cup butter
2 cups sugar
1 8-ounce carton sour cream
1 teaspoon vanilla
½ teaspoon baking soda
⅛ teaspoon salt
2 cups flour
3 egg whites

TOPPING
1¾ cups whipping cream
¼ cup powdered sugar
¼ teaspoon vanilla

Preheat oven to 350°F. For praline layer, grease two round 8-inch pans. In a saucepan combine butter, whipping cream, and brown sugar. Heat until butter melts. Stir in schnapps. Pour evenly into pans. Sprinkle pecans on top.

164 BAKING BLUE RIBBONS

FOR CAKE: In a small bowl stir cocoa powder, boiling water, and schnapps; set aside. In a large bowl beat butter 30 seconds, then beat in sugar. Add cocoa mixture, sour cream, vanilla, baking soda, and salt. Add flour and beat egg whites until stiff. Fold in sour cream mixture. Pour batter evenly into both pans. Bake about 35 minutes. Cool 10 minutes and turn out layers.

Make topping when cakes are cooled. Beat whipping cream until soft peaks form. Blend in powdered sugar and vanilla; beat on high until stiff peaks form. To assemble: Place one layer, praline side up, on a cake plate. Spread with half of topping. Top with second layer, praline side up; spread with remaining topping. If desired, garnish with chocolate curls and pecans. Makes 12 servings.

Joy McFarland, left, and her daughter, Landi McFarland Livingston at the 2018 Iowa State Fair. Joy is holding her First Place Overall cake, and Landi has another of Joy's blue ribbon cakes.

Joy McFarland, Tingley
First Place Overall Cake, 2018

PRESIDENT BILL CLINTON'S HOPE CHEESECAKE

JoAnna Lund created this light dessert with some of President Bill Clinton's favorite flavors, Diet Mountain Dew, southern pecans, and pineapple.

2 8-ounce packages fat-free cream cheese
1 4-serving package sugar-free instant vanilla pudding mix
1 4-serving package sugar-free lemon gelatin
⅔ cup nonfat dry milk powder
1 8-ounce can crushed pineapple, packed in fruit juice, undrained
½ cup Diet Mountain Dew
¾ cup Cool Whip Lite, divided
1 graham cracker crust
¼ cup apricot fruit spread
2 tablespoons chopped pecans

In large bowl stir cream cheese until soft. Add dry pudding mix, dry gelatin, dry powdered milk, undrained pineapple, and Diet Mountain Dew. Mix well, using wire whisk. Blend in ¼ cup Cool Whip Lite. Spread mixture evenly into crust. Refrigerate while preparing topping.

In a small bowl stir spreadable fruit until soft. Add remaining ½ cup Cool Whip. Mix gently to combine. Spread topping mixture evenly over pineapple filling. Sprinkle pecans over top. Refrigerate at least 1 hour. Makes 8 servings.

Primary Pies & Desserts by JoAnna Lund, 1996 Iowa State Fair (See Senator Bob Dole's Double Chocolate Cream Pie in the pie section.)

Pies

ALL-IOWA RHUBARB PIE

The biggest new food contest in 1986 was the All-American Pie Celebration won by Judy Arnold of Indianola. She went on to Nashville to compete for the top American Pie honors with other State Fair winners. Judges agreed that gingerroot and orange flavors took this rhubarb pie to the top.

CRUST
2 cups flour
1 teaspoon salt
2/3 cup shortening
5 to 7 tablespoons cold water

FILLING
1 tablespoon crushed gingerroot
3 tablespoons undiluted orange juice concentrate
1 2/3 cups sugar
1/3 cup flour
4 cups of Iowa rhubarb cut into small pieces
1 tablespoon butter

Preheat oven to 450°F. For crust: Combine flour and salt; mix well. With a pastry blender, cut in shortening and mix until pieces are uniform in size. Sprinkle cold water into mixture, 1 tablespoon at a time, until dough is moistened. Divide dough in half and shape into two discs. With a floured rolling pin, roll first half of dough into a circle 1 inch larger than inverted pie pan. Carefully lift and place in pan.

For filling: Simmer gingerroot in undiluted juice concentrate for 5 minutes. Mix sugar and flour. Add rhubarb to flour and sugar. Strain gingerroot from orange juice and add to sugared rhubarb; mix well. Place rhubarb mixture in unbaked pie crust. Dot filling with butter. Roll second half of dough into a circle and place over filling. Make slits in top of crust to allow steam to escape.

Bake for 10 minutes. Reduce temperature to 350°F and bake approximately 45 minutes more.

Serves 8–10.

Judy Arnold, Indianola
First Place Overall, 1986 All-American Pie Celebration

HARANGUED BY MERINGUE

Jamie Buelt of Polk City is a thoroughly modern businesswoman but loves the nostalgic contests at the Elwell Family Food Center. Her three grown children, Lisabeth, Caroline, and Alexander, also participated in and won Fair food contests. Jamie has emceed many celebrity food events, but her all-time favorite is the Pie + Story contest, where you make a pie and write a story about it.

"I absolutely love the Butterscotch Meringue Pie made by Lana Ross Shope, and I was determined to try to emulate it," she said. Her incredible pie and hilarious poem won honors and laughs from the audience.

HARANGUED BY MERINGUE

BY JAMIE BUELT

Oh, oh, my sweet meringue,
Why do you like to me harangue?
As I beat you from white to fluff,
I ponder why is it so tough.
To make meringue that doesn't weep
So my sanity that I can keep.
Tell me how long should you bake
So that my heart doesn't break.
My feeling is that you'll never tell
From the top of my State Fair pie shell.

I consulted the likes of Lana Ross;
For when it comes to pie, she's the boss.
But pie requires no elocution,'
Just good skills in execution.

So damn you, my sweet meringue;
This story ends without a bang
In a fun cathartic prickly harangue.

*In fact, Jamie's story ended with this beautiful blue ribbon pie,
one we're sure that you must try.*

EMULATING LANA ROSS SHOPE'S BUTTERSCOTCH MERINGUE PIE

CRUST
- 1 cup flour
- ¼ cup cake flour
- 6 tablespoons unsalted butter
- 2 tablespoons lard
- 1 tablespoon ultrafine sugar
- 3 tablespoons very cold water

FILLING
- 1 cup light brown sugar, firmly packed
- ¼ cup butter
- 4 large egg yolks (reserve whites for meringue)
- 4 tablespoons Wondra flour
- ½ cup milk, divided
- 1½ cups heavy cream
- ½ teaspoon pure vanilla extract
- 3 drops butterscotch oil
- ¼ teaspoon cream of tartar
- 1 pinch salt

MERINGUE
- 3 large egg whites
- 1 teaspoon vanilla
- ¼ teaspoon cream of tartar
- ¼ cup granulated sugar

FOR CRUST: Preheat oven to 350°F. Sift dry ingredients and cut in butter until mixture has the consistency of cornmeal. Cut cold lard into pea-size pieces and cut in with pastry cutter. Move mixture to one side of the bowl and, using a fork, take about one-sixth of the dry butter-lard mixture into the other half. Add 1 tablespoon cold water and combine. Repeat with each tablespoon of cold water. Roll out dough and arrange in pie plate. Bake for 30 minutes until crust is brown.

FOR FILLING: Stir brown sugar and butter in a saucepan until butter melts and sugar dissolves. Cook 2 to 3 minutes longer on low-medium heat; remove from heat. Beat egg yolks. In separate large bowl mix egg yolks with half the milk until smooth. Add flour to saucepan with sugar-butter mixture, fold in remaining milk and heavy cream, and cook on low-medium heat until thickened (anywhere from 30–45 minutes), stirring constantly. Remove from heat and blend in vanilla extract and butterscotch oil. Stir in cream of tartar and salt. Stir constantly until blended and slightly warm. Pour into prepared piecrust.

FOR MERINGUE: With a mixer, beat egg whites with vanilla and cream of tartar until soft peaks form. Gradually add sugar, beating until stiff and glossy peaks form and all sugar dissolves. Spread meringue over slightly warm filling, sealing to edge of crust. Bake 12 to 15 minutes. Makes 8 servings.

Jamie Buelt, Polk City
First Place, 2017 Pie and Story Contest

THE MAIN INGREDIENT: HEARTFELT FRIENDSHIPS

The late Chris Montalvo of Windsor Heights, a veteran winner at the Fair, found more than blue ribbons. The real treasure came from heartfelt friendships over 20-some years as an exhibitor.

"We always went to the State Fair when I was young, and I was fascinated with the food competitions," she said in a 2013 interview with *Welcome Home Des Moines* magazine. She got serious about entering in 1995 and found mentors in Emma Whitlock and Marjorie Rodgers, both of Indianola.

In 2011 Chris was diagnosed with breast cancer, and it limited how much she could enter. She learned that it wasn't about gathering ribbons. Instead, it was the camaraderie of fellow competitors. "My State Fair buddies were there for me every step of the way. It was amazing. Virginia Ogren of Osceola, Louise Piper of Garner, Norita Solt of Bettendorf, Cheryl Rogers of Ames, Dianna Sheehy of Audubon, and superintendent Arlette Hollister of Des Moines, among many others, were there for me with weekly cards, calls, and food. It was so special."

Chris was back to pie baking in 2013 and won the Cream Pie Division of the Crisco National Pie Championships in Florida with her Old-Fashioned Butterscotch Cream Pie. Four of her recipes are in *America's Best Pies*.

Chris passed away in 2019. Some of the longtime competitors have cut back on entering, but many of their daughters and other family members have picked up the mantle. "Our circle of veterans has embraced them and taken them in as part of our Fair family," says Cheryl Rogers.

CHRIS MONTALVO'S STONE FRUIT PIE

CRUST
2 cups all-purpose flour
1 cup cake flour
1 cup Crisco
1 whole egg, beaten
1 tablespoon apple cider vinegar
⅓ cup ice water

FILLING
1 cup fresh ripe peaches, peeled and sliced
1 cup fresh ripe nectarines, peeled and sliced
1 cup fresh ripe apricots, peeled and sliced
½ cup sour cherries, pitted
1 cup sugar
¼ cup all-purpose flour
¼ teaspoon ground cinnamon
¼ teaspoon almond extract
¼ teaspoon salt
1 tablespoon butter, cut into pieces
Egg wash: 1 egg plus 1 tablespoon water
Sugar for the top

1980s–1990s

CRUST: In a food processor blend flours together. Cut Crisco into small pieces and add to processor. Pulse until mixture resembles small peas. Transfer mixture to a large mixing bowl. In a small mixing bowl mix egg, vinegar, and ice water. Mix well. Pour over flour mixture in the bowl. Using a fork, combine just until dough comes together Do not overmix. Form dough into a disk, wrap in plastic, and chill for several hours or overnight. Makes two 9-inch crusts.

FILLING: Preheat oven to 425°F. In a large bowl combine all fruit. In a separate bowl combine sugar, flour, spices, extract, and salt. Stir to blend. Pour over fruit and gently blend the fruit and sugar mixture until well mixed. Set aside.

Roll out half of the piecrust. Ease into 9-inch deep-dish pie plate. Spoon the fruit into the prepared crust. Dot with butter. Roll out the second crust; cut out a design in center of crust. Carefully place over fruit. Seal edges and flute. Brush top of pie with egg wash. Sprinkle top with sugar. Bake pie for 15 minutes. Reduce temperature to 375°F. Bake for an additional 45 minutes or until crust is brown and filling is bubbling. Remove from oven. Let cool completely before cutting. Makes 8 to 10 servings.

Chris Montalvo's Prize-Winning Pie, which was entered in Chris' memory by Cheryl Rogers in 2013.

NEVER GIVE UP

When Louise Piper was ten, her neighbor entered a layer cake with swirls of seven-minute frosting at the Humboldt County Fair. It was the prettiest thing Louise had ever seen. Seventy years later, she still remembers it. There were cakes, and breads, and all those cookies on display. "I'd like to do this," Louise thought, but years would pass before she had the chance.

Louise grew up, got married, and had a farm and a family of her own. With three kids and her nursing career, she entered the Iowa State Fair for the first time at age 45. It was worth the wait.

Her first entry in 1984 won a blue ribbon for quick breads. So did her second, a yellow layer cake. Six ribbons later, Louise was hooked.

In her eighties, Louise's peach-apricot-blueberry pie won a best overall for fruit pies in 2019. In more than 35 years of exhibiting, she has won countless prizes. She has appeared on television with Martha Stewart. Her recipes have been featured in magazines, books, blogs, and newspapers across the country. But it wasn't always bright lights and blue ribbons.

Her late husband, Bruce, always supported and encouraged her, even when she was about to give up. "Early on, I entered five or six pies and none of them did well. 'I'm going to quit,' I told my husband. 'They don't like my crusts,'" Louise said.

Bruce patted her leg and told her to swallow her pride and keep trying. It's a good thing she took his advice. Her perfectionism and creativity have led to exceptional pies like this.

PEACH APRICOT BLUEBERRY PIE

3 cups sliced peeled fresh peaches
3 fresh apricots, pitted and sliced
¾ cup blueberries
⅓ cup packed golden brown sugar
¾ cup plus 2 teaspoons sugar, divided
2 tablespoons cornstarch
2 tablespoons plus 1 teaspoon instant tapioca
1 tablespoon orange zest
2 tablespoons butter, cut into small pieces
Pastry for double-crust 9-inch pie
1½ tablespoons milk to brush over top crust
Sparkling sugar for top

CRUST
2¼ cups flour
1 teaspoon salt
⅔ cup vegetable oil
¼ to ⅓ cup cold whole milk

FOR FILLING: Fold together fruits, brown sugar, ¾ cup of the granulated sugar, cornstarch, tapioca, and orange zest. Allow to stand while preparing crust. Spoon into pastry-lined pie plate. Dot top of filling with butter pieces. Cut slits in top to vent steam. Brush milk over crust and sprinkle with sparkling sugar. Put metal pie ring or other covering over pie crust edges.

FOR CRUST: In a large bowl stir together flour and salt. Pour vegetable oil into small bowl and add milk; whisk together. Pour into flour mixture; stir well. Shape into 2 balls. Flatten each into a round. Roll each one out between 2 sheets of wax paper. Place one crust into 9-inch pie plate. Roll out second portion for top crust. Bake for about 50–55 minutes. Cool on wire rack. Serves 8–10.

Louise Piper, Garner
First Place, 2019 Machine Shed Pies—Two-Crust Fruit Other Than Named
First Place Overall, 2019 Machine Shed Pies—Fruit

Louise's Peach Apricot Blueberry Pie

Louise Piper at 2019 Iowa State Fair.

1980s–1990s

SENATOR BOB DOLE'S DOUBLE CHOCOLATE CREAM PIE

JoAnna Lund created this pie with Senator Bob Dole's favorite flavors during the 1996 presidential campaign. There is no mistaking that he loved chocolate, the more the better.

2 8-ounce packages fat-free cream cheese
1 4-serving package sugar-free instant chocolate fudge pudding mix
2/3 cup nonfat dry milk powder
1 cup water
1¾ cups Cool Whip Lite, divided
1 teaspoon vanilla extract
12 2½-inch chocolate graham crackers divided
1 6-ounce chocolate crumb pie crust
1 tablespoon chocolate syrup
Mini chocolate chips

In a large bowl stir cream cheese until soft. Add dry pudding mix, powdered milk, and water. Mix well, using wire whisk. Blend in 1 cup Cool Whip Lite and vanilla. Coarsely crush 9 graham crackers. Add to cream cheese mixture. Fill pie crust evenly with mixture. Finely crush remaining graham crackers. Evenly sprinkle crumbs over top. Refrigerate at least 1 hour. Before serving, combine remaining Cool Whip Lite and chocolate syrup in a small bowl. Drop by spoonfuls on top of pie. Garnish each slice with scant 1 tablespoon chocolate chips. Makes 8 servings.

Primary Pies by JoAnna Lund, 1996 Iowa State Fair

Cookies

A RECORD TO KEEP GOING

Like some other cooks and bakers, Ileen Wallace of Council Bluffs has been represented in nearly every Iowa State Fair cookbook. We want to keep that record going, so here is her winning cookie recipe from 1998. Yes, it calls for a sprinkling of blue sugar over the top. "It's just prettier," she notes. "When you make a white sugar cookie, it looks better with a little color on top. This cookie is the same."

IOWA POTATO CHIP COOKIES

2/3 cup butter or margarine
1½ cups sugar
1 teaspoon maple flavoring
1½ cups crushed potato chips
½ cup chopped pecans
3 cups all-purpose flour
1 teaspoon baking soda
Blue sugar or any color sprinkles

Preheat oven to 350°F. Cream butter, sugar, and maple flavoring. Add potato chips and pecans. Stir in flour and baking soda. Form dough into small balls. Place on ungreased baking sheet; press flat with a fork. Bake 10 to 12 minutes. Sprinkle blue sugar over top. Makes approximately 3 dozen cookies.

Ileen Wallace, Council Bluffs
First Place, 1998 Cookies, Potato Chip

Candies, Snacks & Desserts

FRUITY TOFU ENERGIZER

Here is a flashback energy boost for morning or afternoon, straight from the 1980s health food craze and still fresh today.

1 cup soft tofu
1 cup orange juice
½ cup sliced strawberries
1 banana, sliced
1 tablespoon honey or sugar
1 teaspoon vanilla

Place all ingredients in a blender; blend until smooth. Serve immediately or chill and serve later. Makes 2 to 3 servings.

Diana Duke, Des Moines
First Place, 1989 Cooking With Tofu, Snacks and Appetizers

AHHHH, SWEEEEEEET

Harold Magg of Spirit Lake has won the fudge sweepstakes and numerous candy awards since the mid-1980s. When not making confections, he raises purebred black Angus cattle. He credits his friends and neighbors with encouraging him to enter candies.

"In 1985, I had surgery and was confined to home for a month," Harold explains. He made candies and gave samples away and then took orders. He has been going strong ever since. Harold makes 100-plus pounds during the holidays and mails them around the country. His best advice for candymakers is to be particular since candy recipes and temperatures are so specific. He also insists on using Anderson Erickson cream for his confections. "It's real cream. Sometime when I'm in Des Moines, I will stop at AE and tell them how much I love it."

CLASSIC VANILLA FUDGE

4 cups sugar
4 cups heavy cream
1 tablespoon light corn syrup
Dash salt
1½ teaspoons vanilla
2 tablespoons butter
1 cup chopped nuts

In a heavy saucepan combine sugar and cream. Stir over medium-high heat until sugar is dissolved. When mixture boils, add syrup. Boil until firm ball stage (242°F–248°F) Pour into large bowl. Add salt, vanilla, butter, and nuts. Do not stir. Cool 30 minutes or until lukewarm. Beat with mixer until thick and loses gloss. Pour into greased 9x13-inch pan. Makes approximately 48 squares.

Harold Magg, Spirit Lake
First Place, 1999 Candy, Vanilla Fudge

Building a Blue Ribbon Dynasty
FIVE GENERATIONS OF THE TARBELL-THOMAS CLAN

If you have competed at the Iowa State Fair food competitions any time since the 1960s, you may have come across a clan of culinary wizards that goes back five generations. This is the story of today's Tarbell-Thomas family, which begins at the turn of the twentieth century with a woodstove and one blue ribbon.

ONE BLUE RIBBON

For Eva Horstman, one blue ribbon was enough. Born in 1881, she baked her cakes in a woodstove and adjusted the temperature by opening and closing the oven door. In the early 1900s she entered a cake at the Moulton Festival. Her family never owned a car, so a neighbor took it for her and returned with her first-place ribbon. Eva was proud of that ribbon.

She had no idea that it would launch a baking dynasty spanning five generations and well over 10,000 ribbons. She passed on her culinary skills to her daughter, Mildred Phillips, and granddaughter, Olive Jean Tarbell. The generations that followed have kept the ovens warm and the blue ribbons coming.

LIGHTING THE FIRE

Mildred Phillips turned her mother's woodstove cooking lessons into winning entries at local fairs during the 1930s, '40s, and '50s. When she inquired at the local county extension service about entering the State Fair, they told her not to bother. With champion cooks from all over Iowa, Mildred didn't have a chance.

Their predictions lit a fire in Centerville's best-known baker. Not only did she compete at the state level, she won and won. Mildred retired from competition in 1980 after amassing more than 5,000 prizes. She had some of her ribbons made into family quilts. Mildred was especially proud of her Archway Best Cookie of the Fair peanut butter recipe that placed third at Archway's national cookie competition. At her memorial service in 1992, many of her blue ribbons were given as remembrances to friends and family.

BEST STATE FAIR MEMORY

Fast forward to 2020. Mildred's daughter, Olive Jean Tarbell, shares stories of baking championships. She has appeared in advertisements for Fleischmann's Active Dry Yeast and Folger's Coffee in addition to starring in a Crisco television commercial in 1963. Her winning recipes have been published nationwide. Without the Iowa State Fair, none of this would have happened.

Olive Jean's favorite memories are of family trips to the Fair when she was a child. Her voice lifts as she recalls riding in the back seat with her two younger brothers. Every inch that was not filled with their mother's cookies or canning jars was packed with their dad's potatoes, eggs, sacks of grain—even a live chicken. Camping gear filled the trunk. Best of all was the giant corn stalk strapped to the side of the car, roots and all, ready for the tall corn contest.

"My brothers and I hung out the window, screaming the 'Iowa Corn Song.' 'We're from Iowa. IOWA. That's where the tall corn grows!'" Olive Jean sings as if she still feels the wind on her face. "My brothers and I traveled lots of places," she said. "We never had fun like we did when we went to the Iowa State Fair."

THE MOST RIBBONS

Olive Jean mastered the family recipes and passed them down to her daughter, Robin Tarbell-Thomas, and granddaughter, Molly Thomas. They excel at cakes, canned goods, and any type of bread, but cookies are their specialty. Chances are, if you have exhibited cookies at the Fair in the past 40 years, you have come across a Tarbell-Thomas baker.

Robin is said to have won more ribbons than any exhibitor in the history of the Iowa State Fair Food Department and possibly the nation. In 1997 she won 131 baking competitions, which is believed to be the largest number of blue ribbons ever won at a single Fair. They stopped counting years ago, but her grand total is well over 3,000. She won her first State Fair baking contest in 1975 at the age of 14. Robin's decorated cookies are legendary. She has won the sweepstakes in cookies and canned goods too many times to count. Her pickles have been distributed nationally. Robin says that many of her best recipes come from her Grandmother Mildred and Great-Grandmother Eva.

THE FIFTH GENERATION

Robin's daughter, Molly Thomas, started collecting blue ribbons when she was four with her "most creative ladybug sugar cookie." She continues the family cookie tradition and is also known for her quick breads. In 2019, Olive Jean, Robin, and Molly entered different contests and added to their stash of State Fair silks. Molly won Best of Fair banana bread with her take on her grandmother's recipe. Molly has had great success reinventing family heirloom recipes. Like many State Fair families, 2020 was the first time the Tarbell-Thomas clan had missed the Fair, due to the coronavirus pandemic. Neighbors also missed stopping by during the week to sample cookies, a well-known tradition at their home.

Olive Jean Tarbell passed away at the age of 90 in 2021 a few months after she shared her favorite State Fair memories. The program for her memorial service featured her Best Cookie of the Fair recipe for Molasses Cookies and her photo from the Iowa State Fair banners and advertising in which she was featured in 2016. She was a State Fair icon who loved baking and being a celebrity at the Fair.

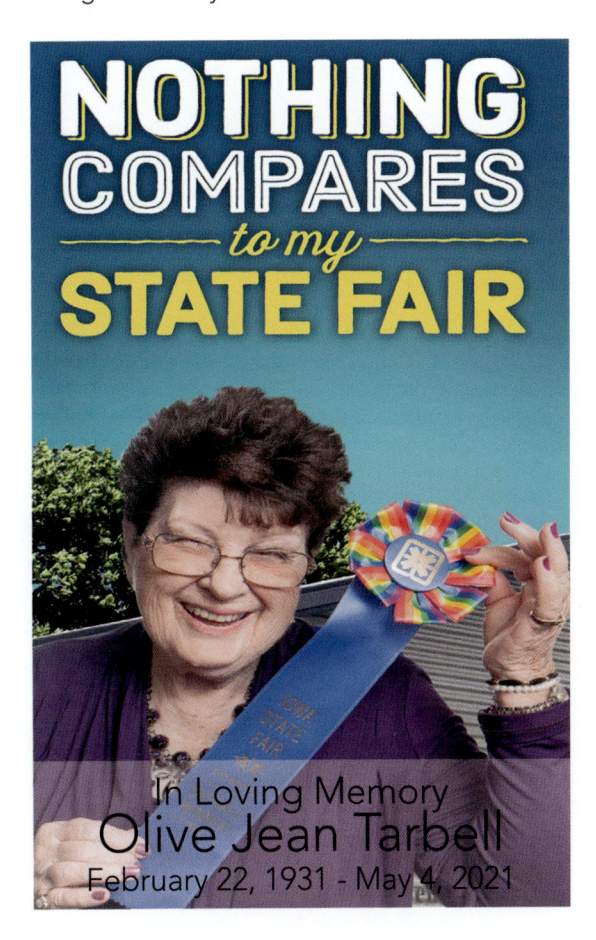

NOTHING COMPARES to my STATE FAIR

In Loving Memory
Olive Jean Tarbell
February 22, 1931 - May 4, 2021

> "My brothers and I traveled lots of places. We never had fun like we did when we went to the Iowa State Fair."
>
> – Olive Jean Tarbell

Favorite Family Recipes

It would be impossible to choose one favorite family recipe, but here are a few to honor the generations.

EVA'S GINGERBREAD BOYS

Olive Jean Tarbell remembers decorating gingerbread boys with raisins in her grandmother Eva's kitchen before chocolate chips were available. Fourth-generation baker, Robin Tarbell-Thomas, updated Eva's early 1900s recipe and won a blue ribbon in 1985 when she was 24 years old.

⅓ cup shortening
⅓ cup brown sugar, packed
1 egg
⅔ cup molasses
1 teaspoon vanilla
2¾ cups flour
1 teaspoon baking soda
1 teaspoon salt
2 teaspoons cinnamon
1 teaspoon ginger

Preheat oven to 350°F. Cream shortening and sugar. Add egg, molasses and vanilla. Mix well.

Sift together dry ingredients. Blend into creamed mixture. Roll dough ¼ inch thick on lightly floured board and cut with gingerbread cookie cutter. Bake for 8 to 10 minutes. When cool, decorate as desired. Makes about 1 dozen.

Eva Horstman Original Recipe, Early 1900s
Robin Tarbell-Thomas, Centerville
First Place, 1985 Iowa State Fair

SOFT PRETZELS

2 packages active dry yeast
2 cups warm water
½ cup sugar
2 teaspoons salt
¼ cup margarine
1 egg
6½ to 7½ cups flour, divided

EGG WASH
1 egg yolk
2 tablespoons water
Salt for sprinkling (and cinnamon-sugar if desired)

Dissolve yeast in warm water (110°F). Add sugar, salt, margarine, egg, and 3 cups flour. Beat until smooth. Add enough additional flour to make stiff dough. Cover bowl and refrigerate from 2 to 24 hours. Turn dough onto lightly floured board. Divide in half; cut each half into 16 equal pieces. Roll each into pencil shape about 20 inches long. Form into pretzels. Place on lightly greased baking sheets.

For egg wash: Blend together egg yolk and 2 tablespoons water. Brush pretzels. Sprinkle with salt. Let rise in warm place, free from drafts, until doubled (about 25 minutes). While dough is rising, preheat oven to 350° F. Bake for approximately 15 minutes until light golden brown. Makes 32 pretzels.

Robin Tarbell-Thomas, Centerville
First Place, 1985

MILDRED'S BEST OF FAIR PEANUT BUTTER COOKIES

1 cup butter (or ½ cup Crisco and ½ cup butter)
1 cup granulated sugar
1 cup brown sugar
1 cup peanut butter
2 eggs
1 teaspoon vanilla extract
2½ cups all-purpose flour
1 teaspoon baking soda
½ teaspoon baking powder
¼ teaspoon salt

Preheat oven to 350°F. In a large bowl cream together butter, granulated sugar, brown sugar, and peanut butter. Add eggs and vanilla extract; mix well. Add dry ingredients; mix well. Shape to 1-inch balls and place on cookie sheet; flatten cookie with a fork, making a crisscross pattern. Bake 10 to 12 minutes. Makes approximately 3 dozen.

Mildred Phillips, Centerville
Best of Fair Peanut Butter Cookies, late 1960s
Third Place, Archway Cookies National Competition

OPTIONAL TOPPING
Solid chocolate wafers, melted
Chopped peanuts

Robin added a decorative and delicious touch to these cookies. Cool cookies completely. Dip one half of a peanut butter cookie in melted chocolate and sprinkle chopped peanuts on top. Let set until dry.

From left: Olive Jean Tarbell, Molly Thomas (front), and Robin Tarbell-Thomas. ©The Des Moines Register – USA TODAY NETWORK, 1999

Olive Jean, Robin, and Molly at the 2019 State Fair

1980s–1990s 177

OLIVE JEAN'S BEST OF FAIR MOLASSES COOKIES

½ cup Crisco
½ cup butter
1½ cups granulated sugar
½ cup molasses
2 eggs
4 cups all-purpose flour
½ teaspoon salt
2¼ teaspoons baking soda
2¼ teaspoons ground ginger
1½ teaspoons ground cloves
1½ teaspoons ground cinnamon
½ cup granulated sugar to roll cookie dough balls into before baking

Preheat oven to 350°F. In large mixing bowl cream together Crisco, butter, and white sugar. Beat in molasses and eggs; set mixture aside. In another bowl combine flour, salt, baking soda, ginger, cloves, and cinnamon. Blend thoroughly with wire whisk. Gradually mix flour mixture into creamed ingredients until dough is blended and smooth. Roll dough into balls and roll in white sugar. Place on cookie sheet. Bake for 10 to 12 minutes. Cool. Makes approximately 4 dozen cookies.

Olive Jean Tarbell, Centerville
Best of Fair Cookie, 2008

HOLIDAY FRUIT BREAD

Molly Thomas is the fifth generation of competitive bakers. Many of her best recipes are those from her grandmother, Olive Jean, which she reinvents with modern twists and unique ingredients. Molly's Holiday Fruit Bread is a great example, like two recipes in one. The base recipe earned her first place overall for Ultimate Banana Bread in 2019. Here she adds a terrific twist with a ribbon of orange marmalade and lots of dried fruit for a rich, versatile loaf—perfect for the holidays or any time of year.

3 medium ripe bananas, mashed
1 cup granulated sugar
1 egg
1½ cups all-purpose flour
¼ cup melted lard (melted butter or vegetable oil may be substituted)
1 teaspoon vanilla
¼ cup orange marmalade
1 teaspoon salt
1 teaspoon baking soda
⅓ cup coarsely chopped candied pineapple
⅓ cup coarsely chopped candied red cherries
⅓ cup coarsely chopped candied green cherries
½ cup coarsely chopped toasted pecans

Preheat oven to 350°F. Combine bananas, sugar, egg, flour, lard, vanilla, marmalade, salt, and baking soda; mix well. Gently fold in candied fruits and pecans. Pour into greased 8½x4½-inch bread pan. Bake for approximately 1 hour. Makes 1 loaf.

Molly Thomas, Centerville
First Place, 2015 Make It with Lard—Fruit Bread
First Place Overall, 2015 Make It with Lard—Quick Breads

Stepping Behind the Blue Curtain
WORDS OF WISDOM FROM IOWA STATE FAIR FOOD JUDGES

Judging in front of live audiences is one thing that sets the Iowa State Fair Food Competitions apart. Walk into the Elwell Family Food Center during any event and listen to what the judges say about the exhibits after slicing, tasting, smelling, prodding, and breaking them apart. They offer expert tips on everything from the right amount of spice for your next batch of chili to why you should roll your bottom pie crust a bit thinner than you might think. Here are a few stories and tips from veterans. We begin with Carol McGarvey, who has worn the judge's badge for 36 years and counting.

IT'S ABOUT THE RIBBONS

Some money in premiums is nice. Some products are a good perk, too. But let's get real. Iowans who enter food contests at the Iowa State Fair are in it for the ribbons—blue if possible.

The judges know that and take their task seriously. It's a big job that goes on for days. Sometimes there are more than 10,000 entries, all judged individually. Some new competitors bring an entry or two; some veterans return year after year with 50, 60, or more.

Come with me to the other side of the judges' table and step behind the blue curtain where final decisions are made.

In 1983, I was asked to be a judge as part of my job at *The Des Moines Register*. Until the pandemic broke my stride in 2020, I had been a judge for 36 years straight. The first year I judged cakes, 98 of them to be exact. My judging partner was a pregnant food editor from Meredith Corporation. Three times she had to go behind the curtain and get sick from having a sugar-high experience. Finally, I whispered to her, "You must leave. You're not being fair to your baby, to yourself, and certainly not to the competitors."

I slowly, slowly finished the task. My younger son, 7 or 8 at the time, asked, "Aren't we ever going to have cake again?" It took a long time.

Since then, I have judged meat casseroles, junior cookies, chocolate concoctions, cooking for college kids, and for the last decade or so, Souper Soups, sponsored by *Welcome Home Des Moines*, for which I'm a freelance writer.

Judges must be trusting. Did any perishable entries come in coolers in air-conditioned cars from Indianola nearby, or did they come in hot trunks from one of the four corners of the state?

Judges can't show emotion. Competitors sit a few feet away. They watch every smile, every nuance. This is serious business. At the end, judges often go behind the curtain to compare notes before naming winners. It's a daunting task.

In earlier times, judging took place under the hot, dusty Grandstand. It is documented that raccoons found their way in every night to have an early Thanksgiving buffet. Later, the competitions took place in the Maytag Family Center and now in the Elwell Family Food Center with refrigerated cases.

Some years back, I was walking to my car after judging, when I stopped in my tracks. With the top prize that year of $3,000 for the Tone's cinnamon roll contest, three women were carrying in their entries, four rolls on white paper plates. They carefully smooshed their powdered sugar icing with their fingers to get the perfect look, then licked it off and did it again. I guess they forgot their plastic knives.

1980s–1990s

It wouldn't work to go inside and tattle. There would be hundreds of white paper plates with rolls. I had to ponder if I would want to know that before I judged. I walked on.

FOR RUTH BECK, THE FAIR IS HER 'HAPPY PLACE'

My judging experiences pale in comparison to the dedication of judges and workers who work before, during, and after the Fair to make the Food Department run smoothly. Take Ruth Beck of Buckingham, for example. For 17 years she came to judge at the Fair and stayed with her older daughter, Mary Ann Beck Wagner of West Des Moines, and her family.

"She came for a week and judged breads, cookies, cinnamon rolls, pies, you name it," Mary Ann says. "I packed a lunch for her so that she would eat something besides the items to judge. That was a really hard job, but she loved it."

Ruth's background suited her perfectly for judging. She was the mother of seven, a 4-H leader, a busy church organist, and a baker of all things yummy for a farmers' market stand in Waterloo each week. She also did custom baking for people in her area.

Mary Ann says her father, the late Don Beck, a farmer, raised vegetables, and Ruth made tons of baked goods to sell at the farmers' market. "They sold out every week." Shoppers always looked for Ruth's items, tied with a red yarn bow.

One State Fair was particularly memorable for Ruth when her granddaughter, Lydia Beck, was named State Fair Queen in 2006. Lydia is now an obstetrician/gynecologist in Iowa City.

Sadly, because of short-term memory issues, Ruth had to stop judging. "But it's still with her," Mary Ann says. "When I called her once and asked what she had been doing, she said she had judged that day at the State Fair."

When Mary Ann mentioned that to her mother's doctor, he said, "It's OK. The State Fair is obviously her happy place."

Ruth Beck passed away February 12, 2021. Thank-you note cards for memorials carried her all-purpose dough recipe.

RUTH BECK'S ALL-PURPOSE YEAST DOUGH

1 package dry yeast, dissolved in ¼ cup warm water
1 cup milk, heated
½ cup shortening
½ cup sugar
1 tablespoon salt
1 cup lukewarm water
2 cups flour
1 egg
4 cups flour

Combine yeast in water, milk, shortening, sugar, salt, and lukewarm water. Cool mixture to lukewarm. Beat in flour and egg. Add yeast mixture to about 4 cups flour. Knead lightly and let rise until doubled. Punch down and use to make loaves, rolls, doughnuts, pull-aparts, pigs in blankets, cinnamon rolls, or buns. Most bake at 350°F until crust is golden brown. Loaves should sound hollow when lightly tapped.

Ruth Beck, Judge's Signature Yeast Dough

CAROL McGARVEY'S PUMPKIN BREAD

This recipe, from a former neighbor at a block party, has been invaluable because of how many loaves it creates. I make it to give to neighbors at holidays. I freeze some to have on hand for hostess gift, or to give when someone has had surgery or needs a pick-me-up present. My younger son used it repeatedly in a high school speech class to make points on many topics. His teacher loved it. —Carol McGarvey

PUMPKIN BREAD
3⅓ cups flour
3 cups sugar
4 eggs
1 cup oil
⅔ cup water
1½ teaspoons salt
2 teaspoons baking soda
1 teaspoon cinnamon
1 teaspoon nutmeg
2 cups (16-ounce can) pumpkin
½ cup chopped nuts (optional)

Preheat oven to 350°F. Blend all ingredients in mixer bowl. Pour into 3 9x5-inch greased loaf pans. Bake 55 minutes.

Note: Makes 3 9x5-inch loaf pans, 6 smaller loaf pans, or any combination thereof, such as 2 larger pans and 2 small ones.

Tips and Tricks from the Judges

Over the decades many dedicated food judges have offered their best tips, advice, and good humor to State Fair food contestants and fans. Here is a tiny sampling of their wisdom.

FOOD COMPETITION

"Competition at the State Fair gets under your skin. You start with a couple of things, and you get a prize and that does it. You start bringing more. The judges make comments and tell you what's wrong and you go home and do better."

—Jeanette Van Peursem, Food Superintendent, 1961–1981

PIES

"An honest-to-goodness home-baked pie has got to have some runniness. Not soupy, just runny enough so one isn't reminded of truck-stop pie at its worst. Some of the ladies out there simply overdid the cornstarch."

"Make that top crust attractive and the bottom crust so it's easily cut with a fork. Try this method of my grandmother's for a never-fail, flakey crust: After preheating the oven and starting the pie at 400 degrees, turn the oven down to 350 degrees after 15 minutes. Makes all the difference in the world."

—Carl Voss, 1970s

BREADS & CAKES

"You can tell a lot about how the bread slices. I always bring my own knife. If a loaf is too heavy, it's probably not done. If it's too light, it rose too fast. Your taste buds get really sensitive. You can taste an off flavor immediately."

"The old-fashioned cakes impress me. They have become a thing of skill. People who show at the Fair really have a standard of excellence. They really care. It's like showing paintings."

For Ellen Thomas, judging at the Fair was her vacation. She judged just about every division and specialized in breads. She would hold a slice to the light and squeeze it for springiness. Then she would taste a dime-size piece. Some claimed that Ellen could always find an air hole if there was one. ©The Des Moines Register – USA TODAY NETWORK, 1976

"I get a kick out of doing it. It's so seldom anymore you find people who really enjoy excellence."

—Ellen Thomas, 1970s and 1980s

BAKING BLUE RIBBONS

COOKIES

Veteran cookie judges Pat Berry, Claudette Taylor, and others offer advice from the 1980s and today.

- Cookies that use oil or butter tend to spread out more while baking.

- Cookies made with solid shortening are puffier than those made with butter. Try using half butter and half shortening for beautifully shaped cookies.

- Make sure the spices you use, like cinnamon, are fresh.

- Be careful how long you leave cookies on the baking sheet once they've been removed from the oven. This can cause overbrowning on the bottom.

- The difference between one chocolate chip cookie and another often comes down to which brand of chocolate chips you use.

- When baking with honey, lower the oven temperature to avoid browning the outside too quickly and undercooking the inside.

Advice for First-Time Judges

TAKE SMALL BITES

"One of the first things judges learn is to take very small portions, even if the apple pie tastes so heavenly, they want to eat the whole slice. I was walking in my first day and a cake judge came dashing out of the room. The Food Superintendent said, 'I told her not to eat such big bites.' That was good enough for me."

—Evelyn Birkby, 1970s cookbook author and food columnist for the Shenandoah Evening Sentinel *for 40 years.*

NO TWISTED FACES

"If you bite into something that makes you want to gag, you're not going to make an awful face. You handle it as discreetly as if you were at a dinner party, but those cases are rare. Practically everything entered is fine, but when you get to the State Fair, you're looking for perfection."

—Dorcas Speer, 1989, former radio and TV personality

©The Des Moines Register – USA TODAY NETWORK
(pages 184-185)

184 BAKING BLUE RIBBONS

PLAY THE PART

"Even though you may feel that you are not as qualified as you would like to be, please give the appearance and confidence that you are."

—*Johanna Beers,* Iowa City Press-Citizen *Food Columnist, 1937–2004. She began her career as a college student and wrote for the* Press-Citizen *until her death in 2004.*

READ THE BODY LANGUAGE

"I couldn't match the faces with the names, but you'd see someone sitting on the edge of her chair and you knew you were looking at one of her cookies."

—*Diana McMillen, food editor for* Midwest Living Magazine, *first-time food judge, 1989.*

IT'S ALL GOOD

"It's a matter of pride. If something doesn't turn out well, they won't bring it to the Fair. I've never encountered something that didn't taste good."

—*Mary Mulry, 1989*

1980s–1990s   185

2000s

THE SWEETEST GIFT AND A LOOK TO THE FUTURE

RECIPES

BREADS
Oatmeal Bread, *Arlette Hollister* **196**

APPETIZERS
Egg Roll in a Bowl Hot Dip, *Sharon Gates* **197**
Basil Tomato Tart, *Suellen Calhoun* **198**
Nacho Dip, *Diane Rauh* **199**
Santa Fe Rice Cups, *Anita Van Gundy* **199**

SALADS
Summer in Iowa Salad, *Ann Carter* **200**
Peas De Resistance Salad, *Jeanne Stall* **200**
Easy Summer Slaw, *Louise B. Cothron* **201**

SOUPS & SIDE DISHES
Roasted Peach and Brown Sugar Soup, *Lana Ross Shope* **202**
All-American Bacon Cheeseburger Soup, *Jacqueline Riekena* **203**
Great-Grandma's Refrigerator Beets, *Bridget Lottman* **204**

MAIN DISHES
Big Mama's Iowa Nachos, *Hadley and Hannah Harvey* **205**
Lasagna for 12, *James Covey* **207**
Tailgatin' Chili, *Kyle Barton* **208**
Iowa Farmhouse BBQ Baskets, *Kelly Barrett* **209**
Bolognese with Homemade Noodles, *Christina McCleary* **210**
Bacon Mac and Cheese, *Brooklynn Sedlock* **211**
Dreamfields Tomato Feta Pasta, *Kay Smith* **212**
Southwestern Sunrise Breakfast Casserole, *Mavis Ward* **213**
Waffle Sausage Strata, *Marion Karlin* **214**

CAKES
Lavender Lemon Cake, *Eileen Gannon* **216**
Red Velvet Cake, *Sally Kilkenny* **217**
Salted Caramel Mocha Cupcakes, *Ann Gillotti* **218**
Best of the Best Lemon Cheesecake, *Janine Knop* **220**
Vanilla Strawberry Cheesecake, *Brian Keul* **221**

RECIPES

PIES
Pillsbury Rustic S'more Pie, *Pam Reynolds* **223**
Strawberry Rhubarb Pie, *Karen McKilligan* **224**

COOKIES
Caramel Apple Cookies, *Brooke Mickelson* **226**
Gluten-Free Monster Cookies, *Emma Scheidel* **227**
Gingerbread House Dough, *Laura Higgins* **228**
Party Animal Cookies, *Micah and Natalie Hunter* **229**
Honey Chocolate and Peanut Butter Candy Bars, *Graham Hutchison* **230**

CANDY, SNACKS & DESSERTS
Reese's Peanut Butter Fudge, *Brian Keul* **231**
Cherry Crispy Rice Treats, *Josiah Derr* **232**
Mocha Mousse, *Mick Wise* **235**

PRESERVES
Violet Jelly, *Rod Zeitler* **236**

2000s: GATHERING IN THE NEW MILLENNIUM

The Iowa State Fair invited everyone to Zero In on Fun in 2000. The Food Department welcomed the new millennium with another record 10,400 entries and 30 new contests, including Live a Little Lighter in 2000 and Men in the New Millennium, Cooking With Beer. The largest State Fair Food Department offered a $59,000 purse and kept pace with judging all those entries in front of live audiences. First-, second-, and third-place winners were displayed. Arlette and her team continued donating many food entries to local shelters.

Roberta Green Ahmanson, benefactor of the Hotel Pattee in her hometown of Perry, sponsored the 10th edition of the ever-popular *Iowa State Fair Cook Book*. Kathie Swift, who served as marketing director and co-editor of the cookbooks for many years, says memories of cold fried chicken, homegrown tomatoes, and homemade chocolate cake inspired Roberta to underwrite the book.

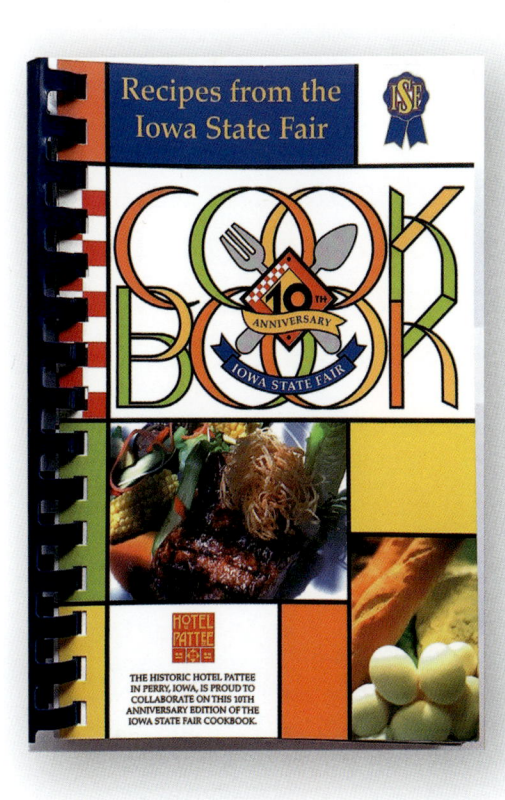

2002: ONE IN A MILLION

For the first time, more than 1 million Fairgoers walked through the gates in August 2002 and started a State Fair attendance trend. The 400-acre grounds offered many new attractions along with our favorite foods-on-a-stick and entertainment on a grand scale.

In the Maytag Family Center, there were 1,000 more food entries than the previous year, including 206 cakes, up from 108 in 2001. *America's Hometown Cookbook* rolled off the presses with winning recipes from 2000 and 2001. Foodies snapped them up and brought that homemade feeling back to their kitchens with creations like Easy Summer Slaw and Iowa Farmhouse BBQ Baskets.

The State Fair's sesquicentennial celebration drew another record million-plus crowd in 2004. The Fair Square, a marshmallow and crisped-rice cereal treat was sold by the Blue Ribbon Foundation and became a new favorite food-on-a-stick. Crispy rice treats have spawned many fun competitions, including one where kids build their favorite State Fair attraction and write a short story about it along with a unique crispy rice recipe.

> *"Minnesota has its lakes, and Colorado has its mountains. But Iowa— it has its State Fair."*
>
> – Gary Slater, Iowa State Fair CEO

2009: THE SWEETEST PRIZE

Iowa State Fair Food contests continued to grow until the thousands of entries were running out of room at the Maytag Family Center. The sweetest prize of all came from Denny and Candy Elwell of Ankeny, who donated $1 million to transform the former Iowa Tourism Building into a new home for the contests. The announcement came in 2007. Expansion and remodeling were complete in 2009, when the family dedicated the Elwell Family Food Center in honor of Denny's parents, Margaret and James, known as "Bud." The building is open, airy, and modern, but the family's State Fair memories go back five generations—and Denny is one of the best storytellers around (Elwell Family State Fair Story, page 194).

Relishing the new space, food superintendent Arlette Hollister made one request. Instead of an office, she wanted a desk in the middle of the action, where she could answer questions and help her team from the sign-in table to awards. Arlette got her wish. Today her wooden desk remains the superintendent's "office" out in the open, where Fairgoers can be part of the contests and meet fellow food enthusiasts and experts from across the state.

Food Department Superintendent Arlette Hollister at her "office."

2016: END OF THE ARLETTE ERA

In 2015, Arlette was named the Grand Marshal of the Iowa State Fair parade. During her years overseeing every aspect of the Food Department, she and her team made Iowa the pinnacle of State Fair culinary contests.

BAKING BLUE RIBBONS

With Arlette's creativity, personal touch, and year-round dedication, the department became a place to gather, learn, and celebrate Iowa through the foods and recipes that bring us together. The Iowa State Fair Food Department grew to well over 10,000 entries annually across more than 200 food divisions and 900-plus contests. A few of the unique competitions in 2015 included the Szathmary Collection of Historic Recipes Contest with an original sponge pudding recipe from 1874, along with Scenic Valley Pumpkin Patch Cookies, *The Des Moines Register's* Hog (and Corn) Heaven, The Great American SPAM Championship, and an international Eggs Around the World competition. The 2016 Fair was Arlette's final year running the department at a remarkable age 86. Thankfully, she had an excellent apprentice.

NEW SUPERINTENDENT WITH A SOUTHERN TOUCH

Karen McKilligan of Ames took over the Food Department in 2017. She had volunteered since 2010 and became Arlette's official understudy in 2016. Arlette had perfected the daily operations, and Karen took copious notes to preserve every detail for future generations.

Karen is a Florida native. Her Southern touch, a love of food and baking, and her ag business background were a perfect match for the job. "The buzz during the Fair when all the exhibitors show up with their entries that they're so proud of. All the stories behind the people. That's definitely the most rewarding part," Karen told the *Des Moines Register* in 2019.

Karen McKilligan of Ames

The food superintendent's job is obvious during Fair time, but lining up new sponsors, judges, and team members happens year-round. Everything must be ready to go by March. One of the things Karen loves about the department is that individuals and families, as well as business of all sizes, sponsor contests. Karen stepped down when the Fair was canceled in 2020, but she continues to volunteer and find ways to get more Iowans involved.

When it comes to her own cooking, Karen likes to make homemade macaroni and cheese, pork loin, biscuits and gravy, breakfast burritos, and lots of pies, including her signature strawberry rhubarb.

"We want to encourage people to come join us because it's fun. If you have a recipe that your family loves, or if you want to try something new and be adventurous, come enter the Fair because there are opportunities to do just about any kind of cooking or baking that you'd like to do."

– Karen McKilligan, Iowa State Fair Food Superintendent, 2017–2020

Iowans did butter sculpting and other events at home when the Fair was canceled in 2020.

NO FAIR

In 2020, the Iowa State Fair was canceled due to the coronavirus pandemic. It was the sixth time in history and the first time since World War II. There were online events to lift Fairgoers' spirits, like at-home butter sculpting, recipe swapping, and a scaled-down youth livestock competition, but nothing could take the place of Iowa's beloved Fair.

When Karen McKilligan stepped down as food superintendent, Pat Berry of Urbandale stepped up and took charge in 2021. The Fair needed someone with unmatched knowledge of the contests. Pat brought experience from every side of the judge's table. Like Mrs. James Dwyer in 1946, Pat oversaw a department with far fewer entries and premiums in 2021, but dedication and enthusiasm from Iowans who were thrilled to be back.

FOOD FAMILY STILL GOING STRONG

For Pat, the Iowa State Fair is more than her favorite place to camp for two weeks every August. It is where friendships have developed over many years. Before she became superintendent, she had been a judge since 1994 and an exhibitor for nearly two decades before that.

"They're like family in the Food Department," she says in an echo of Arlette. "People have moved away and come back every year to judge things. You get together and find out how everyone did during the year and what their kids are doing. You're glad they're back and miss them when they're gone. These are the stories that bring you back every year. I wouldn't miss this. It's a part of me."

After more than 40 years, Pat has stories to tell—like the year she entered 384 food exhibits or when *The Des Moines Register* photographed her making a white chocolate cake and she had to redo it, twice. Then there was the time her dog stepped in a cake when they were loading the van.

IT'S NOT LIFE AND DEATH

"It's a compulsive hobby," she says with a laugh. "You don't do it for the money; you do it because you love it. I don't think I've ever seen anybody have a bitter taste in their mouth that they didn't win a competition and someone else did. It's all done in friendly camaraderie, and it should be. This is not life and death in here. Some years you have a good year, and some you don't."

Pat experiments with the latest techniques and ingredients. Her advice for judges and exhibitors is to stretch your palate. Find new

Pat Berry of Urbandale was named Food Superintendent in 2020.

things and try them at home. When someone wins a ribbon in the Food Department, the prize is more than a piece of silk. Everyone watching learns what took the winner to the top. Food judges continue to give feedback on how to improve a recipe or create a better presentation. During the Fair, the Elwell Family Food Center is like a culinary school where anyone can take seminars, listen to experts, and learn from some of the best home cooks and professionals in the country. As we rebuild for the future, we want to grow the educational aspects that have set us apart for generations.

IT TAKES A VILLAGE

Running hundreds of competitions at the Elwell Family Food Center during the entire Fair doesn't just happen. It takes organization, dedication, miles of walking each day, and the love of making it all come together.

Marilyn and John Martinez of Johnston are two of many behind-the-scenes workers who spend at least 12 days in August carrying out the myriad duties that keep contests on time and running smoothly. About 60 workers make it happen. Some of those live close enough to drive to the Fair each day. Others camp at the fairgrounds or stay with relatives in central Iowa.

"Big contests such as canning and preserves begin several days before the Fair opens," Marilyn explains, "and contests go on throughout the entire run of the Fair." Workers register contestants at the welcome table, serve as writers for the judges' comments, warm items that need to be heated before judging, refresh the judges' stations after each contest, make sure every entry is on the correct table, and record the winners.

Marilyn says she wore a pedometer one day, and it recorded three miles. In 1970 she started participating in the Milk Made Magic contests as a home economist for the Iowa Dairy Council. During the 1980s, she did classes and demonstrations on microwave cooking at Friedman's in Des Moines and on Iowa PBS. "It was my 15 minutes of fame," she says.

After John retired as a bricklayer, he joined her at the Fair. You'll find him checking in judges and answering the two most popular questions in the Elwell Building—"Where is the Ugly Cakes display?" and "Where are the restrooms?"

Marilyn and John Martinez of Johnston are a few of the workers who have helped run the Food Department for years.

Many of the workers get together a couple times each year for lunch or dinner. "It was former superintendent Arlette Hollister's wish that this department would have a family feel," Marilyn says.

"It's fun to see how foods have changed over time. These days, we're more into health foods, and the contests reflect that."

It also has been fun when judges come from, say, New York. "They simply cannot believe the Iowa State Fair. It's amazing."

2000s
STORIES AND RECIPES

For the 2000s, we begin with the inspiration behind the Elwell Family Food Center and end with an invitation to join us at the Fair.

TRIBUTE TO MARGARET AND JAMES "BUD" ELWELL

When Denny Elwell was a boy, the Iowa State Fairgrounds was just a few steps away. At Fair time, he crossed the street from his grandmother's house on East 30th and entered his favorite place in the world. "I walked from her driveway right through the gates," he says. "There was no charge for a five-year-old kid and nothing better than spending an afternoon at the Fair. You would never do this today, but back then I walked the Fairgrounds by myself."

Denny's first stop was the corn dog stand, then the racetrack, where he stood as close to the fence as possible and got sprayed with dirt when the cars whipped around the curve. Brushing off the dust, he wandered through the Fair, always ending at the horse barn to watch the Clydesdales and Percherons.

Those boyhood treks were magical, and Denny wasn't the only one who loved the Fair. His dad, James, who was known as "Bud," made the trip six or seven times every year. When they went as a family, they brought a picnic lunch and bought ice cream for a special treat.

Margaret and Bud Elwell raised their six children on an acreage on Des Moines' east side. Bud drove trucks for Rock Island Motors while Margaret stayed home with the kids. She tended a large garden, raised chickens, and made butter from fresh cow's milk. She canned 500 quarts of vegetables every summer.

When the kids got older, the Elwells moved to Johnston. Margaret and Bud started a grocery business that lasted more than 20 years. During the 1950s and '60s, Denny and his siblings worked there before or after school. By the '70s, his parents sold their stores and began farming full time in Alleman, Iowa.

"My parents were always working for their kids," Denny says, "but they always found time for the Fair."

194 BAKING BLUE RIBBONS

Margaret and Bud Elwell left their legacy with 30 grandchildren and 70 great-grandchildren. The Iowa State Fair remains a summer highlight for five generations and counting. Denny's grandparents' house is gone, but the driveway is still there inside the Fairgrounds. For Denny, walking through the barns and exhibits is like going back in time. He and his wife, Candy, stay at the Fairgrounds each August. Since 1998, they have donated to the Iowa State Fair Blue Ribbon Foundation. In 2007, they announced plans for the Elwell Family Food Center in honor of Denny's mother and father.

"It was the perfect fit for my parents," Denny says. "When we lived on the acreage and out on the farm, and for all the years Mom and Dad worked in the grocery business, this was a great way to honor them."

The Elwells' gift transformed the Food Department, which had grown to nearly 13,000 entries. The Elwells continue to expand and upgrade the space where food enthusiasts gather to cheer their favorite home chefs and be part of the best State Fair Food Competitions in the nation.

Denny and Candy Elwell and family dedicated the Elwell Family Food Center at the Iowa State Fair in 2009. In 2021, the Elwell family expanded its Iowa State Fair legacy with a $2 million gift for the Elwell Family Park, where fairgoers enjoy tractor pulls, monster truck meets, rodeos, barbeque competitions, and other family-friendly events. Denny Elwell is chairman of the eponymous metro Des Moines commercial real estate and development company.

Photos courtesy of the Elwell Family.

2000s

Breads

ARLETTE'S OATMEAL BREAD

Arlette ran the Food Department for 31 years and still found time to bake. At home she was known for Oatmeal Bread, Maple Cinnamon Rolls, and Kringle. On New Year's Day, she always made Lasagna. Arlette passed away in March of 2019 at age 88. Her favorite snack was potato chips and Anderson Erickson Party Dip, which were on the menu at her funeral visitation. Her son, Mark Hollister of Des Moines, and her daughter, Deb Johnson of Ankeny, made sure to put a bag of potato chips in her casket.

To you, Arlette, we raise our wooden spoons and ladles. For your dedication and hard work, we salute you and thank you.

OATMEAL BREAD

2 cups rolled oats
½ cup brown sugar
1 tablespoon salt
¼ cup margarine
2 cups water
2 packages yeast
2 tablespoons sugar
5 to 6 cups flour, divided
½ cup warm water
1 egg
Butter for topping

Place oats, brown sugar, salt, and margarine in a large pan. In another pan bring 2 cups water to boil. Pour over the oat mixture. Stir and let cool until lukewarm. Put yeast, sugar, and 1 cup flour into another bowl. Add ½ cup warm water. Let stand for about 5 minutes. Add to oat mixture. Add egg and beat well. Add 4 to 5 cups flour until you can't stir anymore and it isn't real sticky. Place on a board and knead about 10 minutes. When no longer sticky, put it in a greased bowl. Place greased plastic wrap on top and let rise until double, about 1 hour. Divide into two loaves and put in greased loaf pans. Let rise until double. Preheat oven to 375°F. Bake 35 minutes until loaves are golden brown and sound hollow when tapped. Cool on rack and butter the tops of loaves. Makes 2 loaves.

Arlette takes a quick break for one of her favorite treats at the 2008 Iowa State Fair.

Arlette Hollister, Superintendent Signature Recipe

Appetizers

THE QUEEN OF DIPS

There are many food contests at the State Fair, but only one that honors the Queen of Dips. The Tiffany Family sponsors their contest in memory of Maureen Tiffany of Des Moines, who touched many lives throughout her career with The United Way and other nonprofits. Maureen always had great dips and appetizers on hand. Her sons, Kevin and John Tiffany, and daughter, Mary Cownie, have fun honoring their mom and judging the competition, which has become a fan favorite. As John says, "There are no losers here. If you're bringing a dip, you're a winner!"

EGG ROLL IN A BOWL

Sharon Gates of Des Moines won the hot dip category in 2021 with her Egg Roll in a Bowl. The judges have tasted every dip under the sun, but nothing as unique as this. Sharon started competing in food contests in 2010. Some of her earliest memories are of the Fair in the 1960s and 1970s, when her dad was the superintendent of the exhibitors' campgrounds and her mom worked in the Varied Industries Building. When Sharon was a teenager, she sold tickets at the front gates and has been coming back ever since. She is an avid recipe collector and exhibitor.

1 pound ground meat (your choice beef, pork, chicken or shrimp)
1 sweet onion, diced
1 tablespoon sesame oil
1 tablespoon rice vinegar
2 teaspoons fresh minced garlic
1 teaspoon grated gingerroot
¼ cup soy sauce
1 tablespoon hoisin sauce (optional, but recommended)
1 (16-ounce) bag tri-color coleslaw mix
2 green onions, use both white & green parts, thinly sliced
Salt and pepper to taste

Egg Roll in a Bowl and other dips are ready for the contest.

2000s 197

Heat a large skillet over medium-high heat. Add the ground meat and cook, stirring until it's no longer pink. Drain the fat off and return the meat to the skillet. Add the diced onion, sesame oil and the rice vinegar to the skillet. Cook, stirring for a few more minutes until the onion is tender.

Add the garlic, ginger, soy sauce, hoisin sauce (if using), and coleslaw mix to the skillet. Cook, stirring, for about 5–7 more minutes, or until the cabbage is wilted. Remove the skillet from the heat. Stir in the green onions and season with salt and pepper. Garnish as desired. Sharon uses toasted sesame seeds, both black and white, and scallions. Serve dip hot with wonton chips.

Serves approximately 8.

Sharon Gates, Des Moines
First Place, 2021 Bring Your Best Dip—Hot Dips

Mary Cownie (center) and others judge the Bring Your Best Dip Contest.

BASIL TOMATO TART

Suellen Calhoun has many versatile recipes like this. She has won the Hotel Pattee quick breads and the Tone's sticky caramel cinnamon roll contest to name a few. This tart works well with many combinations, from fresh zucchini and spinach to artichoke hearts and mushrooms. Perfect as a hearty appetizer or light main dish.

1 8-ounce tube refrigerated crescent rolls
1½ cups shredded mozzarella cheese, divided
5 Roma tomatoes or 4 regular tomatoes
1 cup fresh, loosely packed basil leaves, coarsely chopped
4 cloves garlic, minced
½ cup mayonnaise
¼ cup shredded Parmesan cheese
⅛ teaspoon salt
⅛ teaspoon pepper

Preheat oven to 375°F. Roll out crescents on lightly floured surface, patting together to make sure there are no holes. Place dough in a 9-inch tart pan, quiche dish, or pie plate; bake 8 to 10 minutes. Remove from oven; sprinkle bottom of crust with ½ cup mozzarella cheese. Cool on wire rack. Cut tomatoes into wedges; drain on paper towel. Arrange on top of melted cheese. Sprinkle basil and garlic over tomatoes. Combine remaining mozzarella, mayonnaise, Parmesan cheese, salt, and pepper. Spoon over top evenly to cover. Bake 20 to 25 minutes or until golden and bubbly. Cut into wedges. Serve warm. Makes 8 servings.

Suellen Calhoun, Des Moines
First Place, 2003 Creative Crescents, Appetizers

NACHO DIP

Diane Rauh's slow-cooker nacho dip is loaded with flavor, smothered in cheese, and perfect for football games and fiestas.

1 pound bulk sausage
5 small onions, finely chopped
⅓ of a 1.25-ounce envelope taco seasoning
2 tomatoes, chopped
4-ounce can green chile peppers, chopped and drained
2-pound box processed American cheese, cubed

Brown sausage and onions in a skillet; drain. Place all ingredients in a slow cooker; heat on high until cheese melts, stirring occasionally, about 2 hours. Serve with tortilla chips. Makes 3 cups dip.

Diane Rauh, Des Moines
First Place, 2013 Kraft Kreations with Velveeta, Side Dish

SANTA FE RICE CUPS

Anita Van Gundy has won prizes at the Fair and advanced in several national food contests, including three invitations to the national Pillsbury Bake-Off Championships. Here she uses a Pillsbury pie crust as the base for an easy appetizer.

1 8.8-ounce bag Spanish-style ready rice
½ cup black beans
1½ cups shredded Mexican cheese, divided
4 ounces cream cheese
2 refrigerated pie crusts
½ cup breadcrumbs

Preheat oven to 400°F. Mix together rice, beans, 1 cup shredded cheese, and cream cheese; set aside. Cut eight 2½-inch circles from each pie crust. Place crusts in mini muffin pans. Bake 15 minutes. Fill crusts with rice mixture. Mix remaining cheese and breadcrumbs. Sprinkle over top of rice mixture. Bake about 20 minutes more. Makes 16 appetizers.

Anita Van Gundy, Des Moines
First Place, 2011 A Rice Creation, Appetizer

Salads

SUMMER IN IOWA SALAD

Nothing says summer as nicely as this Summer in Iowa Salad with fresh corn. Grilled chicken also makes this a great main dish.

SALAD
4 cups corn, fresh or frozen
1 pint grape tomatoes, halved
8 ounces fresh mozzarella, cut into bite-size pieces
2 cups chopped grilled chicken breast
10 leaves fresh basil, snipped

DRESSING
¼ cup red wine vinegar
¾ cup olive oil
2 cloves garlic, minced
1 teaspoon oregano
1 teaspoon salt
1 teaspoon ground black pepper
3 tablespoons grated Parmesan cheese

Combine salad ingredients. Combine dressing ingredients in a jar; cover with lid. Shake to combine. Pour over salad and mix. Makes 4 servings.

Ann Carter, Carlisle
First Place, 2017 Locally Grown, Iowa Fresh Corn

PEAS DE RESISTANCE SALAD

Jeanne Stall won the salad portion of the Puckerbrush Potluck Contest, which was sponsored by the late Bess Osenbaugh, Solicitor General of Iowa. Bess started the potluck and the food contest to encourage collegiality among women attorneys. Puckerbrush is a scenic area in Lucas County, near her hometown.

2-pound package frozen peas
⅓ cup mayonnaise-style salad dressing
¼ cup prepared mustard
2 tablespoons honey
1 medium red bell pepper, diced
1 medium yellow bell pepper, diced
1 medium green bell pepper, diced
3 ribs celery, chopped
1 medium yellow onion, diced

In large stockpot bring 2 cups water to boil. Add frozen peas; cook over medium to high heat 3 minutes. (Do not overcook.) Remove from heat; drain. Pour cold water over peas to stop the cooking process. In a separate bowl blend together salad dressing, mustard, and honey. Combine peppers, celery, and onions. Drain peas well; stir in diced mixture. Fold in dressing to coat the vegetables Place entire mixture into large serving bowl. Cover and refrigerate until chilled, at least 1 hour or overnight. Makes 8 to 10 servings.

Jeanne Stall, Huxley
First Place, 2011 Puckerbrush Potluck, Salad/Entree

EASY SUMMER SLAW

This recipe highlights zucchini in a fresh version of coleslaw. It works well with grated or chopped spiralized zucchini, which adds liquid to the dressing.

4 cups grated zucchini
¼ cup sweet pepper, thinly sliced
¼ cup chopped onion
1 tablespoon wine vinegar
1 teaspoon honey
1 teaspoon dill weed
¼ teaspoon salt
2 sprinkles black pepper

Combine zucchini, peppers, and onion in a bowl. Mix well and set aside. In separate bowl combine remaining ingredients. Add to zucchini mixture. Cover and refrigerate until ready to serve. Serves approximately 4.

Louise B. Cothron, Kellerton
First Place, 2001 Iowa Fruit and Vegetable Growers' Dishes Made with Iowa Fruits and Vegetables (No Meat)

Soups & Side Dishes

ROASTED PEACH AND BROWN SUGAR SOUP

Lana Ross Shope won with this delightful chilled soup that the judges still remember. Her specialty, however, is pies, where she turned her baking skills from a hobby into a business. Lana also judges many contests at the Fair and has been part of the Food Department for years.

12 cups water
12 ripe assorted peaches
2 tablespoons melted butter or margarine
1¼ cups packed brown sugar
6 cups peach/apricot nectar
1 cup white wine
1 teaspoon ground ginger
¼ teaspoon salt
1 teaspoon raspberry blush vinegar
2 cups light cream

Preheat oven to 425°F. Bring water to boil; drop peaches into boiling water, two at a time. Blanch 1 minute; remove with slotted spoon. Place under cold running water and remove skins. Cut each peach in half; remove pit. Slice peaches and place in roasting pan. Add butter or margarine and brown sugar; stir well to coat peaches. Bake 25 minutes. In pot over medium-high heat combine roasted peaches, peach/apricot nectar, wine, ginger, salt, and vinegar. Bring to boil; let simmer 20 minutes. Remove from heat; purée soup in blender until smooth. Stir in cream.

Place in chilled bowls; refrigerate at least 6 hours before serving. Makes 4 to 6 servings.

Lana Ross Shope, Indianola
First Place, 2013 Welcome Home Des Moines *Souper Soups*

ALL-AMERICAN BACON CHEESEBURGER SOUP

Jacqueline Riekena of West Des Moines took blue ribbon honors at the 2021 State Fair in the Souper Soups contest sponsored by *Welcome Home Des Moines* magazine. She brings lots of experience to entering State Fair contests. Her husband is in the military, so they have moved around a lot. "Wherever we have lived, I try to enter the Fair contests." She has entered the Oklahoma, Texas, Virginia, and Montana Fairs, among others. Her takeaway: "Here in Iowa, ribbons really mean something. They really do."

1 pound ground beef
1 medium white onion, chopped
1 stalk celery, chopped
2 cloves garlic, minced
2 tablespoons all-purpose flour
1 14-ounce can lower-sodium beef broth
2 medium potatoes, scrubbed and coarsely chopped
1 14.5-ounce can diced fire-roasted tomatoes, drained
2 8-ounce packages processed American cheese, cut into small cubes
1 6-ounce can tomato paste
¼ cup spicy ketchup
2 tablespoons prepared mustard
1 cup whole milk
½ teaspoon Himalayan fine white pepper
½ pound bacon, fried, drained, and crumbled
Crispy bacon pieces and sliced chives for garnish
Pickle slices, chopped onion, chopped tomato for garnish (optional)

From left: food judge Carol McGarvey; Jacqueline Riekena, winner; and food judge Gretchen Kauffman. Welcome Home Des Moines magazine, Souper Soups contest, 2021.

Form 5 ground beef patties for grilling on a barbecue grill; grill burgers until pink inside. Remove from grill; cut meat into bite-size pieces. Cover and keep warm. In a Dutch oven cook and stir onion, celery, and garlic over medium heat until vegetables are tender. Return burger pieces to Dutch oven. Sprinkle flour on beef-vegetable mixture; cook and stir 2 minutes. Stir in broth and potatoes. Bring to a boil, stirring occasionally. Reduce heat; simmer, covered, 10 minutes or until potatoes are tender. Stir in tomatoes, cubed cheese, tomato paste, ketchup, and mustard. Cook and stir until cheese is melted and smooth and soup comes to a gentle boil. Stir in milk and white pepper; heat through. Garnish with bacon and chives. If desired, serve with pickle slices, chopped onion, and chopped tomatoes. Makes 8 to 10 servings.

Jacqueline Riekena, West Des Moines
First Place, 2021 Welcome Home Des Moines *Souper Soups*

THAT'S WHAT FRIENDS ARE FOR

Calling themselves "sisters from other mothers," Bridget Lottman and Pamela Reynolds, both of Norwalk, have celebrated their friendship for 25 years at the Iowa State Fair. They're not afraid to enter the same contests, and they celebrate whoever wins. Pamela calls it "friendly competing." They share parking and other expenses to the Fair. They more than make their parking and gas money back with their winnings. They only have about 20 minutes to drop off their foods, so one drives while the other unloads at the Elwell Family Food Center. Pam has entered about 30 to 40 items during a single Fair. Bridget has brought up to 96. They are a winning team with recipes like Bridget's Great-Grandma's Refrigerator Beets and Pamela's Rustic S'more Pie (in the Pies Section).

As Bridget says, "Our friendship is wonderful. Sure, you want to win yourself, but you want the other person to win, too."

GREAT-GRANDMA'S REFRIGERATOR BEETS

12 beets
2 cups cider vinegar
2 cups water
2 cups sugar
1 teaspoon cinnamon
½ teaspoon cloves
½ teaspoon allspice

Wash and clean beets; do not cut off ends. Cut off leaves, leaving about 1 inch of the stems. In a large pan, cover beets with water and bring to a boil. Cook until beets are tender, 45 to 60 minutes, depending on the size of beets. When beets are done, remove from water. Rinse out pan; add remaining ingredients. Bring to a simmer for 30 minutes. When beets are cool enough to handle, cut ends and slip off skins. Cut into bite-size pieces and place in clean jars. When vinegar and spices come to a simmer, pour over beets. Seal and refrigerate at least 3 days before serving. Will keep in refrigerator up to 2 months.

Bridget Lottman, Family Heirloom Recipe

Pam Reynolds (left) with Bridget Lottman

"Our friendship is wonderful. Sure, you want to win yourself, but you want the other person to win, too."

– Bridget Lottman, State Fair Food Exhibitor

Main Dishes

BIG MAMA'S IOWA NACHOS

In 2021, Hannah and Hadley Harvey of Des Moines won the first-ever Tag Team Food Challenge at the Fair. The contest, sponsored by Phil Dicks of Johnston, invited teams of two cooks to select a favorite recipe and improve it in some way. Each entry included a recipe and a brief history of the dish and how it was improved or changed. In the main dish category, Hannah (19) and Hadley (14) took their grandmother's nacho recipe and made it vegetarian with layers of incredible flavor on top of crispy multigrain chips. The sisters love it when their grandmother, Big Mama, comes to visit for dance recitals and to go to their favorite State Fair. They always make her famous Beef Nachos. Now, they have a great new version.

8 ounces Beyond Beef or other meat substitute
¼ cup salsa
Salt and pepper to taste
1 8-ounce can refried beans
1 tablespoon sour cream
1 tablespoon milk

1 package Quinoa and Black Bean Tortilla Chips
1½ cups shredded cheddar cheese, divided
1 cup Mexican shredded cheese, divided
1½ tablespoons chopped onion

DIPPING SIDES:
½ cup salsa
1 tablespoon pico de gallo
1 to 3 avocados

1 tablespoon chopped onion
½ packet guacamole seasoning
Sour cream

Preheat oven to 175°F. In a pan over medium heat brown the Beyond Beef. Add ¼ cup salsa, such as Lola's Fine Sweet & Spicy Mango Salsa. Season with salt and pepper and cook until the salsa is incorporated into the meat. Set aside. Heat the refried beans in a separate saucepan. Once the beans begin to bubble, add 1 tablespoon of sour cream and milk and stir until creamy and well blended. To assemble: in an ovenproof pan add a layer of chips, a layer of beans, and then a layer of half of the meat. Top with half of both cheeses. Repeat the layers and top with a cup of shredded cheese. Sprinkle 1½ tablespoons chopped onion on top. Place in oven for 15 minutes. Increase oven temperature to 220°F and bake for another 15 minutes.

While that cooks, make your dipping sides: A bowl of your favorite salsa, such as a mix of Lola's Fine Sweet & Spicy Mango Salsa and Pico. In a separate bowl add 1 to 3 avocados, diced; 1 tablespoon onion; and half a packet of guacamole seasoning. Mash and mix until all are evenly incorporated. In another bowl add your preferred amount of sour cream. Take the nachos out of the oven and allow to cool for a few minutes. Serve warm with your sides and enjoy with family and friends. Makes approximately 4 main dish servings.

Hadley and Hannah Harvey, Des Moines
First Place, 2021 Tag Team Challenge—Main Dishes
First Place Overall, 2021 Tag Team Challenge

Hadley Harvey (14) of Des Moines accepts the first place overall trophy for Big Mama's Nachos in the 2021 Tag Team Challenge.

LASAGNA FOR 12

James Covey won the Men in the New Millennium Cooking with Beer contest in 2000. Over the years he has entered recipes made with wine, with beer, and with coffee. A decade after his turn-of-the-century creation, he scored with this Sam & Gabe's lasagna, which combines ground turkey with Italian sausage and makes enough for a party.

16 ounces sweet Italian sausage
20 ounces ground turkey
1 tablespoon parsley flakes
1½ teaspoons salt
2 6-ounce cans tomato paste
1 clove garlic, minced
1 tablespoon basil
2 cups chopped tomatoes
1 tablespoon sugar
10-ounce package lasagna noodles
2 12-ounce containers large curd cottage cheese, drained
2 eggs, slightly beaten
½ teaspoon ground pepper
1 tablespoon Italian seasoning, crushed
2 tablespoons salt
2 tablespoons parsley flakes
½ cup grated Parmesan cheese
1½ pounds sliced mozzarella cheese

Preheat oven to 375°F. Grease 12x18-inch pan or two 9x13-inch pans.

In large frying pan brown sausage and turkey together; drain and return to pan. Add parsley, salt, tomato paste, garlic, basil, tomatoes, and sugar. Simmer 30 minutes.

Cook lasagna noodles according to package directions (can use precooked noodles). Drain and rinse with cold water; cool. Mix cottage cheese, eggs, pepper, Italian seasoning, salt, parsley, and Parmesan cheese. Make two or three layers in this order: noodles, cottage cheese mixture, meat sauce, and mozzarella cheese. Cover with foil. Bake 30 to 50 minutes. If desired, prepare in advance and refrigerate until ready to serve. Add additional cooking time if refrigerated, about 30 minutes at least. Remove foil the last 10 minutes to brown the top of the cheese. Let lasagna rest 15 minutes before serving. Makes about 16 servings.

James Covey, Clive
First Place, 2010 Sam & Gabe's Lasagna

KYLE'S TAILGATIN' CHILI

Many of the recipes entered at the Iowa State Fair include basic ingredients—flour, sugar, eggs. When it comes to Kyle Barton's chili, there is always something unexpected. How about chopped black cherries and four different types of chili powder?

Kyle learned to cook with his grandmother. He started entering the State Fair in about 2003, first Mrs. Grimes Chili and then Tone's Cinnamon Rolls contests. He progressed to Ed Podolak's Chili Contest and to the International Chili Contest, which he now runs. "I kept winning the contest, so they had me run it so that others would have a chance at winning," he says.

The sky has been the limit for Kyle, a fierce competitor who absolutely loves the Fair. He also enters photography contests at the Cultural Center and the hog-calling contests, which landed him on the *Today Show, Jimmy Fallon, Steve Harvey, The Gong Show,* and *Jay Leno's You Bet Your Life*.

His best cooking advice came from a writer at the State Fair (a writer keeps track of a judge's comments and writes them on a card for the contestants), who said that he needed to garnish his entries to make them look as great as they tasted. "I did that the next year and won 10 contests." If you are a true chili chef, or want to become one, try Kyle's signature recipe.

TAILGATIN' CHILI

3 pounds ground beef
¾ pound Graziano sausage
1 tablespoon butter
½ cup chicken broth
1 15-ounce can tomato sauce
1 14½-ounce can beef consommé
½ can Mexican salsa (El Patio)
1 10¾-ounce can creamy tomato soup
1 29-ounce can petite cut tomatoes, undrained
1 4-ounce can green chiles
2 white onions, finely chopped
2 green sweet peppers, finely chopped
2 tablespoons chopped black cherries
2 tablespoons Texas chili powder
2 tablespoons New Mexico medium chili powder
1 tablespoon medium New Mexico red chili powder
1 tablespoons ancho chili powder
1 tablespoons pasilla chili powder
2 tablespoons ground cumin
2 teaspoons garlic powder
1 teaspoon chipotle powder
2½ teaspoons sea salt, divided
½ teaspoon Frank's Hot Powder
½ teaspoon ground oregano
2 cans chili beans, undrained
2 cans dark red kidney beans, undrained
2 tablespoons packed brown sugar

208   BAKING BLUE RIBBONS

In a skillet cook ground beef and sausage with butter and a small amount of the chicken broth until meats are no longer pink; drain. In a large bowl combine tomato sauce, consommé, remaining broth, salsa, tomato soup, tomatoes, chiles, onions, sweet peppers, and cherries.

Combine all spices in a bowl, adding 2 teaspoons of the salt. Add half of the spice mixture to the sauce mixture. Then add cooked meat to the mixture. Simmer on low about an hour. Add beans and half the remaining spice mixture; simmer another hour. Add brown sugar, remaining spice mixture, and remaining ½ teaspoon salt. Simmer another 20 to 30 minutes. Makes 10 to 12 servings.

IOWA FARMHOUSE BBQ BASKETS

Kelly Barrett's winning recipe was the perfect sweet and savory comfort food in 2001, with just the right amount of spice. The hamburger bun baskets are a great idea.

1 pound ground beef
5 slices bacon
½ cup western-style barbecue sauce
2 tablespoons honey
½ teaspoon mild chili powder
½ teaspoon cinnamon
1 tablespoon plain yogurt
6 hamburger buns
1 cup shredded cheddar cheese

Brown ground beef in skillet; drain. Fry bacon and crumble into small pieces. Mix barbecue sauce, honey, chili powder, cinnamon, and yogurt in small bowl. Add to meat; heat through. Remove enough bread from buns to form bowls. Scoop mixture into hollowed-out buns. Sprinkle with cheese and bacon. Wrap in foil. Warm in 300°F-oven to melt cheese.

Serves 6.

Kelly Barrett, Cedar Rapids
First Place, 2001 A Taste of Iowa A'Fair–Main Dish

CALLING ALL BEGINNERS

State Fair Food Contests can be daunting for first-time exhibitors. Darrellyn Knight of Des Moines has sponsored the Beginner's Contest since about 2012 to encourage Iowa's home cooks to take the plunge into culinary competitions. Contestants may enter just about any recipe, from main dishes to desserts. The event is a great place to meet other novice exhibitors and learn from the pros at the Elwell Center. In 2021, Christina McCleary of Des Moines won. Brand-new contestants are not necessarily novice cooks, as you can see from her Bolognese with Homemade Noodles.

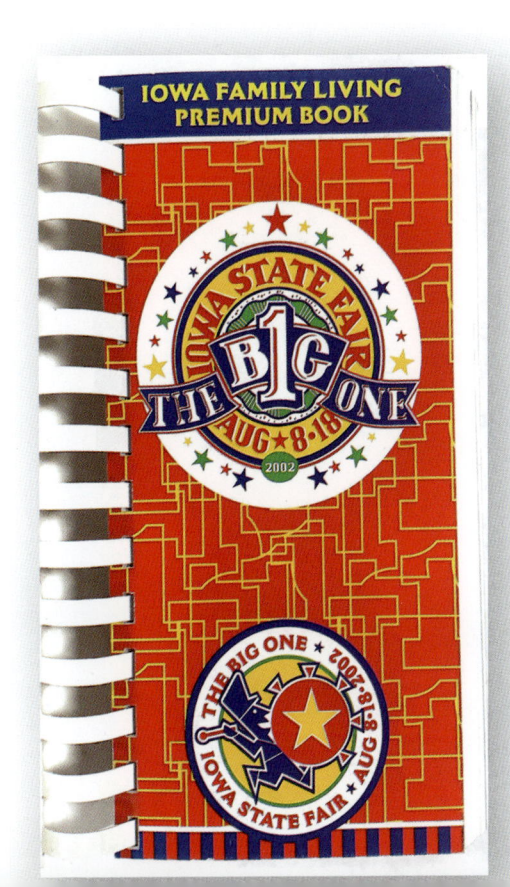

BOLOGNESE WITH HOMEMADE NOODLES

⅓ cup olive oil
1 medium to large peeled and diced carrot
1 small to medium peeled and finely diced yellow onion
2 diced celery sticks
3 to 4 cups chicken stock, divided
1 pound ground beef
1 cup dry red wine (Merlot or Pinot works best)
½ cup tomato paste
Parmesan cheese, grated or shredded

In a sauté pan with lid add olive oil and a pinch of the carrot, onion, and celery. Heat pan to medium heat. When the vegetables start to sizzle, your oil is at a good temperature. Add the rest of the vegetables and sauté for about 5 minutes or until tender. Increase heat a little and add about ¼ cup of the chicken stock and the ground beef. Break up ground beef, cooking until there is no more pink color. The beef doesn't need to be completely browned. Increase heat to high and add the red wine. Cook until the wine evaporates, about 10 minutes, or until you can no longer smell the alcohol. Turn down the heat to low and add the tomato paste. Mix the tomato paste in thoroughly.

Cover and simmer for at least a few hours. Continue adding chicken stock as needed to keep the mixture from getting dry. If making your own noodles, prepare them while the sauce simmers. When ready to serve, add your cooked pasta noodles to the sauce and make sure the noodles are coated. Plate and top with grated or shredded Parmesan cheese.

PASTA NOODLES (Packaged Tagliatelle noodles also work well.)
1 cup flour (00 or all-purpose) plus more for rolling out dough
2 eggs
Salt for boiling water

Add flour to a clean countertop and make a nest. You can do this by making a wheel in the middle of the flour with your hands. Add the eggs to the center. Lightly whisk the eggs with a fork and gradually incorporate the flour from the sides of the nest. Continue until the dough has a sticky consistency and start kneading with your hands. Knead dough for about 5 to 8 minutes until dough holds together and has a smooth texture. Shape dough into a ball and sprinkle with flour; wrap tightly in plastic wrap. Rest dough in refrigerator for at least 15 minutes. Cut the dough into 3 or 4 even pieces and roll into balls. Use a rolling pin, roll out the first dough ball into a circle. The dough should be pretty thin (about ⅛ inch). Cut strips about ½-inch wide to form noodles. Pick up noodles, sprinkle with flour, and set aside. Repeat with the other dough balls until all the noodles are cut. Put a large pot of water on high and bring to a boil. Add a tablespoon of salt. Add noodles and cook for 2 to 3 minutes. Drain and add to the Bolognese Sauce. Makes about 4 servings.

Christina McCleary, Des Moines
First Place, Beginners Contest, 2021.

BACON MAC AND CHEESE

Brooklynn Sedlock of Indianola started baking in her Easy-Bake Oven when she was two. She tagged along to Iowa State Fair Food Competitions with her mom at age three and entered her first contest as a four-year-old. By age twelve, she had earned 139 ribbons, including three Sweepstakes and 53 first place. Her two favorite contests are My Grandparents' Favorite Food because she loves recipes inspired by her family and the Ugly Cake Contest because everyone comes up with fun and gross ideas. Brooklynn's parents are her support team, restocking ingredients and getting entries to the Fairgrounds on time. Brooklynn learns a lot from entering food contests. "I love to get feedback from the judges to help me improve in the kitchen. I have learned so much over the years from their comments and recommendations," she says. Adult competitors are also terrific mentors. "They are great to learn from and very encouraging and supportive."

For the ultimate Iowa comfort food, try Brooklynn's winning Bacon Mac and Cheese.

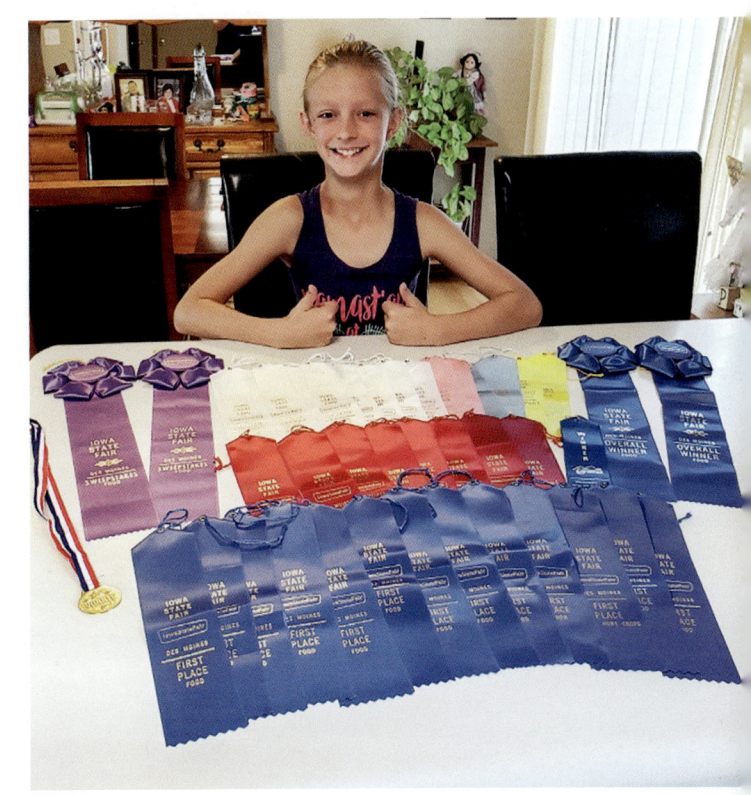

Youth Exhibitor Brooklynn Sedlock and her ribbons.

1 pound box uncooked elbow noodles
8 ounces processed sharp cheddar cheese, cubed
1 cup grated asiago cheese
½ cup cubed smoked Gouda cheese
1½ cups milk
5 tablespoons butter
½ teaspoon salt
½ teaspoon pepper
4 ounces bacon, divided

Cook noodles according to package directions. Drain noodles; add cheeses, milk, and butter. Stir until cheeses and butter are melted and completely mixed. Add salt and pepper; stir until mixed in well. Cut bacon into tiny pieces; fry until fully cooked. Drain well. Mix in three-fourths of the cooked bacon with the macaroni and cheese. Sprinkle remaining bacon on top and serve.

Brooklynn Sedlock, Indianola
First Place, 2019 My Grandparents' Favorite Food–Main Dish/Side Dish
First Place Overall, 2019 My Grandparents' Favorite Food

2000s

DREAMFIELDS TOMATO FETA PASTA

Kay has competed for many years at the Fair, always entering baked goods and never venturing into main dishes. In 2021 she took Food Superintendent Pat Berry's advice and tried something new. The result is this easy and delicious Tomato Feta Pasta bake, which earned her $200 in the Dreamfields Pasta Contest and a lovely blue silk. This is great any time of year and especially when the tomatoes are fresh from the garden or the Farmers' Market.

3 pints cherry tomatoes
12-ounce block feta cheese
½ cup extra virgin olive oil
½ teaspoon fine sea salt
½ teaspoon black pepper
3 teaspoons minced garlic
½ cup chopped fresh basil, plus more for serving
¼ cup basil pesto
1 13.25-oz. box Dreamfields penne or other pasta

Preheat oven to 400°F. Place the cherry tomatoes in a 9x13-inch baking dish. Pour the olive oil on top and season with salt, pepper, garlic, and basil. Toss until combined. Place feta block in the middle of the baking dish surrounded by cherry tomatoes and flip a couple times to coat the cheese with olive oil and seasoning. Bake for 35 minutes, until cherry tomatoes burst and feta cheese melts. While the tomatoes and feta bake, cook pasta in salted water according to package instructions until al dente. Drain. Transfer pasta to the baking dish. Add basil pesto. Toss everything to combine. Garnish with more fresh basil and serve warm.

Serves 6–8.

Kay Smith, Des Moines
First Place, 2021 Dreamfields Pasta

A PREMIUM GIFT

State Fair food winners are generous people. Mavis Ward of Des Moines won many premiums during the 1980s and '90s. She had 22 shoe boxes filled with ribbons. For 17 years, she donated her prize money to the Food Department. Mavis estimates that she returned between $3,000 and $4,000. The money paid for eight lighted display cases in in the Maytag Family Center. Her biggest prize was $1,500 in the Tone's Pride of Iowa Cinnamon Roll Contest in 2001. She tried to donate all of the winnings, but Arlette Hollister would only accept $300, so Mavis used the rest to buy Christmas gifts. Here is her winning Country Lane Breakfast Casserole, complete with Rum Bananas on the side.

SOUTHWESTERN SUNRISE BREAKFAST CASSEROLE

3 4-oz. can diced green chiles, drained
1 pound cheddar cheese, grated
5 green onions, thinly sliced
1 can medium olives, halved
5 to 6 medium, fresh pear-shape tomatoes, seeded and chopped
1 pound crabmeat
9 eggs
2½ cups milk
1 cup flour
¾ pound jalapeño cheese, grated

Preheat oven to 350F. Lightly grease a 9x13-inch baking dish.

Place half of the chiles in an even layer in baking dish. Cover with half of the cheddar cheese, onions, olives, tomatoes, and crabmeat; repeat layering. In blender combine eggs, milk, and flour. Blend until smooth. Pour over layers. Sprinkle jalapeño cheese evenly over batter. Bake 30–40 minutes until center jiggles only slightly when gently shaken. Let stand 10 minutes; cut in squares. Serve with Rum Bananas.

Serves 8–10.

RUM BANANAS

4 large firm bananas
⅓ cup butter
½ cup sugar, divided
1 cup whipping cream
⅛ cup rum
¾ teaspoon vanilla
Dash ground cloves

Peel bananas; sauté in butter until golden brown. Drain on paper towel; place on platter to cool. Sprinkle with half the sugar. Whip cream until stiff; fold in remaining sugar, rum, and vanilla. Cover bananas completely with this mixture; chill. Serve sprinkled with ground cloves.

Mavis M. Ward, Des Moines
First Place, 1992 County Lane Breakfast Casseroles

175 FAIR ENTRIES IN ONE YEAR

Marion Karlin of Waterloo is among the handful of Super Exhibitors who regularly entered 100-plus entries. In 2005 she brought 175. She has won both state and national food contests. Her husband, Leonard, was the official taste tester who made the thumbs-up or thumbs-down call on the recipes that made the trip to the Fair. "If Leonard likes it, it likely will go to the Fair," she said.

Beginning in 1992, the Karlins got into an annual State Fair routine: Pack food items into large boxes, drive 2½ hours to Des Moines, deliver the entries, watch judging, drive 2½ hours back home. Repeat. They racked up many ribbons and even more miles on their car with Marion's winners like this one.

WAFFLE SAUSAGE STRATA

1 pound country sausage
5 7-inch cinnamon waffles, cut into 1-inch pieces
1 cup shredded low-fat shredded cheddar cheese, divided
1½ cups substitute egg product
1¼ cups skim milk
1 teaspoon cinnamon
½ teaspoon ground cloves
Paprika and parsley for garnish

Preheat oven to 350°F. In a skillet brown sausage. Drain, crumble, and set aside. In ungreased 8x8-inch baking dish, arrange 3 cups of the cut-up waffles. Sprinkle 1¼ cups of cooked sausage and ⅓ cup of shredded cheese on top. Repeat layers, reserving ⅓ cup of the cheese for garnish after casserole has been baked. Mix egg substitute, skim milk, cinnamon, and cloves. Pour over casserole ingredients; refrigerate overnight. Bake 35 to 40 minutes or until knife inserted near center comes out clean. Remove casserole from oven; garnish with reserved cheese, paprika, and parsley. Serve warm accompanied by maple syrup. Makes 4 to 6 servings

Marion Karlin, Waterloo
First Place, 2002 Sausage, Breakfast Dishes

Cakes

Eileen Gannon comes from a large family of Iowa State Fair competitors. When it comes to winning blue ribbons, Eileen takes the cake. A competitive baker since the age of twelve, she has won more than 600 awards across the Food Department. Her original recipes stand out with ingredients like culinary-grade lavender and pure honey harvested from beehives in her backyard. Some of her signature creations include spiced caramel cake, cream-filled cupcakes, and elegant Bundt and layer cakes.

Eileen is a Des Moines businesswoman by day and home chef by night. She loves baking with her children, Helen and Graham Hutchison, who have won dozens of State Fair ribbons on their own. In 2018, the mother-daughter duo competed on the *Bake it Like Buddy* TV series, when Helen was ten years old. Eileen has won best overall cake eleven times, but baking with her kids has always been more fun than TV appearances and competitions. Since her cake-winning days, she has moved on to several different food categories, including a first-prize chocolate sauce, which she turned into the Sunday Night Foods line of premium dessert sauces.

Eileen Gannon's 7 Secrets to Beautiful Cakes

1 Set the timer for 5 minutes before your cake should be done to ensure a moist and more flavorful cake. Often the flavor bakes out in those last 5 minutes.

2 Stand at the oven for the last 2–3 minutes of baking to check for overbrowning—at this stage every second counts.

3 Test layer cakes with a toothpick or cake tester inserted about an inch from the center—not directly in the center as most recipes say. The toothpick should still have a few crumbs clinging to it, not clean. By the time it's clean in the center, the cake is likely overbaked.

4 Add 1 teaspoon of fine instant coffee to chocolate cakes to create deeper, richer flavors.

5 For white cakes, 1 teaspoon of almond extract adds more complexity.

6 Never fill a cake with frosting. Instead, use a filling that will add dimension and improve the flavor, like lemon curd, preserved fruit, chocolate ganache, or something that complements the recipe. For layer cakes, this is an opportunity to make it stand out and add moisture, not just more sugar.

7 Create new recipes by taking your favorites and changing them up with these tips and your own unique flavor combinations.

LAVENDER LEMON CAKE

¾ cup unsalted butter, softened
1½ cups sugar
4 large egg whites
2 teaspoons vanilla
3 cups cake flour
4 teaspoons baking powder
¾ teaspoon salt
1 cup milk

LEMON BUTTERCREAM
1 teaspoon culinary lavender
5 large egg whites
½ teaspoon cream of tartar
1 cup sugar, divided
¼ cup water
2 cups unsalted butter, softened
4 drops yellow food coloring
¾ cup lemon curd

Preheat oven to 350°F. In a large bowl cream butter and sugar until light and fluffy. Add egg whites one at a time, beating well after each addition. Beat in vanilla. Sift together dry ingredients. Add alternately to cream mixture with milk. Pour into two 8-inch cake pans that have been greased and floured. Bake 25 to 35 minutes or until cake tester comes out with a few crumbs. Let cakes cook in pan for 10 minutes, then remove to wire racks to cool completely.

Eileen Gannon (holding microphone) announces the finalists in the Helen Gannon Memorial Contest, which she and her siblings sponsor in memory of their mother who was a 40-year State Fair food contestant from 1968–2008.

FOR BUTTERCREAM: Mince lavender in a coffee grinder. Set aside. Whip egg whites with cream of tartar and ¼ cup sugar until stiff peaks form. Place remaining sugar and water in small saucepan and stir and cook until firm ball stage (248°F) Remove immediately and pour ⅓ of syrup over egg whites. Beat 10 seconds. Stop mixer. Repeat steps twice until all the syrup is incorporated. Beat on low until cool, about 2 minutes. Beat in butter 1 tablespoon at a time. Add yellow food coloring and mix well. Stir in lemon curd. The buttercream will be thick and glossy. Divide in half. Add lavender to ½ of buttercream.

Split cake layers horizontally. Fill with lavender buttercream. Frost sides and top with reserved Lemon Buttercream. Makes approximately 12 servings.

Eileen Gannon, Des Moines
First Place, 2001 Iowa State Fair Softasilk Cake Championship

RED VELVET CAKE

Like most Super Exhibitors, Sally Kilkenny has won ribbons across a wide variety of foods. This Red Velvet Cake that took the Hy-Vee Smiles in Every Aisle Cake crown in 2013 is just the beginning.

CAKE
3½ cups cake flour
½ cup unsweetened cocoa powder
1½ teaspoons salt
2 cups canola oil
2¼ cups sugar
3 large eggs, at room temperature
Red food coloring
1½ teaspoons vanilla
1¼ cups buttermilk
2 teaspoons baking soda
2½ teaspoons white vinegar

CREAM CHEESE FROSTING
2 8-ounce packages cream cheese, at room temperature
1 cup butter, at room temperature
2 teaspoons vanilla
6 cups powdered sugar

Preheat oven to 350°F. In a small mixing bowl combine flour, cocoa powder, and salt; set aside. In large mixing bowl beat oil and sugar until well blended. Beat in eggs, one at a time, mixing well after each addition. Carefully stir in desired amount of food coloring, mixing well. Stir in vanilla. Add flour mixture in three batches, alternating with buttermilk, beating just enough to combine. In small bowl combine baking soda and vinegar; stir into batter, beating for 10 seconds. Divide batter among three greased and floured 9-inch round cake pans. Bake 40 to 45 minutes or until toothpick inserted near center comes out clean. Remove pans to wire racks; cool 10 minutes. Invert pans to remove cakes; cool completely. Place one cake layer on serving platter. Spread top with Cream Cheese Frosting. Repeat with second layer and frosting. Top with third layer, frosting sides and top of cake. Garnish as desired. Makes 14 servings.

For frosting, beat cream cheese and butter in mixing bowl until light and fluffy, about 2 minutes. Beat in vanilla. Gradually add powdered sugar, beating on low speed to combine.

If too soft, chill 10 to 15 minutes before using.

Sally Kilkenny, Granger
First Place, 2013 Hy-Vee Smiles in Every Aisle Cakes, Red Velvet Cake

WHEN THINGS GO WRONG, IMPROVISING WINS THE DAY

Ann Gillotti of Ankeny won a blue ribbon for her first entry at the Iowa State Fair in 2017, but it wasn't beginner's luck or perfection that took her to the top. The ganache for her original mocha cupcakes flopped at the last minute. With no more chocolate chips, she substituted Hershey's salted caramel chips for the filling—and the Salted Caramel Mocha Cupcake was born. This rich dessert wowed the judges and earned her a blue ribbon for filled cupcakes and second place overall for single layer cakes in the Hy-Vee Smiles in Every Aisle contest as well as the Beginner's Dessert contest. If you are looking for unexpectedly elegant cupcakes, your search is over.

SALTED CARAMEL MOCHA CUPCAKES

3 ounces bittersweet chocolate, finely chopped
⅓ cup unsweetened cocoa powder
¾ cups strong hot brewed coffee or espresso
¾ cup bread flour
¾ cups sugar
½ teaspoon salt
½ teaspoon baking soda
6 tablespoons vegetable oil
2 large eggs
2 teaspoons white vinegar
1 teaspoon vanilla extract

Preheat oven to 350° F. Line standard-size muffin pan with baking-cup liners.

Place chocolate and cocoa in a medium bowl. Pour hot espresso over mixture and whisk until smooth. Set in refrigerator until completely cooled, about 20 minutes. Whisk flour, sugar, salt, and baking soda together in medium bowl and set aside. Whisk

BAKING BLUE RIBBONS

oil, eggs, vinegar, and vanilla into cooled chocolate-cocoa mixture until smooth. Add flour mixture and whisk until smooth.

Divide batter evenly among 12 muffin pan cups. Bake on middle rack for 15–17 minutes, or until cupcakes are set and firm to the touch. Cool cupcakes in pan until cool enough to handle, about 10 minutes. Carefully lift each cupcake from muffin pan and set on wire rack. Cool to room temperature. Makes one dozen cupcakes.

SALTED CARAMEL GANACHE:
1 cup Hershey's salted caramel chips
¼ cup heavy cream
1 tablespoon brewed coffee or espresso, warm
1 tablespoon powdered sugar

Place ganache ingredients in a microwave-safe bowl and microwave for 1 minute. Stir until ingredients are combined and smooth. Place in refrigerator for 1 hour to cool down and thicken. Remove from refrigerator and whip with a hand mixer until ganache lightens in color and becomes fluffy. Using a pastry bag, squeeze ganache filling into center of cupcakes until they bulge slightly.

ESPRESSO BUTTERCREAM:
1½ cups (3 sticks) unsalted butter, softened
3 cups powdered sugar
3 tablespoons strong brewed coffee, or espresso, chilled
3 tablespoons milk
12 chocolate covered espresso beans, for decoration

Beat butter in bowl of electric mixer on medium speed until fluffy, about 1 minute.

Reduce mixer speed to low. Add powdered sugar, 1 cup at a time, beating for a few seconds after each addition. Increase mixer speed to medium and mix for about 3 minutes. Add coffee and milk; beat on low to combine. Scrape down sides and bottom of the bowl. Increase mixer speed to medium and beat until fluffy, about 4 minutes. Pipe frosting onto cupcakes and top with a chocolate-covered espresso bean for garnish.

Ann Gillotti, Ankeny
First Place, Hy-Vee Smiles in Every Aisle—Filled Cupcakes, 2017
First Place, Beginner's Dessert Contest, 2017

BEST OF THE BEST LEMON CHEESECKE

Janine Knop, a longtime Fair supporter, turned her love of baking cheesecakes and other delights into a bakery and restaurant, Miss Nini's Fine Desserts. Her winning lemon cheesecake is a fine dessert, indeed! The recipe bakes ultralight and fluffy, like a cross between a soufflé and a cheesecake while it is in the oven. The result is this beautiful spring-yellow confection.

CRUST
1½ cups graham cracker crumbs
3 tablespoons sugar
½ teaspoon cinnamon
¼ cup butter, melted

FILLING
3 8-ounce packages cream cheese, softened
1¼ cups sugar
6 eggs, separated
1 pint sour cream
⅓ cup all-purpose flour
2 teaspoons vanilla
Grated rind of 1 lemon
1⅓ tablespoons lemon juice
Powdered sugar for dusting

CRUST
Preheat oven to 350°F. Combine graham cracker crumbs, sugar, cinnamon, and melted butter. Stir to blend. Generously grease 9x3-inch springform pan. Press three-fourths of the graham cracker mixture into bottom and up sides of pan. Chill prepared crust while making filling. Reserve remaining crumb mixture for topping.

FILLING
Beat cream cheese until soft. Gradually beat in sugar until light and fluffy. Beat in egg yolks, one at a time, until well blended. Stir in sour cream, flour, vanilla, lemon rind, and juice until smooth. Beat egg whites until stiff peaks form. Fold whites into cheese mixture until well blended. Pour into prepared pan. Bake 70 minutes or until top is golden. Turn off oven heat; leave cake in oven 1 hour. Remove cake from oven; cool on wire rack at room temperature. Sprinkle remaining crumbs on top. Chill overnight before serving. Dust with powdered sugar for garnish. Makes 16 servings.

Janine Knop, Atlantic
First Place, 2003 Cheesecake, Baked Cheesecake
First Place Overall, 2003 Cheesecake

VANILLA STRAWBERRY CHEESECAKE

Brian Keul is a standout baker who specializes in cakes and cheesecakes. His attention to detail in recipes and execution comes through in his flavors and presentations. He started baking as a kid with his mom and grandmother on the family farm north of Osceola. He made cakes for birthdays and family gatherings. Everyone encouraged him to enter the Fair, and he has racked up many blue ribbons since his first entry. He loves being part of the Food Department and watching and learning from judges as well as helping others with their ideas and recipes. Brian contributed this terrific cheesecake winner from 2021 and also helped with many test bakes for this book. His comments and experience were invaluable.

CRUST
2 cups Oreo cookies with cream center removed, finely ground
¼ cup unsalted butter, melted
2 tablespoons sugar

CHEESECAKE FILLING
4 8-oz. packages cream cheese, room temperature
1⅔ cups sugar
3 tablespoons all-purpose flour
¼ teaspoon salt
4 large eggs
2 egg yolks
1½ teaspoons pure vanilla extract
¼ cup sour cream

STRAWBERRY GLAZE
1 cup frozen strawberries, thawed
3 tablespoon water
2 tablespoons sugar
1 teaspoon cornstarch
red food coloring
1 pint fresh small strawberries, washed and hulled

Position oven rack in the middle of the oven and preheat to 325°F. Put a tea kettle or large pot of water on the stove to boil for the water bath. Mix the crust ingredients and press into 9-inch springform pan. Bake crust for 7 minutes and set aside to cool. In a large bowl beat together the cream cheese, sugar, flour, and salt until smooth. If using a mixer, mix on low speed. Add the whole eggs and the egg yolks, one at a time, beating well (but still at low speed) after each addition. Beat in the vanilla and sour cream. Pour the batter into the springform pan on top of crust. Place the springform pan in a larger roasting pan. Fill the roasting pan with the boiling water until it reaches halfway up the sides of the springform pan. If your cheesecake pan is not leakproof, cover bottom and sides securely with foil before adding water.

Bake until the cheesecake is firm and slightly golden on top, 70 to 80 minutes.

Brian Keul with his winning cheesecake at the Elwell Family Food Center, 2021.

Remove the cheesecake from the water bath and cool to room temperature. Cover the cheesecake with plastic wrap and refrigerate until very cold, at least 3 hours or overnight.

For Glaze: Puree frozen strawberries in a small food processor. Press blended strawberries through a fine-mesh strainer into a small saucepan. Add water.

In a small bowl mix sugar and cornstarch. Stir into the puree in saucepan. Bring to a boil, stirring constantly. Continue cooking and stirring until thickened and clear. Add food coloring to give vibrant red color. Cool to room temperature.

Arrange strawberries in a single layer around the cooled cheesecake. Drizzle cooled glaze evenly over cheesecake. Using a pastry brush, brush glaze over strawberries to coat each berry. Store, covered, in refrigerator until ready to serve.

Yields 8 servings.

Brian Keul, West Des Moines
First Place, 2021 Cheesecakes

Pies

PILLSBURY RUSTIC S'MORE PIE

CRUST
1 9-inch Pillsbury Pie Crust for single-crust pie
7 rectangular graham cracker boards (reserve 1 teaspoon for topping)
2 tablespoons packed light brown sugar
¼ cup (½ stick) unsalted butter (melted)

CHOCOLATE FILLING
2 eggs at room temperature
¾ cup buttermilk
¼ cup heavy whipping cream
2 ounces cream cheese
2 tablespoons granulated sugar
1/10 teaspoon (about 2 pinches) salt
½ teaspoon pure vanilla extract
1 cup semisweet chocolate chips
1 tablespoon unsweetened cocoa powder

MARSHMALLOW TOPPING
3 large egg whites
2 tablespoons corn syrup
¾ cup granulated sugar
⅛ teaspoon salt
½ teaspoon unflavored gelatin
½ teaspoon pure vanilla extract
1 teaspoon (reserved) finely ground graham cracker crumbs

Heat oven to 400°F. Press 9-inch Pillsbury Pie Crust into the bottom of a 9-inch cast iron skillet or pie plate. Grind graham crackers in food processor until fine crumbs are formed. Transfer to bowl and mix in the brown sugar and melted butter. Layer on top of pie crust. Bake for 10 minutes or until crust is slightly brown. (Cover crust with aluminum foil to bake.) Cool for 10 minutes.

FILLING: Reduce oven temperature to 350°F. Beat eggs in a small bowl; set aside. Combine buttermilk, cream, cream cheese, sugar, and salt in a medium saucepan over medium heat until simmering. Remove from heat and add vanilla, chocolate chips, and cocoa powder; stir until combined and smooth. Stir 1 cup of the chocolate mixture into the beaten eggs, stir the egg mixture and add it back into the saucepan to chocolate mixture. Pour filling into the cooled pie crust. Bake for 30 minutes. It should look glossy. Cool completely on a wire rack.

TOPPING: Bring 1 inch of water (in the bottom of a medium saucepan) to a simmer, Combine egg whites, corn syrup, sugar, unflavored gelatin, and salt in a metal bowl that can sit on top of the saucepan. Whisk constantly in the metal bowl over simmering water until sugar is dissolved and eggs have reached 160°F.(3 to 5 minutes; do not overcook; the eggs could scramble. Pour mixture and vanilla into the bowl of a stand mixer fitted with wire whisk attachment and beat on high speed until fluffy, about 5 minutes and set aside.

Heat broiler. Spoon marshmallow topping on cooled pie and sprinkle lightly with 1 teaspoon finely ground graham cracker crumbs. Broil until topping is slightly brown, 2 minutes on high (watch carefully). Makes 8 to 10 servings.

Pamela Reynolds, Norwalk
First Place, 2012 Pillsbury Pie Crust

KAREN McKILLIGAN'S STRAWBERRY RHUBARB PIE

Karen McKilligan took over for Arlette Hollister in 2017 and brought her own passion to the Food Department. "I love that food is such a legacy in Iowa. Teaching our kids and passing along food favorites is so special. It's a way to spread the love of food, and it celebrates our culture."

Her signature pie recipe is perfect for summer celebrations—and entering at the Fair!

STRAWBERRY RHUBARB PIE CRUST
4 cups all-purpose flour
1 tablespoon sugar
1 teaspoon salt
1½ cups shortening
1 large egg
1 tablespoon cider vinegar
½ cup ice-cold water

FILLING
2 cups fresh sliced rhubarb
2 cups fresh sliced strawberries
1¼ cups granulated sugar
½ teaspoon salt
2 tablespoons tapioca
⅓ cup flour

ASSEMBLY
2 piecrusts
2 tablespoons butter
Sanding sugar

For crust, combine flour, sugar, and salt. Cut in the shortening. Combine egg, vinegar, and the water. Sprinkle the mixture over dry ingredients. Stir gently with a fork to combine. Divide into 3 equal balls. Each will make 1 crust. Pastry may be refrigerated or frozen for later use. Makes 3 single crusts.

For filling, preheat oven to 425°F. Combine rhubarb and strawberries. Combine granulated sugar, salt, flour, and tapioca. Gently fold dry ingredients into fruit mixture. Roll one crust to $1/8$-inch thickness and place in a 9-inch pie pan for bottom crust. Place filling mixture on top of crust. Dot with butter. Cover with top crust, rolled about $1/8$ inch thick. Brush top with water and sprinkle with sanding sugar. Bake 15 minutes. Lower temperature to 350°F. for 45 minutes or until filling is bubbly and pie is done. Makes 6 to 8 slices.

Karen McKilligan, Superintendent's Signature Recipe

"No one else has its own food building, even the larger fairs such as Minnesota and Texas. So often food is housed in the same building as the arts or needlework entries."

– Jen Cannon, Iowa State Fair Competitive Events Manager on the opening of the Elwell Family Food Center

Cookies

GIVING BACK WITH COOKIES AND T-SHIRTS

Brooke Mickelson of West Des Moines loves the Food Department. "Whether I'm entering a food contest or sponsoring one, it's just a happy place," she says. "So many of our mothers, grandmothers, and aunts were good cooks, but you know what? So are the cooks of today. We must celebrate and encourage them, and the Fair is the perfect place to do that."

Brooke sponsors the "My Favorite Birthday Cake" contest since her birthday falls during the Fair and "What to Take a Friend in Need" in honor of her late mother. She is a busy mom of four sons and a social media influencer and motivational speaker. Her intent is simple: "If people can combine their talents and work together for a greater goal, there's nothing that can stop them."

A great example of this is the University of Iowa "Wave" T-shirts, which Brooke developed with Meighan Phillips and Lori Willis. The shirts raise money and celebrate the tradition of football fans at Kinnick Stadium who wave to patients at the Stead Family Children's Hospital at the end of the first quarter during home games. Brooke's youngest son and Meighan's daughter both received treatments at the hospital, and this is a special way to say thank you. Sales of the shirts have raised nearly $2 million for the hospital and counting. Her Caramel Apple Cookies are perfect for fall football—and waving to the kids in Iowa City.

CARAMEL APPLE COOKIES WITH BROWN SUGAR ICING

¾ cup butter
½ cup sugar
¼ cup apple butter
½ teaspoon cinnamon
2 teaspoons vanilla
½ teaspoon salt
2¼ teaspoon baking powder
2¼ cups flour

ICING
3 tablespoons butter
¼ cup cream
½ cup brown sugar
2 cups powdered sugar
1 teaspoon vanilla

Preheat oven to 350°F. Cream butter and sugar. Mix in apple butter, cinnamon, vanilla, salt, baking powder, and flour. Roll dough into balls and bake for 8 minutes. Cool and frost.

For frosting, melt butter in a saucepan over medium heat. Combine cream and brown sugar with butter and let cool Add powdered sugar and vanilla. Cool completely before icing cookies. Makes 12 to 18 cookies.

Brooke Mickelson, West Des Moines
Sponsor's Signature Recipe

Brooke Mickelson

GLUTEN-FREE OATMEAL MONSTER COOKIES

Eleven-year-old Emma Scheidel of Ankeny won first place for her Gluten-Free Monster Cookies in the 2021 Casey's Creations Contest. Emma cannot eat gluten and she loves to create recipes that she can enjoy and share with family and friends. These are her favorite. The recipe uses oatmeal instead of flour, which makes it hard to tell that they are gluten-free.

½ cup butter, softened
1 cup packed brown sugar
1 cup sugar
1½ cups creamy peanut butter
3 large eggs

2 tsp. baking soda
1 tsp. vanilla extract
4½ cups gluten-free rolled oats
1 cup semisweet chocolate chips
1 cup plain M&M's

Preheat oven to 350°F. With an electric mixer, cream together butter, sugars, peanut butter, and eggs until light. Add baking soda, vanilla extract, and oats. Mix on low speed until well blended. Stir in chocolate chips and M&M's. Use a cookie scoop and place dough on cookie sheets,. 12 cookies per sheet. Bake at 350°F for 12–15 minutes until the edges are golden brown. Let cookies cool and enjoy! Makes approximately 36 cookies.

Emma Scheidel, Ankeny
First Place, 2021 Casey's Creations Gluten-Free Monster Cookies

2000s

GINGERBREAD MEMORIES

Laura Higgins is one of the most creative gingerbread house builders at the Fair. She has the blue ribbons to prove it, but for Laura it's not about prizes. It is the experience of building something together with people you love, and laughing, and having fun. Some of Laura's best memories are of making gingerbread houses and decorating cakes with her sister, Sharon Higgins, who taught her how to cook and bake when they were growing up.

Sharon passed away in 2015. Laura wanted to honor her in a fun and special way, and the gingerbread house contest seemed like a perfect match. The Iowa State Fair needed a new sponsor, and in 2021 Laura brought it back in Sharon's memory. Laura continues the tradition with her family and hopes that the gingerbread house event will get others to give it a try. "If I do anything with this contest, it's to encourage people to do something together as a family. Just have fun and create." Here is a gingerbread recipe that Laura recommends for building your masterpiece.

A prizewinning gingerbread house from 2021.

GINGERBREAD HOUSE DOUGH

Structural gingerbread is used for building gingerbread houses. Although edible, it is not typically meant to be eaten. This recipe has little or no leavening agents; makes a stiff, strong dough; and is designed to hold up your house and all its decorations.

4½ cups flour
1 tablespoon ground ginger
1 tablespoon ground cinnamon
1 teaspoon ground nutmeg
1 teaspoon baking soda
1 teaspoon salt
1 cup vegetable shortening
1 cup sugar
1 cup molasses

Sift dry ingredients (flour, ginger, cinnamon, nutmeg, baking soda, and salt) together in a large bowl and set aside. Melt shortening in large saucepan and whisk in sugar and molasses. Remove from heat and stir in the flour mixture until just combined. Dough should be slightly crumbly, but not sticky. Turn dough out onto a large piece of plastic wrap, wrap tightly, and let cool slightly for about 10 minutes. Preheat oven to 325°F, line baking sheets with parchment paper, divide dough in half, and roll slightly warm dough out on parchment paper to ⅜ inch thickness. Cut out desired shapes, remove extra dough from the edges, and bake for 30 minutes. Transfer to wire rack and cool completely before assembling your structure and decorating.

PARTY ANIMAL COOKIES

Brother-sister duo, Micah (8) and Natalie Hunter (6) won the 2021 Tag Team Challenge for desserts and snacks with their Party Animal Cookies. With a little help from their mom, they transformed their favorite spritz bakery cookies into a new recipe. They kept the fun sprinkles from the original but changed the tea cookies into large, soft treats with pieces of frosted animal crackers baked in and topped with white chocolate. The baking team believes that their recipe makeover turned basic tea cookies into "a birthday party taste celebration," and the judges agree. The combination of soft, buttery cookie and animal cracker crunch is a yummy surprise.

1 cup (2 sticks) salted butter, softened
2 cups granulated sugar
2 large eggs
1 teaspoon vanilla extract
3 cups all-purpose flour
½ teaspoon baking soda
½ teaspoon cream of tartar
1½ cups crushed Circus Animal Cookies (leave some larger pieces, like halves)
¼ cup sprinkles
2 ounces white chocolate (candy dipping chocolate wafers preferred)
Additional sprinkles for garnish

Combine butter with sugar and beat on medium speed until well creamed together. Add eggs and vanilla extract. Mix into butter and sugar until eggs are well beaten. In a separate bowl combine flour, baking soda, and cream of tartar. Slowly add into batter and beat on medium low speed until well combined and dough forms. As the dough is thickening, add in the crushed Circus Animal Cookies and sprinkles and continue mixing until they are thoroughly mixed.

Refrigerate dough for a minimum of 45 minutes and as long as 24 hours. Before baking, preheat oven to 350°F. Use a large cookie scoop (3 tablespoons) and scoop cookie dough onto a parchment paper-lined baking sheet. Place about 2 inches apart and let rest for 10 minutes prior to baking. Bake 10–12 minutes. Allow cookies to cool on the baking sheet for several minutes and then transfer to a wire rack to cool completely.

For the white chocolate drizzle, microwave at 50% power for 30 seconds at a time. Stir the chocolate after each 30 seconds so that it does not burn. Use a piping bag to drizzle the white chocolate over the cookies and add a couple of sprinkles on top. Set these on a piece of parchment paper to allow the drizzle to harden. Makes 16–18 cookies.

Micah and Natalie Hunter, Waukee
First Place 2021 Tag Team Challenge—Desserts and Snacks
Second Place Overall, 2021 Tag Team Challenge

Micah (8) and Natalie (6) Hunter with their trophy for the Tag Team Challenge—First Place Cookies and Second Place Overall.

HONEY CHOCOLATE AND PEANUT BUTTER CANDY BARS

These 4-layer bars are packed with everything we love about candy bars: chocolate, caramel, peanut butter cups, peanuts, and shortbread. The many layers may seem challenging, but the shortbread is made from buttery crackers, so they are easy enough for kids to make. Youth exhibitor Graham Hutchison won with this recipe in 2016. These are his favorite treats because he loves candy bars, especially peanut butter cups. "These bars are fun to make because I get to use my favorite candy and make it into something even better."

Youth exhibitors Graham (8) and Helen (9) Hutchison baking in 2016.

8 ounces rich rectangular crackers, such as Club crackers
¾ cup unsalted butter (1½ sticks)
¾ cup honey
1 cup packed brown sugar
⅓ cup whipping cream
2 cups finely crushed graham crackers
1 teaspoon vanilla
2 cups (9 oz.) chocolate-covered peanut butter cups, chopped into ½-inch pieces
2 cups dry roasted peanuts

TOPPING
1½ cups milk chocolate pieces
⅓ cup butterscotch-flavored pieces
⅓ cup peanut butter

Line a 13x9x2-inch baking pan with nonstick foil, extending foil over the edges of the pan. Arrange half of the crackers in a single layer over the bottom of the prepared pan. In a medium saucepan combine butter, honey, brown sugar, and cream. Bring to boiling, stirring constantly. Add graham cracker crumbs, reduce heat to a simmer, and continue to cook mixture for 5 minutes, stirring constantly. Remove from heat and stir in vanilla. Pour half of the caramel mixture over the crackers in the prepared pan, spreading to cover. Sprinkle with chopped peanut butter cups and peanuts. Pour remaining caramel over. Arrange remaining crackers in a single layer over the caramel, pushing slightly to secure.

For topping, in a medium microwave-safe bowl combine chocolate and butterscotch pieces. Microwave for 1 to 2 minutes or until melted, stirring every 30 seconds. Stir in peanut butter until smooth. Spread chocolate mixture over cracker layer.

Chill bars for 2 hours or until completely firm. Using the edges of the foil, lift the uncut bars out of the pan. Cut into small bars.

Graham Hutchison, Des Moines
First Place, 4-layer bars—Youth Class in Adult Division, 2016

Candy, Snacks & Desserts

BUD ELWELL'S OLD-FASHIONED FUDGE CONTEST

Denny Elwell's father loved the Iowa State Fair and was known for making fudge the old-fashioned way. "Sometimes he would be up at 3 a.m. making his fudge to put in the refrigerator to get it cold," says Denny. "With six kids, he kept it in his room under the bed and would have a piece in the middle of the night. You knew he liked you if you got a piece of that fudge." Since 2009, the Elwell Family has sponsored a fudge contest in Bud's honor. Here is one of our favorites from this annual tradition.

REESE'S PEANUT BUTTER FUDGE

½ cup butter
2 cups brown sugar
½ cup whole milk
1¼ cups creamy peanut butter
1 teaspoon vanilla extract
2½ cups powdered sugar
20 Reese's Peanut Butter Cup Miniatures, cut into quarters

Line an 8x8-inch pan with foil and spray with nonstick spray. In a large saucepan melt butter over medium heat. Stir in brown sugar and milk. Bring to a rolling boil; cook for 2 minutes or until mixture reaches 234°F (soft ball temp), stirring frequently with wooden spoon. Remove from heat. Add peanut butter and mix to combine. Add vanilla extract and mix. Transfer the mixture to the bowl of your mixer. Add powdered sugar, 1 cup at a time, mixing between additions. After all the powdered sugar is added, mix well to incorporate. Press the mixture into the prepared dish. Sprinkle quartered Reese's Peanut Butter Cup Miniatures over the fudge and gently press them down. Let stand at room temperature for 20 minutes. Chill in the refrigerator for an hour or until firm, then use the foil as handles to lift the fudge out of the pan and cut into small squares. Cover and refrigerate until ready to serve. Yields approximately 16 squares.

Brian Keul, West Des Moines
First Place, Bud Elwell's Old-Fashioned Fudge Contest, 2019

A PINK PIGLET WINS BLUE AT THE FAIR

When ten-year-old Josiah Derr saw a new contest to build crispy rice treats into his favorite thing at the Fair, he couldn't wait to enter. "I had never made or even had a rice crispy treat before. It was really fun learning how to make them," Josiah said after winning first place out of both adult and youth contestants. Going to see the piglets at the Knapp Learning Center is his favorite thing to do at the Fair. His pink piglet stole the show at the first Edible Art Contest in 2021. His sister Ashlyn (13) took second in the youth division with her crispy rice bee sculpture and theme of bee-ing at the Fair.

CHERRY CRISPY RICE TREATS

6 tablespoons butter
1½ tablespoons cherry gelatin powder (not sugar-free)
16 oz. marshmallows
7 cups crispy rice cereal

Melt butter and cherry gelatin powder together in a large saucepan. Add marshmallows and stir until mixture is smooth and marshmallows are melted. Add crispy rice cereal and stir until cereal is thoroughly combined. Sculpt into your favorite Iowa piglet using the decorating ingredients below or place the marshmallow mixture into a 9x13-inch pan. Allow to set. Cut into 2-inch squares and enjoy! Makes approximately 12–15 extrathick crispy treat squares.

To sculpt Josiah's winning pig, scoop out about half the mixture and form into a large three-dimensional oval shape for the body and a pink ball for the head. Wrap these it in parchment paper and put them in the freezer for about 20 minutes so they will harden quickly. Roll out logs for the legs. When they are firm, cut the logs into equal sizes for the pig to stand on. Add the following elements to complete the creation with the face, ears, tail, and, of course, the mud and blue ribbon stand for a classic Iowa piglet!

Melted chocolate (for pig's mud puddle)
Black fondant (for eyes)
Water and powdered sugar icing (for decorating eyes and the ribbon stand)
1 extra marshmallow (cut diagonally in half for ears)
Pink sugar (for inside of ears)
Pink food coloring (to color tail and ears)
1 uncooked spiral pasta noodle for the tail

Josiah Derr, Clive
First Place Overall, 2021 Crispy Rice Edible Art Contest

Josiah Derr (10) and sister Ashlyn (13) accept trophies at the 2021 Iowa State Fair for their winning piglet and bee-ing at the Fair edible art sculptures.

233

MOOSE ON THE LOOSE

There's yummy Chocolate Mousse, a classic French dessert to serve at dinner parties. Then there's the life-size Chocolate Moose that was the hit of the Elwell Family Food Center at the 2012 Iowa State Fair. Master chocolatiers at Chocolaterie Stam U.S.A. in Des Moines created "The World's Largest Chocolate Moose in Captivity."

According to Ton Stam, head of the company, "We sponsored a food contest for chocolate mousse at the Fair that year, and we thought this would be fun." Visitors who flocked to see the rich creation agreed, including President Barack Obama, who came to the Fair that year and saw the chocolate statue.

From hooves to antlers, the moose's stainless-steel frame weighed 320 pounds. It stood 10 feet, 6 inches tall and was 118 inches long. The head and the body were constructed separately. Ton Stam says hundreds of pounds of Dutch chocolate were applied in layers. Glucose was added to give the chocolate more resilience.

A real moose might weigh more than 850 pounds, and the chocolate on this one would make about 4,250 Stam chocolate bars. David Stam, Ton's husband, was creative director of the huge project, and Lynn Sprafka was the artist.

Hot August weather and chocolate probably aren't a good combination. "We built the moose in Ankeny and moved it on a flatbed trailer in the middle of the night, the coolest part of the day," Ton Stam says.

We found a winning Mocha Mousse to celebrate this giant food exhibit.

MOCHA MOUSSE

5¼ ounces bittersweet chocolate, coarsely chopped
14 ounces cold heavy cream
3 large egg whites from pasteurized eggs
1 ounce granulated sugar

Place chocolate in a large bowl set over double boiler at a low simmer. Stir chocolate until melted. Remove from heat; let stand. Beat cream over ice until soft peaks form. Set aside; hold at room temperature. Whip egg whites in mixer until soft peaks form. Gradually add sugar; continue whipping until firm. Scrape chocolate into large bowl and use whisk to fold in egg whites all at once. When whites are almost completely incorporated, fold in whipped cream. Cover and refrigerate 1 hour or until set.

SWEETENED WHIPPED CREAM
1 cup heavy cream
1 teaspoon vanilla
1 tablespoon powdered sugar
Shaved bittersweet chocolate

In large bowl whip cream until stiff peaks are just about to form. Beat in vanilla and powdered sugar until peaks stand up straight. Do not overbeat. Serve with mousse. Garnish with shaved chocolate if desired.

Mick Wise, Des Moines
First Place, 2014 Chocolate Mousse

Preserves

ROD ZEITLER WINS COVETED HOLLISTER AWARD IN 2021

Dr. Rod Zeitler, a general internist for the University of Iowa Hospitals and Clinics in Iowa City, is a man of many talents. He has exhibited canned goods at the State Fair for more than 20 years.

In 2021 he took home 93 first-place ribbons and 53 red ribbons. His most prized ribbon is a two-toned purple silk that he received for the Arlette Hollister Food Supreme Sweepstakes Award. He is the second recipient of the award that honors the pursuit of excellence and can-do attitude that Arlette herself exhibited. The first went to Louise Piper of Garner. Although his mother canned produce, Rod didn't start until he was an adult.

"He is a great presenter and exhibitor in the world of preservation," Pat Berry, Food Superintendent, told the *Cedar Rapids Gazette*.

VIOLET JELLY

8 cups firmly packed violet flowers
5 cups boiling water
¼ cup lemon juice

4 cups sugar
44 grams dry pectin

Pick violet flowers that have not been exposed to spray. Wash the violet flowers. Place flowers in a saucepan; add 5 cups boiling water. Return to a boil; stirring to cover the flowers well. Remove from heat; cover and let stand overnight at room temperature. Strain the flowers from the liquid with 4 layers of damp cheesecloth; measure 3¼ cups of liquid; place in a flat bottomed stainless-steel pot. Add ¼ cup strained lemon juice. Whisk in the dry pectin. Bring the infusion to a full rolling boil, stirring frequently. Add sugar, whisking until dissolved. Return to a full rolling boil and cook for 1 minute, stirring continuously with a wooden spoon; then remove from heat. Skim off foam. Ladle mixture into hot, sterilized half-pint jars, leaving ¼ inch head space. Wipe rims with a clean, damp cloth. Apply hot lids and tighten rings. Process in a boiling-water bath for 5 minutes if processing at an altitude of less than 1,000 feet. If the altitude is 1,000 feet or higher, process for 10 minutes. Remove from the water bath and place on a towel and let the jars cool. They will seal on their own.

2000s AND BEYOND: HELP US BUILD THE FUTURE

We've covered State Fair Food history, stories, and recipes, but the most important ingredient for the future is YOU. We hope you, and your family and friends, will join us. Whether you enter foods every year, or this is your first time, please stop by the Elwell Family Food Center. Check out the displays and see which food categories you might want to enter. Observe contests and listen to judges' comments. Ask questions. Take a seminar. The Superintendent and staff are here to help, and you can learn a lot from exhibitors. If you are an Iowa resident and you're ready to enter, here are key dates and tips for success.

How to Enter the Iowa State Fair Food Competitions

1. **Get an *Iowa State Fair Food Premium Book*.** In April the new *Premium Book* is available online (www.iowastatefair.org) or by mail. It has everything you need to know about the Food Competitions, from eligibility and parking to completing entry tags, and delivering your exhibits to the Fair. Contests are listed by category, date, and time. Read through this amazing list and choose your contests.

2. **Register by the deadline.** The Food Department deadline is typically July, when you must register the number of competitions you plan to enter. You have until Fair time in August to decide which recipes to bring. Tags, stickers, and a blank entry list are mailed, along with a 15-minute parking pass for unloading at the Elwell Center.

3. **Follow the Rules.** The Premium Book has detailed instructions on how to enter your exhibit, including the criteria for judging each contest. If you have questions at any point, call or email the Food Superintendent listed at the top of the Premium Book.

4. **Attach Your Tags, Stickers, and Recipes** to each entry so we know it's you when the winners are announced.

5. **Leave Extra Travel Time.** If it takes an hour to get to the Fair, give yourself two in case you are delayed by traffic or the trains that pass near the Fairgrounds. You don't want to miss your check-in time.

6. **Check-In Your Entries.** Unload your prizeworthy bakes in front of the Elwell Center and head for the welcome table. Staff will make sure that you have everything labeled and ready before your entries are whisked off to the judging areas.

7. **Have Fun.** If you made it this far, you're already a winner. Whether you're at the Elwell Family Food Center as a contestant or a fan, soak in the atmosphere of America's #1 State Fair Food Department.

See you at the Fair!

COUNTING THE DAYS 'TIL THE NEXT IOWA STATE FAIR

Geraldine Tait of Des Moines reminds us why we love it so much in her prizewinning poem from 1975.

HEY, MOM! YOU KNOW WHAT I SAW AT THE FAIR?

I saw
Dogs and rabbits and chickens and sows,
And sheep and horses and big black cows,
And combines and bailers and balloons filled with gas,
And raccoons and ducks and even a bass!
I saw Duane Ellett and Floppy and Bill Riley, that's true,
And I rode a real pony and that big Ferris Wheel, too!
I rode on a boat where it was all dark and scary,
Then I won this here teddy bear, just the right size to carry,
And I saw a punkin' this great, great big,
And I saw that buttered cow and that lard pig,
And I saw all-l-l them apples, so I just et one,
Then this here mad guy says, "Don't do that, son!"
You know when that glider thing stopped, I could see the whole fair,
But was I ever glad when that fire truck got me down from up there!
Boy! I was so hungry that I et a whole sack of that candy that's sticky,
Then I et some hotdogs and popcorn 'til I felt kinda icky,
Then I looked around and I was all-l-l alone,
Then this policeman bought me this here ice cream cone,
And, Mom, when you came, was I ever glad!
Gee, Mom, this is the most fun I ever had!

—Geraldine Tait, 1975
Reprinted with permission.

ACKNOWLEDGMENTS

Baking Blue Ribbons has been an incredible project. It is an honor to bring this slice of Iowa history to life. For all of the people, stories, and recipes in these pages, there are countless others, which could fill many books. Thank you to the home cooks and bakers, past and present, for your enthusiasm and dedication and to those who celebrate Iowa's State Fair food traditions today and into the future.

Writing this book began with weekly meetings at a picnic table in Greenwood Park in Des Moines. During 2020, *Baking Blue Ribbons* became our pandemic project. Our outdoor office and phone calls kept the book moving forward and our love of the Food Department alive when the Fair had to be canceled. Along the way, many who love the Fair and food contests as much as we do were an enormous help.

Denny Elwell and his daughter, Brianna Kinsley, were supportive from the moment we shared the idea. Their encouragement and gift from their family foundation helped to bring *Baking Blue Ribbons* to print.

We are grateful to everyone at the Iowa State Fair and the Blue Ribbon Foundation for their stories and generosity, including Gary Slater, Jen Cannon, Peter Cownie, Robin Taylor, and Drew Sniezek. For years, our friends at the Food Department have shared their expertise, including current and past superintendents Arlette Hollister, Karen McKilligan, and Pat Berry, as well as former State Fair marketing director, Kathie Swift.

We also appreciated ideas and encouragement early on from food and history fans like Jamie Buelt, Eileen Gannon, Phil Dicks, Lisa Holderness Brown, Jill Means, Wini Moranville, and others.

Our gratitude to Mary Kay Shanley, our friend and writing mentor, who introduced us at one of her writers' workshops and who worked with Carol at *The Des Moines Register*.

We found countless historical gems thanks to research librarians at Des Moines Public Library and archivists and historians who helped us on many fronts. We dug deep into the Iowa State Fair archives and State Historical Library with guidance from Kelsey Berryhill, Sharon Avery, Delpha Musgrave, and Leo Landis at the State Historical Society of Iowa in Des Moines and Hang Nguyen Ph.D., in Iowa City.

Encouragement and input from readers and editors of our early chapters was invaluable. Our gratitude goes out to Annie Williams, Joanie Seabrook, Lisa Kingsley, Jill Olson, Beth Burgmeyer, Archana Venugopal, Erin Johnson, and others. We could not have published without line-editing expertise from Gretchen Kauffman and guidance from Diane Penningroth.

We appreciate the time that Kassie Ricklefs and Matt Warner-Blankenship, attorneys at Dentons Davis Brown PC, donated to help us navigate copyright and publishing questions, along with Carol Hunter at *The Des Moines Register*.

Enormous thanks to Brian Keul, who lent his expertise and passion for baking with numerous cakes and photographs, and to Ann Gillotti and Jacqueline Riekena who also baked and photographed recipes.

We received a treasure trove of period photos from Living History Farms and food photography from Eileen Gannon at Sunday Night Foods. Sherry Failor, publisher, and Amber Loerzel, art director, of Home Productions, Inc., also provided images for the book from *Welcome Home Des Moines* magazine. Everyone who donated family photos—from 1909 through 2021—made the book complete.

It has been wonderful working with our creative partners at Sigler who brought *Baking Blue Ribbons* to life with gorgeous design work by Michelle Stephenson and Jenny Butcher, and the leadership of Cindi Doornenbal. Their teamwork and generosity helped to make this book possible.

Carol thanks her husband, Tom McGarvey, for his ever-present love and support and their son, Matt McGarvey, for his expertise and encouragement.

Kay thanks her husband and chief taste-tester, Elliott Smith, for his love and support, along with their kids, Freddy and Sarah. Their encouragement was invaluable, from the first spark of an idea to stepping back in time through research, writing, and baking.

Many thanks to you, our readers. Proceeds from *Baking Blue Ribbons* will benefit the Iowa State Fair Food Department and help to keep it going strong for future generations.

MEET THE AUTHORS

Kay Fenton Smith has been winning ribbons at the Iowa State Fair Food Department since 2007. As a kid in upstate New York, she and her brother and sister loved the State Fair in Syracuse.

She graduated from Cornell University and began her first career in advertising and marketing at Leo Burnett, U.S.A. and Hyatt Hotels Corporation in Chicago. There she met her husband, Iowa native Elliott Smith. They moved to Des Moines, where Kay continued her career at Meredith Corporation. She and Elliott raised their family and enjoyed many trips to the Iowa State Fair through the years with their children, Freddy and Sarah. Kay stayed home with the kids and began a home-based business and freelance writing career.

Her first book, *Zakery's Bridge*, shares the immigration journeys of families who came to Iowa from around the world. She teaches creative writing and cultural arts workshops inspired by the book. *Baking Blue Ribbons* brings together her passions for writing, baking, and history.

Carol Marlow McGarvey decided in middle school that she wanted to be a journalist and storyteller. She was born in Boone, Iowa, and moved to Perry, Iowa, at age 10. She is a proud graduate of Perry High School and of Iowa State University in Ames, where she majored in home economics journalism.

Her career as a features reporter for *The Des Moines Register* spanned 33 years. As an adjunct instructor, she taught reporting at the Drake University School of Journalism for 10 semesters. She has enjoyed a freelance career for magazines and books, writing about homes, food, landscaping, and people.

At the Iowa State Fair, she has been a food judge since 1984 and has interviewed many of the talented cooks and bakers who make the food competition so special each year. Carol has written three small cookbooks, coauthored *The Des Moines Register Cookbook,* and wrote *What a Ride,* a book of 40 essays for her children and friends.

She and her husband, Tom, are proud parents of Matt, Andy, and Molly and grandparents to seven fabulous grandchildren.

The Gazette, (Cedar Rapids, Iowa), August 27, 1964.
Sioux City Journal, June 20, 1965.
Ames Daily Tribune, June 24, 1966.
The Des Moines Tribune, August 22, 1967.
The Des Moines Tribune, July 17, 1968.
Ames Daily Tribune, March 6, 1970.
Sioux City Journal, July 10, 1972.
The Des Moines Register, August 29, 1977.

Chapter 6: 1980s–1990s: A Match Made in Food Heaven
The Des Moines Register, August 15, 1980.
The Des Moines Register, August 6, 1982.
The Des Moines Register, August 14, 1983.
The Des Moines Register, September 6, 1984.
The Des Moines Register, June 30 and August 21, 1985.
The Des Moines Register, June 8, 1986.
Iowa City Press-Citizen, October 15 and October 18, 1986.
Iowa City Press-Citizen, June 10, 1987.
The Des Moines Register, July 3, 1988.
The Des Moines Register, June 11 and August 2; August 23, 1989.
The Gazette, (Cedar Rapids, Iowa), July 10, 1990.
The Des Moines Register, August 12, 14, 15, 1990.
Iowa City Press-Citizen, August 22, 1990.
The Des Moines Register, August 8, 1995.
The Des Moines Register, August 17, 1996.
The Gazette, (Cedar Rapids, Iowa), August 16, 1998.
The Des Moines Register, August 11, 2015.

Chapter 7: 2000s: The Sweetest Gift and a Look to the Future
Quad-City Times, (Davenport, Iowa), June 14 and August 30, 2000.
The Des Moines Register, June 14 and 18, 2000.
Iowa City Press-Citizen, June 21 and July 19 and August 30, 2000.
Iowa City Press-Citizen, June 6, 2001.
The Des Moines Register, August 16 and 22, 2001.
The Gazette, (Cedar Rapids, Iowa), August 13, 2002.
Iowa City Press-Citizen, August 21 and September 11, 2002.
The Des Moines Register, August 8, 2006.
The Des Moines Register, May 24 and June 20, 2007.
The Des Moines Register, August 3 and 12, 2008.
Quad-City Times, (Davenport, Iowa), September 2, 2009.

The Des Moines Register, August 16, 2010.

The Des Moines Register, June 6, 2011.

The Des Moines Register, August 5, 2012.

The Gazette, (Cedar Rapids, Iowa), June 20, 2013.

The Courier, (Waterloo, Iowa), August 8, 2014.

The Des Moines Register, June 2 and August 11, 2015.

The Des Moines Register, August 17, 2016.

The Des Moines Register, August 11, 2017.

The Des Moines Register, March 27, 2019.

The Gazette, (Cedar Rapids, Iowa), August 12, 2019.

PHOTO CREDITS

Photos are attributed clockwise, beginning with A in the upper left corner of the page. FC. represents the front cover. BC represents the back cover.

Courtesy of Barb Bare 34, 42

Courtesy of Ruth Beck Family 180

Courtesy of Chocolaterie Stam 234A-B

The Daily Iowa Capitol, (Des Moines, Iowa) 13B

The Daily Gate City and Constitution Democrat (Keokuk, Iowa)43B

The Daily Times, (Davenport, Iowa) 59

Courtesy of Heather Derr 233A, B, D

Des Moines Public Library 66, 82, 87B, 105A, 105B, 105C, 16A, 16B, 16C, 16D, 17A, 17B

The Des Moines Register – **USA TODAY NETWORK** 12B, 38A, 39B, 40, 54A, 64B, 85, 86A, 89, 109, 113, 116, 117, 124, 130, 143, 147, 152, 177A (David Peterson), 182, 184B, BCG

The Des Moines Tribune – **USA TODAY NETWORK** 49B, 49C, 54B, 86B

The Evening Journal, (Wilmington, Delaware) 64A

Courtesy of the Denny Elwell Family 194, 195B, 195C

Kay Fenton Smith FCB, FCD, FCE,12A, 25, 44, 46, 47, 50, 51, 62, 65, 67, 68,69, 71A, 71B, 73, 77, 86C, 87A, 91, 92, 93A, 93B, 93C, 95, 96, 99A, 101, 102, 103A, 111A-B-C, 115A, 119, 120A-B-C, 127,129, 131, 132, 133, 144, 145, 148, 158, 171A, 171B, 183, 185B, 186, 189B, 197, 198A, 198B,199, 203A, 203B, 205, 206, 208, 212A-B, 227B, 228, 229, 233A-B, D, 236, BCD

Courtesy Eileen Gannon and Sunday Night Foods (sundaynightfoods.com) 97, 98, 118, 216, 230, 235, BCC, BCE

Ann Gillotti 24, 28, 29, 139, 218B, 219

Courtesy of Matthew Harvey Family 206

Courtesy of Julia Hunter 186, 229

245

Iowa City Press-Citizen – USA TODAY NETWORK 123, 185A

Iowa State Fair FCC, FCE, FCF, viii, xiii, xiv, xv, xvii, 2, 9, 11A, 18, 22, 38B, 38C, 39A, 52, 55, 58, 100, 105, 108A, 108B, 114, 115B, 140, 146, 153, 158, 184A, 189, 192, 195A, 201, 233C, 240, BCD, BCF

Brian Keul FCA, 45B, 128A, 128B, 217, 218A, 220, 221, 222A-B, 231, BCB

Living History Farms (lhf.org) 5

Courtesy of Norma Lyon Family 112A

Courtesy of Marilyn and John Martinez 193

Courtesy of Joy McFarland Family 165

Courtesy of Carol McGarvey 112B, 149, 203, 241B

The Mount Pleasant News 99

The Muscatine Journal 49A

The Muscatine Journal and News-Tribune 61A

The Nashua Reporter 57

News-Journal, (Mansfield, Ohio) 43C

Press and Sun Bulletin, (Binghamton, NY) 43A, 45A

Quad-City Times, (Davenport, Iowa) 13A, 103B, 162

Jacqueline Riekena 138

Courtesy of Pam Reynolds and Bridget Lottman 204

Courtesy of Carrie Scheidel 227B

Jennifer Sedlock 211

Sigler, (Ames, Iowa) 8, 15B, 48, 159, 173, 214

Sioux City Journal 106, 122

The Sioux County Index, (Hull, Iowa) 78

Smithsonian Open Access, Creative Commons Zero (CC0) 7

State Historical Society of Iowa, Des Moines 4, 11B, 14A, 14B, 15A, 17A, 84, 55, 75, 80, 88, 104, 110, 134, BCA

State Historical Society of Iowa, Iowa City 17B

Courtesy of Robin Tarbell-Thomas 103C, 150, 175, 177B, BCG

Welcome Home Des Moines magazine (welcomehomedesmoines.com) 32, 155, 169, 191, 193A, 224, 225, 226, 227A
  (Ben Lochard); 157 (JJ Grinvalds); 144, 190, 196 (John Johnson)

Courtesy of Annie Williams 241A

Courtesy of Dianna Zaiger Sheehy 135A

Courtesy of Rod Zeitler 236

"I'm a great swimmer!"

"You all are! Your tongue is able to roll up at the back of your mouth to stop you from swallowing water while you snooze at the bottom of the swamp. Did you know that you can sleep underwater for up to two hours at a time and that your eyes are designed to work like swim goggles?"

"That's super cool!"

"Grandmother, how old are you?"

"I am fifty years old, my dear."

"Whoa! That's really old!"